THE SCOTT AND LAURIE OKI SERIES
IN ASIAN AMERICAN STUDIES

THE SCOTT AND LAURIE OKI SERIES
IN ASIAN AMERICAN STUDIES

From a Three-Cornered World: New and Selected Poems
by James Masao Mitsui

*Imprisoned Apart: The World War II Correspondence
of an Issei Couple* by Louis Fiset

*Storied Lives: Japanese American Students
and World War II* by Gary Y. Okihiro

Phoenix Eyes and Other Stories
by Russell Charles Leong

Paper Bullets: A Fictional Autobiography
by Kip Fulbeck

Born in Seattle: The Campaign for Japanese American Redress
by Robert Sadamu Shimabukuro

*Confinement and Ethnicity: An Overview of World War II
Japanese American Relocation Sites*
by Jeffery F. Burton, Mary M. Farrell,
Florence B. Lord, and Richard W. Lord

*Judgment without Trial: Japanese American Imprisonment
during World War II* by Tetsuden Kashima

*Shopping at Giant Foods: Chinese American Supermarkets
in Northern California* by Alfred Yee

SHOPPING AT
GIANT FOODS

Chinese American Supermarkets
in Northern California

ALFRED YEE

UNIVERSITY OF WASHINGTON PRESS

Seattle and London

This book is published with the assistance of a grant
from the Scott and Laurie Oki Endowed Fund
for the publication of Asian American Studies,
established through the generosity of Scott and Laurie Oki.

Copyright © 2003 by the University of Washington Press
First paperback edition, 2013
Printed in United States of America
Design by Pamela Canell

Library of Congress Cataloging-in-Publication Data
Yee, Alfred.
Shopping at Giant Foods : Chinese American supermarkets
in Northern California / Alfred Yee.
p. cm.—(The Scott and Laurie Oki series in Asian American studies)
ISBN 978-0-295-99294-5 (alk. paper)
1. Supermarkets—California, Northern.
2. Chinese Americans—California, Northern.
I. Title. II. Series.
HF5469.23.U63C29 2003   381'.148'0899510794—DC21   2003040288

CONTENTS

v

PREFACE

WRITING ABOUT WHAT ONE KNOWS BEST helps to make an interesting and engaging topic. For over twenty years I was solidly involved in the Chinese American grocery and supermarket business. After graduating from college with a bachelor of science degree in 1973, I went to work for a Chinese American supermarket chain in the Sacramento area. This was meant to be a temporary job while I searched for a professional career that was congruous with my education. In reality, the job provided a welcome suspension in decision-making about the direction of my life. Getting a job in a supermarket was not difficult, because I had many years of experience working in a grocery store. This "temporary" job lasted fifteen years. I was employed at Jumbo Markets from 1975 to 1989 as a courtesy clerk, cashier, stock clerk, warehouseman, and head clerk (third person in charge under the manager and assistant manager). While at Jumbo, I was also a shop steward for the Retail Clerks Union Local 588 for a short period.

The job provided a solid middle-class income and outstanding health and welfare benefits, which were won by the hard negotiating of the local retail clerks union. Life was comfortable, to say the least, for a full-time clerk with union wages and benefits. It was easy to drudge on for years, leaving work behind each day when quitting time arrived. For a young person, the routine physical work was not very challenging, but it could be stupefying. On the other hand, the rapport between clerks and customers and the camaraderie among the clerks helped mitigate much of the mental monotony. I knew I would not remain a lifetime grocery clerk, but I procrastinated for a long time before I made the break, returning to college to pursue additional degrees for a career as a college instructor.

During those years as a clerk, I learned much about the supermarket business, in particular the Chinese American operations. I met countless people who talked and gossiped about who did what recently or in the past. Among them were store employees, managers, owners, salesmen, deliverymen, vendors, and so forth—people who were in the business for decades and people who owned or worked for competing stores. There were always plenty of anecdotes and stories, the veracity of which ranged from factual to exaggerated to fabricated. But carefully scrutinized and cross-checked, they contributed to a fairly accurate account of the workings and histories of the various Chinese American operations.

Prior to my employment at Jumbo Markets, my family and I had already been involved in the grocery store and supermarket business. My late father worked in the Sacramento area as a "butcher" (nowadays called a meatcutter) for a few years in General Food Market before becoming a minor partner in Fine Food Market from 1956 to 1964. Established in 1939, Fine Food Market was one of the earlier Chinese American supermarkets and a member of Famous Food Markets, a cooperative providing purchasing, advertising, and promotional services. While a young teenager, I worked part-time at Fine Food Market for two summers, my first undertaking in the grocery business. From 1967 to 1975, my father operated a small supermarket, Florin Market. I worked in Florin Market during my high school and early college years— after classes, on weekends, and during summers. Later, while I was at Jumbo, my two brothers and other partners operated a four-supermarket chain during the early 1980s. Although my brothers had over thirty years of experience between them, the stores were not successful for reasons similar to those detailed in this study. My older brother then ran two other small supermarkets until he retired in the mid-1990s. For a few years I worked weekends and summers in one of them while attending graduate school. My younger brother has since become a vendor for a national snack food company. Most of the people I socialized with and knew before I reentered college were people in the grocery store and supermarket business. It was from this background that I thus began research for this study. I knew as much or more about the details and nuances of nearly every aspect of the grocery business as the people I interviewed. Hence, they were comfortable recounting their experiences, feeling that I understood their sentiments. Their anecdotes and stories provided material to construct histories that heretofore have not been recorded.

I have met many people who exclaimed after learning about my family's business background that Chinese American supermarket operators were well-to-do. There is some truth to this common perception, but the reality is much more mixed. Some did become very successful, but many others made modest or meager profits or failed altogether. The stories of the few who became wealthy were the ones that were the loudest and most remembered. In all cases, the grocers worked long, hard hours that were weighted with a never-ending series of problems and ongoing concerns. Ask any past or present grocer and he or she will say that there is no such thing as easy money in the grocery and supermarket business. It was thus no surprise that nostalgia was not prevalent in the oral interviews that were used to construct this history of Chinese American supermarkets.

ACKNOWLEDGMENTS

THIS ENDEAVOR HAS HAD ITS SHARE of intellectual and emotional vicissitudes. At times I felt overwhelmed and discouraged, but many friends and colleagues encouraged and prodded me along. I must thank Steven Avella, Bing Fun Cheng, Sandra Chim, Rosemary Flemmer, Kenneth Luk, and Lewis Robinson. My mentor, Kenneth Owens, gave me invaluable insight and advice.

I wish to thank my graduate school adviser at Ohio State University, Professor Warren R. Van Tine, for his support, encouragement, and patience, which made this work possible. He was truly a "white knight" during my darkest hours. Other professors who gave me reassurance and help include Samuel Chu, Yan-shuan Lao, and James Bartholomew. Gratitude for administrative assistance goes to Joby Abernathy.

Naomi Pascal at the University of Washington Press gave professional guidance and was much more patient and persevering than I was through the steps of publication. Also assisting me at the press were Lorri Hagman and Mary Ribesky.

I am indebted to George Quan, Jr., who introduced me to his network of associates, all fruitful resources. His knowledge and eagerness greatly facilitated my research. I am very grateful to Leland Lee, who provided invaluable details and nuances with straightforwardness and enthusiasm, making the material come to life. Bill Wong and George Wong were very informative and helpful. It was awakening to listen to the late George Chan, whose revelations were provocative.

Appreciation must also be extended to Susie Chan, Henry Fong, Earl Joe, Lewis Kassis, Jimmie Lee, Louis Lee, Bill Lew, Joe Tang, Rose Yee, Gene Yee, and Art Yim, all of who made this research so engaging. And finally, I would like to give special thanks to my friend the late Anna W. Lee, who eagerly assisted me with her vigilant search for resources.

SHOPPING AT GIANT FOODS

Introduction

EMERGING DURING THE 1930S and securing a competitive market share for about the next four decades, Chinese American supermarkets were prominent operations in small, medium, and large cities throughout Northern California. Until recently, they were so well established that there were very few residents who did not shop in one of them or know about them. These supermarkets were located in nearly every community and were able to prosper and compete directly with national chains, local chains, and independent operations. In 1960, for example, Chinese Americans operated 91 of 223 supermarkets and grocery stores in the city of Sacramento.[1] Their competitors were very aware of their presence. As one recalled, "It was hell to pay if you had Chinese grocery stores as competition." Their prominence was also evident in their one- or two-page weekly advertisements in newspapers from the 1950s to 1970s, in which shoppers looked forward to comparing prices of featured sale items of competing supermarkets. Invariably, the Chinese American supermarkets offered the lowest prices. The businesses ranged from single-store to multiple-store operations, and were owned by Chinese American families, partnerships, or corporations. It must be underscored that from the start, the stores did not sell ethnic foods and merchandise in ethnic enclaves, but sold American groceries, meat, and produce to mostly Euro-American customers who generally accepted the stores in their neighborhoods at a time when racial prejudice and segregation were prevalent. In due course, these stores, with their Chinese American personnel, helped erode social barriers. No other minority ethnic group since has achieved such prominence in the grocery business in Northern California.

Some multiple-store operations began as a small grocery store that expanded in size and number into a small chain of supermarkets. Many single-store supermarkets secured niches in local markets and did adequate business, although not enough to warrant expansion into chain operations. Well-known

Chinese American supermarket chains included the forty Farmers Markets, four Giant Foods, nine Centr-O-Marts, eleven Jumbo Markets, eleven Dick's Markets, seventeen Bel Air supermarkets, and the Famous Food Markets.[2] None of these prominent chain supermarkets remain in operation under the original owners or partners. A small number of independent supermarkets are still in the hands of Chinese Americans, but they are not competing in large markets. Many of the factors that facilitated the rise and prosperity of the supermarkets also contributed to their decline and passing. Basically, most of the operators were unwilling or unable to adapt to the rapid changes of the retail food industry. Some operators tried to keep up with trends and to weather the vicissitudes of the business, but only a few succeeded. A combination of trends and changes caused most of the supermarkets to become insolvent, although not before their operators had succeeded in achieving what they set out to do, that is, to make money.

Three phases of Chinese American supermarkets can be discerned: their modest beginnings, their proliferation and prosperity, and their decline and passing. The prominence of Chinese American supermarkets was exclusive to Northern California, notwithstanding numerous operations scattered in Central and Southern California and in Arizona and Texas.[3] Even in San Francisco, the locale of many narratives of the Chinese American experience, the retail food business by Chinese Americans did not extend beyond "mom-and-pop" grocery stores.

AN OVERVIEW

Since the mid-nineteenth century various means of livelihood have existed for Chinese Americans, which for the convenience of this study refers to both foreign-born and American-born Chinese Americans. The businesses and occupations in which Chinese Americans engaged depended upon the circumstances and opportunities afforded to them by the larger community and by their own intergroup relationships. Essentially, Chinese Americans sold goods or services to the majority group or to members of their own group. Clearly, supplying goods or services to the majority group netted a greater economic reward because the needs of the majority group were more extensive than the smaller Chinese American population. In *The Chinese in the United States of America*, Rose Hum Lee listed eight categories of businesses and occupations undertaken by Chinese Americans during their first hundred years in America. One of these was "selling American goods, [with] Chinese service, [for an] American clientele."[4] This category included the operation of laundries, cafes and restaurants serving American dishes, truck farms and produce markets, and grocery stores in urban areas. For a short period, Chinese Americans also operated a small number of rooming houses, taverns, and nightclubs in the larger cities. Some of these enterprises, such as the laundries, began during the gold rush era, while others, such as the nightclubs, emerged in the 1930s. For most contemporary Chinese Americans, two or more generations removed from their immigrant forefathers, these enterprises have long ceased to be their means of livelihood. Recent Asian immigrant groups such as Asian Indians, Koreans, and Southeast Asians, however, have engaged in these enterprises in their modern forms, albeit some aspects of their operations are reminiscent of those under past Chinese American proprietorships.

By the 1920s, many Chinese immigrants, for various reasons, had decided not to return to China as earlier sojourners did. If they did return to China, it was for a short visit to see one's wife and family or to get married. Later they would seek the means to bring wife and family over to settle, and consequently, this usually meant finding better livelihoods to build their futures. It was clear to them that an entrepreneur selling products was a better occupation than a worker selling labor because the former offered the possibility of increased rewards from increased effort. And selling American goods like groceries, meat, and produce offered the most potential for profit and economic security at a time when the population and economy in California were rapidly expanding. In the meantime, new immigrants came to the United States to become permanent residents.

For a host of reasons, prejudice and hostility toward Chinese Americans were decreasing. Much of this prejudice was redirected toward other recent Asian immigrant groups, in particular the Japanese. More and more residents from the community at large were patronizing Chinese American businesses, primarily because they offered lower prices for services and products than their competitors. But offering lower prices was nothing new; that was how the ubiquitous laundries remained viable for decades. In addition to vendors who sold produce from the back of their trucks or produce stands, an increasing number of Chinese Americans opened meat shops that sold fresh and cured products. This trend was a natural extension of the restaurant business, where cooks and entrepreneurs received preparatory training. Experience in produce or meat retailing would serve as the genesis for most Chinese Americans entering the small grocery store business.

Until the advent and spread of the combination grocery store, consumers purchased groceries, meat, and produce separately from stores that sold only those items, or from the different concessionaires under one roof. With the onset of the combination grocery store in the 1930s, Chinese Americans were ready and willing to take advantage of new opportunities.

Chinese Americans started their small grocery businesses by purchasing an existing operation or by building a store from scratch. They rented or erected buildings, put in equipment, and bought inventory. Each and every one financed their venture with money that they had saved from working in previous occupations or from operating former businesses. A few borrowed additional funds, usually from their family or relatives, and sometimes from close friends. Banks would not give them loans, but Chinese Americans did not seek capital from financial institutions. Neither did they borrow money from family or district associations in their communities. They tried to keep all money matters simple by avoiding written contracts and dealing with cash whenever possible. Personal integrity was their guarantor. Often a primary proprietor took on one or more partners to help capitalize and operate the grocery store. They were generally relatives or close friends who shared the risks as well as the profits, which were usually divided at year-end.

In family-owned stores, the proprietor and his family did most or all of the work. The children were expected to help out after school and on weekends. In partnership stores, the partners were usually the workers, and the hiring of employees was avoided to minimize expenses. In all stores, family members or partners were preferred as workers because they were presumed to be trustworthy, reliable, and hardworking. Payroll expenses for family-owned stores were almost nonexistent because of unpaid labor, but family members occasionally drew money when it was necessary. In sum, the family-owned store epitomized the concept of mutual responsibility and collective welfare. On the other hand, the payroll expenses for partnership stores depended upon the arrangement among the partners. Each partner, for example, regularly drew minimal wages and received his share of the year-end profits. Any practice of mutual responsibility and collective welfare depended upon the relationship among the partners and the attitude of the individual partners.

Generally, the grocery store neophytes learned how to run their businesses while on the job. Nearly everyone became capable at every task because these early stores were small and simple to run. But there was usually a division of labor and responsibility. By one account, one family-owned store was managed "by the seat of our pants" (using experience, instinct, and guesswork). They would often visit nearby competitors to see how they operated, and priced their products accordingly. Or they would ask grocery product salesmen for such information. Chinese American operators almost always kept their stores open for business longer. Whether open for business or not, a whole day off for anyone was rare because there was always work to be done.

During the Depression, the national chain companies closed their small outlets or enlarged and remodeled them to open combination grocery stores, the forerunners of the larger supermarkets. Chinese Americans also increased the space of their grocery stores if possible, and installed additional equipment and stocked fresh meats and produce to keep up with the competition. During this period the grocery business in Northern California was uneven; some stores remained profitable while others became insolvent. Business was much better during the war years, although some stores had to close because of a shortage of manpower. The wartime economy put more money into people's pockets, and rationing and shortages of products created a high demand for nearly everything.

When Chinese American operators did hire employees, the latter were nearly always relatives or friends from the same home village or district in China. During the 1930s to 1960s, when employment opportunities were still limited, Chinese Americans preferred working in grocery stores or supermarkets rather than toiling on farms, sweating in laundries, or laboring in restaurants. Compared to their Euro-American counterpart working in a grocery store or supermarket, the employees' work was not so much demanding in efficiency as it was demanding in time. Employers paid their employees a fixed sum for working long hours during a six- or seven-day workweek, much like they expected from their own family members. Following traditional employment practices in Chinese society, employees were provided room and board if needed. But the trade-off, again like old-world ways, was that employees were expected to be loyal and obedient to their employer, especially when the latter sponsored the immigration of the former. Hence, when the labor unions tried to organize Chinese American clerks in the late 1940s and early 1950s, they had virtually no success. A history of discrimination by labor unions, which generated distrust from Chinese American workers towards them, also caused employees to side with their employers. Thus, employers worked their employees for long hours, which kept their labor costs lower and profits higher compared to their competitors.

Looking to increase profits, Chinese American owners opened more supermarkets. These were either new independent supermarkets usually interrelated through common partners, or additional supermarkets within the same operation. The latter type became a chain of supermarkets under the same ownership. To finance expansion, they used their profits, secured credit from equipment sellers and grocery wholesalers, and took on new partners.

Often the new partners were former employees. Some operators purchased existing supermarkets and renamed them after remodeling. Others built everything from the ground up after purchasing real estate at promising locations, modeling their stores and operations along the lines of the national supermarket chains.

It was not unusual for employees to strike out on their own and form partnerships without the involvement of their former employers. A partnership not only brought title and profits for an entrepreneur, but also employment. In other words, many Chinese Americans bought into partnerships in new or existing operations in order to secure jobs. Because there were numerous partners, it was not unusual for conflicts to erupt over the management of a store or the company's chain of stores. These differences invariably affected the operation and success of the store or company. The discords were compounded by the fact that many partnerships were originally drawn up by verbal agreements and consummated by handshakes, if at all. In addition, the common practice of partners employing family members, relatives, and close friends in their supermarkets sometimes brought on other problems, such as how to manage them or hold them accountable when they were not productive. Discharging them for indolence or even theft was difficult because of the traditional sense of obligation the Chinese have for the welfare of family members, relatives, and close friends.

With a flourishing economy and a population boom, the two-and-a-half decades after World War II were very profitable for Chinese American supermarkets. This era can be described as its "golden times." However, just when it appeared that business could not be better, business began to get progressively more difficult. Competition from the national chain supermarkets intensified. The trend in the retail food industry was for bigger and bigger stores, which were increasingly more expensive to open and operate. The national chain companies seemed to have unlimited capital for closing unprofitable stores, remodeling old stores that still had potential, opening new stores in prime locations, and acquiring the latest equipment for efficiency. For the Chinese American operators, the cost of keeping up with the national chain companies was too high, especially when profit margins were narrowing as expenses rose steeply. Recessions occurred frequently, cutting down or wiping out whatever slim profits the Chinese American supermarkets were able to net. Managing the supermarkets became exasperatingly complicated because of the increasing complexity of the business. Labor unions gained strength, making it possible for the unions to enforce work rules and to negotiate higher wages and benefits for store employees. Concurrently, the relationship between employees and employers gradually turned from cooperative to adversarial as the attitude of both changed in the face of intense competition and pressure in the industry. With employees siding increasingly with labor unions, the labor costs for Chinese American supermarkets rose, negating the competitive edge they once had. Over the decades, once youthful neighborhoods were maturing and changing such that business and profits for the supermarkets that served them were in decline or stagnant. As the owners and partners themselves became older, many became indifferent or less vigilant about maintaining their stores' competitiveness. And the recurring conflicts among the partners would not end.

With all these forces working against them, Chinese American owners gradually sold or eventually closed their supermarkets. The "handwriting on the wall" was apparent by the mid-1960s. Many of the former owners or partners went into retirement, while others engaged in other types of business, employment, or investments. Some of their employees did the same, but most found employment in other supermarkets. In the 1970s and 1980s, the remaining chain operations expanded the number of their supermarkets and managed to survive the vicissitudes of the business by adopting different management techniques. But neither profits nor operations would be the same again. In 1992 the owners of the last Chinese American supermarket chain in Northern California sold their operation to a major competitor. They were the only Chinese Americans to leave the business while their company was on the ascent.

One Chinese American supermarket, however, still commands attention. Owned and operated by the same family in the small city of Colusa, California, since 1921, Chung Sun Grocery (Market) was the launching point for other Chinese American supermarkets that opened in the 1930s, 1940s, and 1950s. Many operators throughout Northern California owed their start to Chung Sun Grocery, where they acquired business apprenticeships, capital, and future partners. Chung Sun's longevity is extraordinary, given the intense competition and the unpredictable changes of the supermarket business. Family members continue to work the supermarket, enabling the store to remain solvent, although the store is not as profitable as in past years. Despite a loyal customer base, which has helped Chung Sun ward off competition from national chain supermarkets, recent developments in the retail food industry and the community have rendered its future uncertain.

Chinese American supermarkets in Northern California were built and maintained by an ambitious and industrious group of people whose success gave Chinese Americans a sense of accomplishment and place in their greater communities. Much of the storeowners' success was due to timing, hard work, and luck. For decades, they prospered in an industry that has always been extremely competitive. By not resigning themselves to an ethnic-niche service or trade, they made a big step toward social assimilation through economic means. Profits and earnings from the supermarkets enabled employers and employees to build secure foundations, which in turn allowed their progeny to start their ascension toward loftier goals and rewards. Thus, the passing of Chinese American supermarkets should be regarded not so much as a failure or loss, but as a triumphal step up the socioeconomic ladder of the American dream.

COMMUNITY DEVELOPMENT

The emergence and operation of grocery stores and supermarkets advanced the socioeconomic development of the Chinese American community and its relationship with the greater community. Nearly all of the early operators were not from the mercantile class of traditional society whose power and wealth were based in Chinatowns that served a primarily Chinese clientele. They were from the peasant class who immigrated to America with little or no money, started out as employees at restaurants, laundries, farms, and other small businesses, and saved enough capital to start their own small enterprises located mostly outside ethnic enclaves. Furthermore, the influence of the traditional merchants—who usually headed family and district associations to which nearly every Chinese American belonged and who often acted as intermediaries between the Chinese and the majority population—was fading or minimal on these later immigrants who lived in communities throughout California. These immigrants were more akin to the truck gardeners and tenant farmers of the late nineteenth century. Store operators were less dependent on ethnic solidarity for survival than earlier Chinese Americans, although their success was still due in large part to old-world practices.

Chinese Americans considered operating retail food stores more desirable than operating restaurants, laundries, farms, and other small businesses because stores provided more reliable income and better working conditions. Their prospect for long-term financial security was also comparatively good, which justified the higher investment, but in turn required a sustained commitment. Small-scale businesses such as the laundry, on the other hand, were inexpensive to start and easy to operate and liquidate, factors preferred by sojourners. Likewise, Chinese Americans sought employment in grocery stores and supermarkets because they offered better income and working conditions than most other occupations available to them. Even after World War II, employment opportunities were still limited for Chinese Americans in the professional, craft, technical, clerical, and sales fields. This occurred for a variety of reasons, including lingering discrimination. Entrepreneurship or employment in grocery stores and supermarkets thus offered one of the best means for Chinese Americans to become middle-class residents. This business opportunity stood in contrast to the transience and insecurity of the enterprises and occupations available to Chinese Americans in earlier times.

Most of the Chinese American grocery stores and all of the supermarkets were located outside their owners' and workers' primary residential areas. Because they largely served Euro-Americans and, in many instances, a mixed ethnic clientele, including Mexican Americans, these businesses reflected a growing acceptance, if not tolerance, of Chinese Americans in their greater communities after decades of hostility and discrimination. But there were still obstacles. As late as the mid-1960s, landlords and realtors in some urban neighborhoods refused to rent and sell homes to owners and employees. Some customers who would not hesitate to patronize Chinese American stores operating in their neighborhoods would not accept Chinese Americans living next to them. In rural communities, the situation generally was slightly better. Chinese Americans there had a history of socioeconomic tolerance dating back to the nineteenth century, when they were an integral part of the agricultural economy.

Working in grocery stores and supermarkets considerably facilitated the acculturation of Chinese American individuals and families. Unlike sojourners and Chinatown residents, Chinese Americans in grocery stores had to have some proficiency in English because of their extensive contact with the general public. Wives of store proprietors who had recently immigrated to America, for example, learned English on the job. Lifestyles and friendships could not help but expand because of exposure to the American way of life and to the American public. Profits or wages provided the means for many immigrants and American-born young men to marry, raise families, and purchase homes in communities outside their old neighborhoods. By and large, they could afford to buy into the American dream and to affix the suffix "American" to their identity. Their earnings provided the resources and opportunities for their children to attain higher educations and pursue professional occupations. Unfortunately, quite a few private-sector occupations—skilled, white-collar, managerial, and professional—remained largely inaccessible to Chinese Americans, even those who were American-born and had college degrees, until after the civil rights movement of the mid-1960s. Assimilation took longer than acculturation.

In sum, grocery stores and supermarkets helped advance the socioeconomic status of Chinese Americans. They formed an integral part of an evolving Chinese American community from the end of World War I to the mid-1960s. From the mid-1960s onward, the make-up of nearly all Chinese American communities became very complex and dynamic because of the tidal wave of Chinese immigrants who arrived from China and East Asia. These immigrants possessed a wide degree and variety of resources, education, and occupational skills. Until then, one of the most salient characteristics of Chinese Americans in Northern California was their prominence in the supermarket business.

THE HISTORICAL RECORD

Most of the historical record of Chinese Americans from the end of World War I to the mid-1960s tends to focus on the Chinatowns in large cities. Tong wars, immigration, the Diaspora, labor strikes, and political activities garnered the bulk of the attention. But almost unnoticed are Chinese Americans outside the Chinatowns and the development of their communities. Aside from political rallies tied to events in China, very little has been recorded and analyzed about these communities. There are many references and anecdotes about family grocery stores in the general histories and memoirs of Chinese Americans, but no in-depth studies about the supermarkets and the people who operated them have been done, even though there were at least three thousand Chinese American grocery stores and supermarkets in California in the early 1960s.[5] Neighborhood grocery stores were generally listed along with hand laundries, restaurants, curio shops, and farms as the primary businesses in which Chinese Americans were engaged, and large supermarkets were noted simply as a phenomenon on the West Coast.

This scarcity about the history of grocery stores and supermarkets is due in large part to the lack and limited value of primary resources for research. Government censuses and studies and newspaper articles that are used to provide details, statistics, and accounts about Chinese American grocery stores and supermarkets are very few, nonexistent, or of little help. The U.S. Census Reports of 1940, 1950, and 1960, for example, provide Chinese population totals for California's counties but no specific type and numeration of businesses and occupations of the Chinese. Their numbers are grouped under "other races" or "nonwhite," which includes Japanese, Filipino, Indian, and other races outside the Euro-American and Negro groupings. Yearly business directories tend to list only those grocery and supermarkets that pay for their listings. County records of licenses and owners of Chinese American grocery stores and supermarkets record only those names the owners or partners want to make public. Even the trade journal *Supermarket News* includes a disclaimer about the accuracy of its findings on the market share of supermarkets, publishing figures, and trends based on data that were gathered from incomplete surveys and secondary sources.[6]

Ideally, the bulk of the primary sources ought to come from the stores' operational records. But it became apparent through the course of this research that most operators kept very few if any documents about their business dealings, especially from the 1930s to the early 1960s. Whatever operational records they did have, such as account books, contracts, and invoices, were not saved for posterity. If the former owners or partners still possessed any, they could not provide them when asked, claiming to have misplaced them long ago. Even the Retail Clerks Union Local 588, whose labor contracts with the supermarkets greatly affected their operations and profits, did not keep old labor agreements. An old contract, which stipulated hourly wages and labor rules, was routinely discarded when a new contract was negotiated and implemented.

Another problem in gathering information was rooted in the type of ownership. The stores were private enterprises, not public companies or corporations whose business practices were open to scrutiny and thus whose records were saved. The owners or primary partners themselves tended to be secretive about their operations and plans in order to keep their competitors, the government, labor unions, and even their minor partners, employees, and wholesalers from knowing much about them. The same applied especially to their income tax records. If tax records are available, they should be examined with skepticism, because Chinese American operators tended to practice "creative bookkeeping" when it came to reporting revenues, expenses, and other information. It must be pointed out that such practices have never been exclusive to any particular business or group of people, as made evident by history and recent events. "Creative bookkeeping/accounting" or "cooking the books," from small mom-and-pop businesses to large multinational corporations, has always been more prevalent than the general population thinks.

If documentary evidence is unavailable or unreliable for analysis, then how can the claim that Chinese American supermarkets were prominent operations be substantiated? Basically, it was common knowledge among the people in the industry that they were leaders during the period under study. The claim relies on anecdotal and empirical evidence. Grocery shoppers will point out the ubiquity of the supermarkets. Merchandise vendors and truck drivers for grocery, meat, produce, or dairy wholesale orders will say that generally they delivered more products to the Chinese American supermarkets than to their nearby competitors. Product salesmen who were familiar with the business of competing supermarkets because of their regular contacts with them commented frequently about the higher sales volume of Chinese American supermarkets when compared to their competition. And at any location where supermarkets operated by a national company, local chain, and Chinese Americans competed directly against each other, often it was the national company or local chain that first went out of business. But more important in this study is understanding how Chinese Americans began their supermarkets, what led to their prominence, and why they are no longer in business. Getting the answers to these questions requires another approach.

Details and nuances must therefore come primarily from the owners or partners themselves, their immediate heirs who worked closely with them, and from those associated with the operations, the store employees, product salesmen, and union representatives. But most of these people have passed away, taking with them their experiences. And the majority of the surviving ones are in their seventies or older. Therefore, the history of the Chinese American supermarkets takes on a sense of urgency if these prominent enterprises and the people who operated and worked in them are not to remain primarily a notation in historical writings.

The principal material for this history came from oral interviews of the former owners, partners, and employees. But relying on oral interviews, especially when the interviewees were elderly, had its shortcomings. Memories were faded, selective, and colored, and details were forgotten or confused. Hence, recollections had to be analyzed with reservation, and follow-up interviews were conducted to clarify information and retrieve overlooked points. It was often possible to verify an interviewee's account with reference material—directories, newspaper advertisements, and journal articles—and with information drawn from other interviewees. Accounts were further measured against the broader context in which they occurred to test for plausibility. Ultimately, even if the particulars of the stories were somewhat embellished, inaccurate, or incomplete, they were not as important as the indelible contours of history the interviewees recalled. Although a useful number participated, some former supermarket owners, partners, and employees who would have contributed greatly to this study did not want to be interviewed. The past was not something about which they wanted to reminisce. The reasons will become apparent as the narratives unfold. Those who did participate were enthusiastic and candid, even though they were queried repeatedly and sometimes relentlessly for details.

The owners, partners, employees, and salesmen interviewed and the supermarkets studied were representative, serving to elucidate the workings of various operations and the socioeconomic context in which they occurred. This study was not intended to be a directory that lists all the past and present Chinese American–owned grocery stores and supermarkets in Northern California, Southern California, Arizona, Texas, or anywhere else in the United States. To have done so would have been tedious, to say the least. Nor was this study intended to be a celebration of "Who's Who" in Chinese America, which would have interested mostly those in the ethnic community. Instead, this study is meant to present a history of a business phenomenon that heretofore has never been examined. Hopefully, it will serve as an impetus and reference for similar research.

1 / Supermarkets

SUPERMARKETS ARE SO PROSAIC and ubiquitous that historians have largely ignored them as institutions worthy of study. This is a serious oversight, because supermarkets are barometers of the local communities in which they do business. Supermarkets reflect their communities' status, developing and evolving in step with local socioeconomic conditions. They fulfill the needs and desires of customers, and sometimes create them.

During the two decades following World War II, which were characterized by the explosive growth of families and suburbs, shopping in a supermarket was one of the duties of the exemplary housewife and mother. Food from the supermarket was the nucleus of the family dinner. Supermarkets became social gathering-places of the neighborhoods in which they were located, places where shoppers often ran into their neighbors and friends. Shoppers purchased an increasing variety and quality of products made available by new technology. Supermarkets, in the meantime, continued to expand to accommodate new products and services. In sum, the history of supermarkets is as much a study about the communities in which they operate as about the industry itself.

It was through the operation of supermarkets that Chinese Americans in Northern California quickly became part of the mainstream economy and gradually became part of the mainstream society. The supermarket was an American phenomenon that Chinese Americans opportunistically seized during the industry's early development. They were able to do so because of a combination of fortuitous and propitious factors. Their supermarkets were not very different from their competitors. Chinese American operators of supermarkets were not trendsetters, but astute followers of the industry's standards and innovations. They selectively adopted management and merchandising methods and spent only enough capital on equipment to meet basic needs, increase sales volume, and beat or match the competition. They had one chief advantage that their competition did not have: low-cost labor. It resulted from labor practices based on employer-employee mutual obligations carried over from the old world. The operation of their supermarkets was the quintessential combination of Eastern and Western business practices, by which they were able to reap very good profits. Before narrating their history, highlighting the emergence and growth of the supermarket industry will illuminate the road markers that Chinese Americans followed.

COMING TOGETHER

Although the supermarket was not a completely innovative enterprise, all of its components came together in 1930. Until then, separate small stores made up the bulk of food retailing: stores selling only groceries, meat and seafood markets, confectioneries, bakeries, fruit and vegetable markets, delicatessens, and dairy stores. These food stores were located close to the customer and offered a variety of services such as credit and delivery. There were already chain stores, which were comprised of a group of stores under common ownership with centralized and standardized management. Located in city neighborhoods, chain stores were spreading, but they were small and often one-person operations. The trend toward combination stores was well under way by 1929, but these stores, which were created by joining two or more specialty stores like grocery and meat, represented only about one-fifth of all food stores.

During the 1920s, parts of the supermarket concept were used in many areas of the country. Cash-and-carry, for example, was rapidly replacing credit and delivery as a more expedient and less expensive means for grocery purchasing by customers. Self-service, standardization, and simplification were practices that were synonymous with the Piggly Wiggly chain, which was founded in Memphis, Tennessee, in 1916. "Drive-in markets," stores where customers drove their automobiles right up to the buildings and parked in free parking spaces, were common in the West and Southwest. The concept of one-stop shopping, which was based on large city markets that had separate retailers selling specific foods under the same roof, was gaining popularity among shoppers. Selling non-food products was a business identified with the general store, which also did approximately 60 percent of its sales volume in food products.[1] Except for free parking, the objectives of these retailing methods were to reduce operating costs and selling prices, and consequently to bring in more customers and increase sales. During the Depression era, combining these features was a good business strategy because shoppers were looking for stores that offered low prices.

In 1930, in Jamaica, Long Island, Michael J. Cullen opened what the public called a "warehouse grocery" in an abandoned garage with all the elements that defined a supermarket. He had proposed his retailing concepts to his previous employers, Kroger Grocery & Baking Company and A & P, but his ideas were rejected as impractical because they were untested. Cullen had suggested that they open a large no-frills store in a low-rent district on the outskirts of town to cut operating costs, a store that would symbolize bargain prices and offer free parking. He also favored selling national brands at cost and at low markups, which would yield razor-thin profit margins but would attract crowds of shoppers. To make it a complete one-stop shopping store, concessionaires would sell meat, produce, dairy, deli, and household items. Lastly, he wanted to use bold price-oriented advertising to solicit customers. Although his ideas were initially rejected, he was able to apply them in his own store. Other entrepreneurs quickly followed suit, and the age of the supermarket began.[2]

Reflecting the mood of the Depression era, the interior of these new supermarkets typically had crude floors, bare ceilings, no partitions, unpainted fixtures, glaring lights, gaudy signs, and merchandise piled everywhere. One of the earliest supermarkets was the Big Bear Store, which opened in a former automobile factory in Elizabeth, New Jersey, in December 1932, amidst aggressive ads and promotions.[3] These new stores' reduced selling prices were formidable when compared with established food retailers. This was reflected in their promotional names on signs on the front of the stores and in newspaper advertisements; for example, King Kullen the Price Wrecker and Big Bear the Price Crusher.[4]

Prior to 1930, some of the supermarket concepts used in the East were in development in Texas and Southern California. Besides the drive-in markets, there were self-service food stores in which independent concessionaires operated under a central management. The earliest documented self-service food store was the Groceteria of Los Angeles, founded in 1915 by Albert Gerrard. He would later open the Alpha-Beta stores, in which grocery items were arranged alphabetically to help shoppers find items. Another self-service store in downtown Los Angeles was Ralph's Grocery Company, which by 1929 had grown to sixteen large, attractive supermarkets. Established in 1872, the company built a flourishing business by offering clerk-service and delivery, but began converting to self-service in 1926, when it recognized self-service's advantages, chief of which was lower labor costs. It was about this time, the late 1920s, that the term "supermarket" first became associated with the large self-service food stores. It was a marketing invention that through usage became synonymous with this type of food retailing. In 1933, William H. Albers founded Albers Super Market, formally adopting the appellation "super-market" for the first time.[5]

Drive-in markets appeared about 1925 and were located primarily in the outlying areas of Los Angeles and in some of its neighborhoods. A drive-in market was comprised of a group of food stores in a one-story building with parking immediately adjacent. Although each of the food stores was individually owned and operated, shoppers regarded the large market as a single entity. The development of the drive-in market can be attributed to at least two factors. First, expansive Los Angeles did not have a good public transportation system, which forced individuals to use private automobiles to get about and go shopping. This fact was reflected by a higher percentage of automobile ownership among its population than the national average. The other factor was the limited and restricted parking in Los Angeles's central business district. This prompted entrepreneurs to build stores in outlying areas where land was plentiful and cheap, and where space was available for parking.[6]

During the 1930s, economic progress within the country was generally slow and sporadic. There were national trends, however, that affected the development of the supermarket. The number of trucks and automobiles on the road was increasing, as was the number of miles of roads. This trend made local products available to distant markets and national products available to local markets, and made it possible for shoppers to travel to out-of-the-way supermarkets to get the best bargains. The radio became a common fixture in the home; consequently, commercials on the radio increased the awareness of and the demand for national brands which supermarkets readily stocked. Advertisements in mass-circulation magazines rendered the same results. By the mid-1930s, competition among local newspapers heightened due to the availability of news wire services. This prompted the newspapers to offer additional spreads such as "food day" editions, which published recipes, food buying suggestions, and supermarket advertisements. More and more homes were wired to electricity, enabling occupants to use household appliances such as refrigerators, irons, mixers, and clothes washers, which gradually became necessities rather than luxuries. These appliances in turn stimulated the development of and demand for new grocery products and necessitated the enlargement of the kitchen space, which encouraged the family to buy more on shopping trips and allowed them to stock up. Thus, supermarkets were destined to become larger and larger to accommodate more products as well as more customers.[7]

The influence the automobile had on the shopping habits of customers and on the development of supermarkets was considerable. Because the automobile made going to the store easier, shoppers went more often. With more exposure to merchandise, shoppers were more likely to make impulse purchases and large purchases. Because of large purchases, the stores' cost-effectiveness increased, prompting management to stock more merchandise and a greater variety of merchandise. Since the automobile enabled shoppers to travel to different and distant stores to get the best bargains, it helped increase the competition among food retailers as they fought for the same customers. Store management had to plan for weekly sales and labor costs as customers shopped throughout the week. Finally, the automobile made the size and layout of parking lots increasingly important in the planning of supermarket construction or enlargement.[8]

GROWTH AND DEVELOPMENT

As the number of supermarkets grew, small independent grocery stores and combination stores found themselves increasingly squeezed between the large food markets and the powerful chain stores. While some went out of business, others expanded and became supermarkets on their own. Often it was the wholesale food distributors who helped bring these small grocery stores and combination stores into the supermarket business. Small operators usually did not have the expertise or resources to do it on their own, but wholesalers were usually willing to help finance expansions and devise merchandising strategies. Without a doubt the wholesalers were looking after their own interests in the wholesale food trade, supplying exclusively their merchandise to the new supermarkets. These affiliations were typical of 1930s wholesale-retail alliances or associations, which increased and strengthened in future years. When the vast explosion in supermarkets began in the 1950s, many small independent operations were thus able to expand and keep pace as supermarkets.[9] If small independent operations did not become large supermarkets, they converted into non-super combination markets, or "superettes," which were similar to supermarkets but more modest in scale. They managed to remain profitable by reducing their operating expenses, largely because wholesalers let them purchase products at a small percentage above what they charged alliance members. In addition, many superettes found niches in local markets that big companies considered unprofitable for their own operations.[10]

The early supermarkets were successful primarily because they sold groceries at 8 to 15 percent below the price level of the traditional service grocery store. Plain no-frills interiors and self-service along with low rent and overhead allowed for low prices that attracted customers, but these stores also tended to be disorderly and confusing. Its critics, for example, called the Big Bear Store in New Jersey a massive 50,000–square-feet "circus-like emporium."[11] The experiments in the early 1930s of converting abandoned warehouses, factories, garages, and other large buildings into supermarket operations were soon discontinued in favor of smaller, more orderly supermarkets. Starting in 1935, supermarkets that were attractive inside and outside were opened, and soon the "cheapy" lost favor among shoppers. With the concept of the supermarket proven sound, new capital began flowing into the retail food industry and attractive supermarkets began multiplying in better locations with larger investments in equipment and buildings.[12]

National supermarket chains began laying out model floor plans that illustrated the location of work areas as well as the general arrangement of the sales floor. The next generation of supermarkets was planned from the ground up, starting with parking lot layouts and contemporary designs for the exterior of the buildings. Interiors were designed for space and order. Better refrigeration and freezer equipment, new prepackaging materials like cellophane, and improved lighting, shelving, and signs were used. The sales of meat, produce, dairy, bakery, and non-food products, which in the past were handled by separate concessionaires in the earlier supermarkets, were consolidated into the grocery operation, allowing shoppers to purchase all items at one checkout stand for their convenience. This advanced the concept of customer self-service while supermarkets benefited from lower overhead and increased efficiency and profitability. These aims were further maximized by an innovation that came into widespread use by the late 1930s, the grocery cart. The grocery cart enabled shoppers to carry more items than the handheld "market baskets" that were commonly used in earlier stores, and consequently, supermarkets gained grocery sales.[13]

Like most other sectors of the domestic economy, supermarket development and expansion were very limited during wartime. In 1941 and early 1942, however, the number of supermarkets increased by about two thousand when many chains and independents tried to beat the impending building restrictions as the country was entering World War II. During the war, food retailers enjoyed robust business, selling nearly everything they stocked because product shortages and rationing pushed up demand and prompted hoarding. This did not, however, mean that all supermarkets reaped huge profits. The percentage of increase in sales for independents was double that of the chains. Under closer government control than independents, the chains could not expand to compete because of material and labor shortages, and their buying power was reduced because of product shortages and price controls.

The chains also had serious labor shortages when many of their male employees entered the armed forces or went to work for better wages in defense plants. The independents, on the other hand, were less closely monitored, which afforded them more opportunities to evade regulations. They were able to develop a "gray market" for products by maintaining a close if not surreptitious wholesale-retail customer relationship. The independents were also more flexible during labor shortages because owners or managers could use their family members to work or could employ less qualified workers, such as retired people, to work part time. Despite the advantages of the independents, the chains did increase sales and profits, and the industry as a whole emerged from the war period in very good condition.[14]

There were a few notable legacies from the war period. Because of the scarce supply of food products and price controls, stores began selling nonfood items such as health and beauty aids and general merchandise to supplement their sales volume. These additions were successful in profits and customer acceptance, and were retained after the war. Stores also began selling more national-brand products than private-brand products because the former returned higher profits and were more available than the latter. Consequently, national brands made substantial gains in market share as customers increasingly shopped for those products. Lastly, the male labor shortages led to an increase in the number of women employed in the retail food industry, an inroad first witnessed at the checkout counter and that quickly became standard practice.[15]

POSTWAR DEVELOPMENTS

When the country reverted back to a peacetime economy, pent-up consumer demand ignited an economic explosion. Consumers went on a buying spree using their savings accumulated from years of labor and rationing. The boom in spending was fueled further by an enormous growth in the population. This was the beginning of good times for the supermarkets. With the experimental phase over and the modern supermarket defined, independent and chain operators began constructing in earnest new stores with larger floor space and parking facilities. Many older stores were remodeled. The national chains had already closed hundreds of small clerk-service stores in the prewar years, and thousands of small, family-owned grocery stores had closed during the war when the head of the family left to join the war effort. In other words, the country was going supermarket shopping.[16]

In the early 1950s, suburbs sprouted around every urban center in America, helping to relieve the housing shortage that resulted when American veterans looked to settle down and raise families. The availability of home mortgages with small down payments and low interest rates assisted young families in purchasing their first single-family houses in suburban developments such as Levittowns. These types of developments offered new, spacious, and affordable mass-produced dwellings in planned communities located away from aging, congested, and expensive central cities. The exodus to suburbia was helped by a tremendous increase in automobile ownership and by an extensive highway building program throughout the country. By 1960, for example, at least four out of five households had an automobile.[17]

The migration of people usually took the general direction of north to south and east to west, as did the relocation of old industrial and manufacturing plants and the location of new ones. Along with housing developments, shopping centers were built, usually around a new supermarket. Of course, it was good business acumen to follow the population movement, but builders of shopping centers and supermarkets were also able to take advantage of the low-cost land and less restrictive building ordinances of unincorporated areas.

Generally, there were three types of shopping centers. The smallest was the neighborhood type, which had a maximum of ten stores on five to ten acres with one major store, usually a large supermarket, to attract shoppers. The second type was the intermediate community shopping center, which included an additional large retail outlet, often a small department store. This ten- to fifteen-acre development needed at least five thousand families for support. The third type was a regional center, which had a minimum of thirty-five acres serving a hundred thousand people. Although supermarkets were everywhere, they tended to be concentrated in the growth areas of Arizona, California, Colorado, Florida, Louisiana, and Nevada, where they accounted for more than 70 percent of the grocery sales.[18]

Just as the supermarket became standardized in the retail food industry, so did the way of life for middle-class Americans in their suburbs. The 1950s may be stereotypically but correctly described as a period of conformity and consumerism for the millions of people who lived in mass housing, bought from mass markets, and worked in mass corporations. Two of the most distinctive aspects of this period affecting the development of the supermarket were the "baby boom" and "domesticity." The surge in the birth of babies in the 1950s contributed to a national population increase of about 30 million, a change of approximately 18 percent from 1950 to 1960. In California, the population rose about 5 million, a change of approximately 48 percent from 1950 to 1960. This was due to an increase in migration into the state as well as more births. Among the 15,717,204 residents in California, over 34 percent were age eighteen years and under, which translated to a large expenditure of family income on food for growing families.[19]

Closely related to this demographic phenomenon was the exultation of motherhood. The media glorified the role of the dedicated housewife at home with her children. Print and radio advertisements and television programs often pictured the ideal mother in the kitchen. Accordingly, one of the chores that fulfilled this role for the housewife was shopping in the supermarket for her family. Furthermore, supermarket operators themselves promoted the shopping center and the stores in them as a social gathering-place for the American family to increase business. Hence, the 1950s were times of growth and prosperity for supermarkets. From 1950 to 1958, for example, the number of supermarkets increased from 14,217 to 20,413, a 43 percent change. Although they represented only 5.5 percent of all food stores, their sales accounted for 57 percent of the total food sales in the country.[20]

In addition to suburbanization, population growth, and idealization, there were other factors that contributed to the growth and prosperity of supermarkets. Notable was the 80 percent increase in the median income for families and individuals from 1950 to 1960.[21] This enabled people to spend more money, and food stores captured a large portion of it, mostly through the sale of costlier food items and nonfood merchandise. Since the late 1920s, there had been a shift in the dietary habits of Americans from less expensive bulk foods, such as potatoes and grain products, toward more expensive leafy green vegetables, fresh fruits, and meat and dairy products. This change, plus an increase in sales volume of those products, benefited the supermarket because these products netted larger profit margins. Other profitable products that were amply stocked and highly promoted in supermarkets included convenient ready-to-eat foods, such as baby food in jars and frozen foods developed from new manufacturing and processing techniques. In addition to the fact that new products required more space for display, changes in packaging, such as different sized packaging and multiple packaging, also increased the number of products in the store. These developments required stores to carry larger inventories and put sizable investments in refrigeration and freezer equipment, all of which benefited mainly the larger supermarkets rather than the smaller operations, which generally lacked space and financial resources.[22]

SUPERMARKET OPERATIONS

Like mass-produced suburban communities, supermarket designs were based on simple, functional designs that could be constructed quickly. But the stores were expensive to build. Electrical systems, specialized lighting, and large refrigeration and freezer units were some of the factors that drove the cost of building a new supermarket dramatically up from prewar days. Independent operators were behind in the race to build modern supermarkets, but the support and guidance of food wholesalers bolstered the independent segment of the business. This maintained a competitive balance between the chains and independents. The alliance between wholesalers and independent retailers enabled the latter to contract lower wholesale prices, which were passed on to customers. It also enabled retailers to benefit from up-to-date planning, store financing, central accounting, and cooperative advertising, which were mostly managed by the wholesalers, who had greater expertise and resources.[23]

As more supermarkets were built with standardized features, the customer's decision about which one to patronize was determined more by prices than by an allegiance to a specific chain or independent operation, notwithstanding convenient location. Price was a tenuous factor for supermarket management when formulating strategies to secure customer loyalty. There were other shopping trends which management had to take into account. Similar to the pre-supermarket days, customers started to patronize food stores less frequently. More people shopped just once a week, usually on Friday or Saturday. Consequently, their expenditure per visit increased substantially. Furthermore, people were willing to travel farther to shop. And where people shopped was greatly influenced by sales advertisements in newspapers, by means of which customers could compare prices. In general, shoppers tended to go to those stores that they believed would give them the best deal in making all of their purchases. In their weekly advertisements, supermarkets often featured "loss leaders," products that sold at or below cost for the sole purpose of attracting customers. But it was not unusual for shoppers to visit more than one supermarket to stock up on bargain items. Supermarket operators tried to counter this activity by attractively and strategically displaying high-profit products to stimulate impulse buying—the purchasing of items that customers did not intend to buy—as customers entered and navigated the store for sale items.[24]

Shoppers still gave consideration to a supermarket's conveniences when making their decisions about where to shop, features that especially enhanced self-service shopping. They presumed correctly that self-service reduced a supermarket's operating cost, which in turn was passed on to them. For a supermarket, lower prices attracted customers, which helped to increase its competitiveness. With some exceptions, supermarkets were completely self-service by 1960, when meat departments converted. Grocers also turned to other areas of the store to attract customers. A source of irritation for customers was waiting in long lines at the checkout counters. To speed up checkouts, the counters became mechanized. For additional efficiency and convenience, the stores employed clerks whose primary duties involved bagging groceries and carrying them to the customers' automobiles.[25]

In the operation of a supermarket, the essential emphasis was on sales volume. A supermarket's low prices necessitated a minimum level or better in sales volume to compensate for small gross-margin mark-ups and for even much smaller net profits. In addition, competition forced supermarkets to continuously invest capital to upgrade their equipment and to reorganize their operations, preventing most supermarkets from operating at fixed levels for long periods, which would yield the greatest profit return. Hence, supermarkets were constantly seeking ways to maximize their sales volume, minimize wholesale prices, and optimize their operations to increase profits, remain competitive, or just to survive. The various techniques used to increase sales volume have been mentioned earlier: price appeal, display techniques, self-service, attractive and convenient facilities, advertising and promotion, large but well-managed inventories, and diversified lines of merchandise.[26] But sales volume, no matter how high, became pointless if supermarkets did not turn a profit because of excessive sales of "loss leaders" and the insufficient sales of regular-price merchandise.

The chain, large independent, and small independent supermarkets utilized various means to minimize wholesale prices. Chain supermarkets and large independent supermarkets integrated their wholesale-retail operations by performing more wholesale functions and engaging in some manufacturing capacities. As a result, their merchandise cost less than that of small independent supermarkets that purchased from regular wholesalers. In the extremely competitive, high-volume, and small-profit margin supermarket business, even a 10–cent price advantage on a case of tomato catsup, for example, was significant. Small independent supermarkets reduced their wholesale prices by joining voluntary or cooperative wholesale-retail alliances to procure merchandise at reduced prices. As mentioned earlier, depending upon the relationships, additional benefits for the small independent supermarkets were available from the wholesalers.[27]

There were basically two types of buying affiliations. One was the wholesaler-sponsored voluntary association, which was owned by its wholesale and retail members. It managed many activities, including contracting with manufacturers to pack merchandise for its wholesalers, making large purchases from manufacturers, and arranging discounts for retail members. The largest of these affiliations was the Independent Grocers Alliance of America, commonly referred to as IGA. The other principal buying affiliation was the retail-sponsored cooperative association, in which a group of retailers formed a cooperative to purchase some or all of their common merchandise from wholesalers. In some cases, the cooperative owned and operated its own warehouse; for example, United Grocers of Sacramento. Members purchased merchandise at cost, plus an association fee and transportation expense.[28]

To optimize supermarket operations, management diligently tried to reduce expenses. The major expenses of supermarkets were payroll, salaries, rent or real estate costs, advertising, and store supplies. But management invariably targeted payroll because the other costs tended to be fixed or much less adjustable in the short term. In the supermarket business, big profits or losses could occur quickly from small adjustments. Cutting labor costs took into account the amount of business projected for a coming period, the result of which was often contingent upon what the competition was doing. With the cost set, a supermarket's profit was realized when the sales volume exceeded the break-even point. As sales rose, the profit percentage and the absolute dollar profit increased until some additional costs incurred.[29]

COMPETITIVE PRESSURES

Supermarkets continued to prosper and expand in the 1960s because of a healthy economy and a growing population, but the decade ended with increasingly fierce competition. The average number of items carried by supermarkets grew from 5,900 in 1960 to 7,800 in 1970 as new products filled the shelves. The stores became larger, with the space of the sales floor ranging from 16,000 to 20,000 square feet and some reaching 30,000 square feet. The "standard" model store gave way to supermarkets that were carefully planned for specific neighborhoods, appealing to particular types of customers. New departments such as service bakeries, delicatessens, and prescription drug counters were added to the typical supermarket to cater to the busy lifestyles of families with working spouses and large disposable incomes, saving them time and labor. Installing larger-capacity refrigeration and freezer units became necessary as more convenience food products came into market. All of these changes, of course, required considerable investments, which the chain and large independent operations usually had the means to do. Older and smaller supermarkets, on the other hand, acutely felt the competitive pressures because they were unable or unwilling to change due to the lack of resources, expertise, or other reasons.[30]

The 1960s ended with a notable trend. National chain companies led discounting on a total-store scale, reducing overall price margins by 2.5 to 3.0 percentage points to attract more customers and to retain their shopping loyalty. The result was a greater growth in sales for the chains compared with independents. Independents, on the other hand, were not able or willing to discount their products as rapidly as the chains. They lacked the managerial and technical expertise for a transition of such magnitude. Because they had exceptional sales and profits in previous years, some came to believe that discounting was not an immediate concern. Independents that did discount had to rely almost totally on wholesalers to plan and execute the selective price reductions.[31]

Technological advancements and government regulatory changes benefited both supermarkets and shoppers. The use of computers in data processing cut costs in operations at the retail level as well as food distribution in the wholesale level, enabling the whole system to run more efficiently. Shelf space, for example, was evaluated and assigned on an item-by-item basis. Government regulations required unit pricing, open code dating, and other measures that provided consumers with relevant shopping information. Supermarkets initially resisted these impositions, citing increased costs to implement them, but when consumers responded favorably, supermarkets embraced the regulations.[32] But as progressive as these technologies and measures were, they necessitated large investments. The vicissitudes of the retail food business, especially for small independent supermarkets, did not guarantee their cost-effectiveness. Over time, however, stores that invested in new technologies usually found their business firm, if not more profitable; stores that did not invest usually encountered difficult times. Nevertheless, there were some small independent supermarkets that remained profitable because they found niches in local markets that did not demand the latest supermarket trends.

Prior to the 1960s, companies opened stores in unserved locales or remodeled smaller stores that still had good business. Direct supermarket-to-supermarket competition was generally avoided because of easy opportunities. After years of building, however, nearly every community had a supermarket, saturating the markets and limiting the possibilities for expansion. The companies then started competing directly with one another, opening supermarkets at the same locations.[33] This new competition tended to favor the larger companies. Some supermarkets, however, did not face any direct competition because their local markets were too small or their locations offered limited potential for other companies. These stores were usually located in old or impoverished neighborhoods.

Traditionally, company earnings and creditors' capital financed the building of new supermarkets. As supermarkets became larger, borrowing became
the principal means of financing. This was possible largely because a bigger
percentage of the total assets of the supermarket was now in fixed assets such
as equipment and building, which was preferred collateral for creditors, rather
than in inventory, as was common in the past.[34] Inasmuch as good profits
encouraged companies to expand, expansion was necessary to continue
steady profits in the high-volume-sensitive industry. In expansion, large companies had an inherent advantage over small ones in that they were able to
spread the liabilities of their new or unprofitable operations over more outlets and over a wider geographical area until those operations became
profitable or had to close. Accordingly, their ability to borrow money was
easier and cheaper than that of small companies. Furthermore, the rates they
paid for capital were less than the profits that accrued from the use of the
capital. Hence, the more profits the company made, the cheaper the loan. In
large companies, the amount of the creditors' capital was often greater than
the owners' or shareholders' stake. And large companies had more marketable
securities to acquire additional capital. In contrast, small companies found
it difficult to secure outside capital, especially when interest rates were high
and rising, which forced them to rely primarily on retained earnings to open
new supermarkets.[35]

When small companies, particularly local chain operations, wanted to lease
sites in shopping centers to open new supermarkets, they found it nearly
impossible. The huge insurance companies that invested in the development
of most prime-location shopping centers wanted national or regional chain
supermarket companies as tenants under long-term contracts. Consequently,
small local chain companies were usually shut out by leasing practices from
expanding into preferred shopping centers. In addition, the economy-of-scale
favored the expansion of national chain and regional chain companies. They
could better utilize their warehouses, transportation equipment, and manufacturing facilities by spreading their costs over many outlets acquired
through building, acquisition, or merger. A simple example of economy-of-
scale was the spreading of their weekly newspaper advertising costs over many
stores. In sum, as the supermarket industry progressed, everything appeared
to be stacked against smaller companies, the small local chain as well as the
independent. The trend was toward bigger in terms of store size, sales volume, and number of stores, imparting credence to the adage "big begets big."[36]

In Northern California, the supermarket business reflected the national
trends of the industry, and more. The 1970s and 1980s witnessed what appeared

to be frantic attempts to capture shoppers' patronage amid the vicissitudes of local economic and market conditions. National and local companies tried a variety of means to hold onto their regular customers as well as to bring in new ones. Some were successful, while others proved ineffective and faded within a short period.

National chain companies offered total-store discounts and a moderate price decrease on all merchandise. This became one of the most successful marketing strategies and was soon copied by most competitors. National chain companies were able to implement total-store discounts because of their access to financial resources, which were used to purchase or lease expensive computers. Closely related to the discount method, which came and went depending upon the economy, was the warehouse shopping experience, in which customers shopped from a reduced variety of deeply discounted merchandise and bagged their purchases themselves.

On the other end of the cost scale, some local companies revived the awarding of savings stamps for purchases, but the use of premiums was not effective. A short-term promotion that many stores used was the sale of discounted non-food merchandise, usually dishes or kitchenware, when customers made large purchases. Small local chain and independent companies offered raffles and in-store coupons to their customers, an inexpensive strategy. Many of the small companies also continued to advertise "loss leaders" in their weekly advertisements in newspapers to distinguish themselves from other grocers. National chain and large local companies, on the other hand, promoted their numerous departments, abundant selection of merchandise, and customer services that only they could afford and offer to shoppers.

The vast complexity, high capitalization, rapid changes, and intense competition in the supermarket industry were very apparent by the end of the 1970s. These factors eventually took a toll on many small and large companies, including nearly all of the Chinese American supermarkets that were major competitors in Northern California. In the early years of the supermarket industry, Chinese American operators were able to implement many successful methods of management and merchandising because their operations were simple and inexpensive. They opened stores in large low-rent buildings located away from urban centers and offered one-stop shopping that included meat, produce, and dairy as well as national brand-name groceries. They used bold price-oriented advertising to bring in customers. They formed cooperatives to lower purchasing costs from wholesalers and to share advertising costs. During the postwar period, they imitated the layout of national chain supermarkets in planning, constructing, and equipping their stores. But what distinguished Chinese Americans' supermarkets from their competitors were their lower selling prices, which resulted from lower labor costs. Combined with an expanding customer base, it was no wonder that Chinese American supermarkets were highly competitive and profitable in the 1950s and 1960s. During subsequent decades, however, they gradually lost their competitiveness to the national chain and large local chain companies. Unwilling or unable to keep up, Chinese American operators began selling or closing their old supermarkets. The few remaining operators developed small or medium-sized shopping centers, in which they located their supermarkets, or became tenants in new shopping centers in new suburbs. But most of these shopping centers were not at prime locations. Like their predecessors, they eventually succumbed to the costs, changes, and competition in the industry.

2 / Community, Employment, and Enterprise

CHINESE AMERICANS IN SACRAMENTO and other Northern California communities lived fairly quiet lives from the 1930s to the mid-1960s. Their population increased slowly because of disproportionate gender ratios and restrictive immigration laws, and then rose quickly in the years following World War II, primarily because of changes to these social and statutory checks. Other than political activities in support of the Chinese's effort to fight the Japanese invasion of China during the 1930s and 1940s, Chinese Americans may be noted for their initiatives and efforts to achieve economic advancement, seizing business opportunities and building upon them. The economic foundations upon which future generations would support themselves in their climb up the socioeconomic ladder were laid by immigrants who settled and invested for a future in America rather than by sojourners who clung to their homeland ways. The disposition of the latter may be explained in part by their wariness of anti-immigration statutes that could be used to deport them and their cognizance of the naturalization laws that kept them outside of mainstream society. These laws reminded them daily of the need to maintain ethnic solidarity and traditions, which had helped them endure the hostilities of the past. Later immigrants and their families also utilized old-world practices, however, from which they benefited.

Later generations of Chinese Americans would seek assimilation into the greater community, but prior to the mid-1960s, the dominant population generally did not want them in their neighborhoods and workplaces. Yet there were exceptions. Most Chinese Americans in Sacramento lived within a defined area where they eked out a livelihood in the few occupations and businesses available to them. Their coworkers, employers, or clientele were usually other Chinese Americans. But others in the city and throughout Northern California's rural communities resided in neighborhoods where they established family businesses catering to non-Chinese clienteles. While laundries and restaurants were common, some families operated small grocery stores, which they would later expand into supermarkets and chain operations. Usually the quarters behind or above their businesses served as their residences. Their children attended nearby schools, and they seldom left their businesses or households except to travel within their community or to another community to socialize with others like themselves. In other words, these families did not live and work in homogeneous ethnic enclaves. While many Chinese Americans endured prejudice, discrimination, and segregation, others did not. Some elderly Chinese Americans recalled that everyone got along in their communities or neighborhoods, but that venturing beyond familiar territory was sometimes an ordeal. Basically, the socioeconomic experiences of Chinese Americans depended largely on where they lived. Thus, it is only safe to say that their experiences were mixed.

After the passage of anti-immigration laws that restricted their immigration and reduced their population, Chinese Americans gradually ceased being primary scapegoats for politicians, labor unions, and competing businessmen. Japanese American immigrants supplanted them as Asian targets of political and economic campaigns in California. Aside from some biographies, very little has been written about the socioeconomic institutions of Chinese Americans in Sacramento and other Northern California communities from the 1930s to the mid-1960s. A summary about the people and their communities, employment, and enterprises during this period is in order to understand the circumstances in which Chinese American supermarkets developed and prospered.

STATISTICAL PROFILE

According to U.S. Census reports, the Chinese American population in California, including native- and foreign-born, increased from 37,361 in 1930 to 58,324 in 1950. The 1960 census recorded a population of 95,600, a large gain that can be attributed primarily to the increased immigration of Chinese females allowed under an amendment to the 1945 War Brides Act, which consequently increased the number of families and birth of children. The effect of internal migration into the state was minimal, accounting for less than 10 percent of the total population.[1] The population in Sacramento County was 2,792 in 1930, 3,852 in 1950, and 6,457 in 1960, following the trend in the state.[2] At best, these figures show statistical "snapshots" without describing the dynamics of the population.

Additional data helps explain the development of the Chinese American community, revealing their gender ratio, places of residency, and occupational and economic characteristics. As the population rose, the ratio of males to females became increasingly balanced due to an increase in the immigration of females and birth of female infants. The number of males per one hundred females in California, for example, was 298.6 in 1930, 161.9 in 1950, and 127.8 in 1960. In the city and county of Sacramento, however, the ratios were more balanced: for example, 234.0 in 1930 for the city and 147.7 in 1950 for the county.[3] The increasing number of females to males indicated an increasing number of females available for marriage. The smaller ratio of males to females in the city and county of Sacramento compared to the state average also suggests that there was a smaller sojourner population in the Sacramento area. Sizable numbers of sojourners were usually found in large Chinatowns and in farming communities, the first of which the city did not have and the second of which the county did have. This conclusion is supported by the slightly higher male-to-female ratio in the county than in the city.

Additional figures point to the fact that there were a large number of males and females of childbearing age and a correspondingly large number of young, American-born children. In other words, there was a trend in the Chinese American community toward marriage, family, and permanent settlement. Although data is not available for 1930 and 1940, the census for the Sacramento metropolitan area in 1950 shows that the predominant age groups for females were ages under 5 years and 20 to 34 years; in 1960, ages under 14 years and 25 to 39 years. Comparatively, the predominant age groups for males in 1950 were under 5 years and 25 to 64 years; in 1960, under 14 years and 30 to 44 years.[4] The large number of children under 14 years of age in 1960 indicates a group that was born in the current and previous decade, characterized by slightly more males than females. The large number of elderly males in 1950 indicates a shrinking vestige of the old sojourner society. In other Northern California areas there were very few statistical details published about Chinese Americans from 1930 to 1960.

IMMIGRANTS

Prior to World War II, many sojourners returned to China, consequently decreasing their numbers in the community. Others who changed their plans and stayed, by choice or necessity, grew old and passed away in America without ever marrying or bringing over their families. Annual reports of the U.S. Immigration Office revealed that from 1903 to 1943 almost twice as many Chinese had departed (90,299) than were admitted (52,561) in the United

States. In that period, there were only seven years in which the number of admittance exceeded the number of departures. There were a few reasons for this trend. The 1882 Chinese Exclusion Law and the 1924 Immigration Act combined to discourage many Chinese from settling permanently, especially when the laws made it difficult, if not impossible, for most of those already in America to send for their wives. Interestingly, the anti-immigration laws had the unanticipated effect of narrowing the gap in the gender ratio. Those who were not married had little chance to marry Chinese women, since there were so few of them in America. In addition, the economic depression of the 1930s discouraged the Chinese from immigrating or staying because it lessened their chances of making a decent living.[5]

The immigration of Chinese, nonetheless, continued. During the early decades of the twentieth century, economic and political disorder in China "pushed" those with the means to leave, and the economic opportunities in America "pulled" those with the ambition to come. To circumvent the immigration laws, immigrants purchased "papers" from American citizens of Chinese ancestry or from Chinese merchants, two groups who were allowed unrestricted entry into the country. Whether born in China or the United States, the children of citizens and merchants received the same privilege. After the 1906 San Francisco earthquake and the ensuing fire that destroyed countless records, many Chinese immigrants seized the opportunity to re-register as U.S. citizens. As citizens they subsequently reported to American authorities that they had fathered numerous children, which may or may not have been true, during their periodic visits to their families in China. The children were usually sons, and the reports created "slots" available for their immigration to the United States. The fathers were thus able to bring their children to America or to sell the slots to those wanting to immigrate. Merchants who left families in China also took advantage of this type of scheme: making periodic trips home, claiming the birth of children, and selling slots. Those who sold slots were often close or distant relatives or friends of buyers from the same or nearby villages or districts. In other words, there was a network in place for immigration to America for those who could afford to buy into the scheme. Those who purchased the slots became "paper sons" or "paper daughters" and entered the country claiming to be the children of citizens or merchants. Thereafter, these immigrants and their descendants, if they decided to settle permanently, would live in America with "paper names." Unlike most of the earlier sojourners who came as laborers, the status of these later immigrants allowed them to reenter America after leaving. By 1920 the majority of young men immigrating to the United States had purchased papers, and they continued to do so until the passage of the 1965 Immigration Act, which greatly increased the number of immigrants allowed into the country. The immigration laws also provided to the wives of merchants the same rights that their husbands had, but not without some difficulty at first in securing them. Until the repeal of the exclusion acts in 1943, the situation for the wives of citizens was inconsistent, "depending upon the exclusion laws, judicial interpretations, and administrative enforcement."[6]

Some bachelor immigrants dutifully returned to their home villages in China, fulfilled marriage contracts their parents had arranged, and reentered the United States to continue earning money. Often these new husbands fathered children during their visits. Some immigrants decided to become permanent residents in America, bringing their families with them or sending for them at a later time. During the time when males far outnumbered females, American-born bachelors were also expected to return to their parents' villages, marry native girls, and bring their wives back to America with them.

The large increase in population during the two decades after 1943 reflected the repeal of the 1882 Chinese Exclusion Law in December of that year and the implementation of a number of special acts after World War II. The repeal did not directly lead to a large increase in immigration because of the standing annual quota for Chinese, a minuscule one hundred and five, but it did grant the right of naturalization for those already in the United States. Many who took advantage of this privilege sponsored others to immigrate, as did Chinese Americans who served in the armed forces during World War II and gained their citizenship. The War Brides Act of December 1945 and "An Act to Place Chinese Wives of American Citizens on a Non-Quota Basis" of August 1946 provided for the admittance of Chinese wives of U.S. citizens under a non-quota basis, resulting in a tremendous immigration of women from 1947 to 1953. In five of those years, women accounted for about 90 percent of Chinese immigrants, most of them as wives. In succeeding years, a variety of other immigration acts facilitated the entry of family members of citizens and of persons in possession of certain skills.[7] A more balanced sex ratio certainly facilitated the formation of family life. Furthermore, the increase in the number of wives contributed to the rise in the birth of children, evident in the large population of young American-born children in the Sacramento area in the 1950s and 1960s.

Before World War II, most of the young men immigrated with the intention of earning money to remit to improve their families' economic situation at home. They hoped to return home with enough money for financial security for themselves and their families, but changing circumstances at home and in America often caused them to alter their plans. Some were unable to earn enough for subsistence let alone for remittance, and subsequently left the United States permanently. Their number was probably not large, since there was a socioeconomic network assisting the newcomer in immigration, housing, and employment. Some sojourners earned just enough money to remit home but not enough to send for their families to settle in America or for them to return to their home in China to retire. They were destined to remain in the United States for the rest of their lives to toil to help support those at home. Some sojourners saved what they thought was enough money and returned home, but ended up reentering the United States to earn money again after their savings ran out. Undoubtedly, there were some young men who immigrated with the intention of settling permanently.

How many returned home, changed plans, or settled permanently remains unknown. There are no reports or surveys available, only biographies and anecdotes to recount the numerous varieties of experiences. But America's opportunities for economic betterment certainly prompted many Chinese to immigrate. If these immigrants were successful through hard work and good luck, they had many options available to them, including family life and permanent settlement in America.

Most of the immigrants who settled in Sacramento and many in other Northern California communities came from very impoverished villages in the Sze Yup (four districts) region, located in the southwestern part of the Pearl River Delta in the Guangdong (Kwangtung) Province of southeast China. (A district is comparable to a county in the United States.) They maintained cultural solidarity through their family, district associations, and a strong socioeconomic network established through decades of immigrant experience in "Gold Mountain" (America). Up until the mid-1960s, when a flood of immigrants from Hong Kong and other parts of China arrived, more than 80 percent of the Chinese Americans in Sacramento could trace their roots back to the Sze Yup region, in particular the Toishan and Hoiping districts. The dialect commonly spoken in Sacramento originated from these two districts.

The large number of Chinese Americans in Northern California and their collective resources made a difference in the competitiveness of their businesses against national and local companies in terms of the availability of labor and capital. Individually, their lives of endless toiling on farms or as day laborers for bare subsistence in their villages ingrained into them a work ethic that served them well in America.

EMPLOYMENT AND BUSINESS

From the 1930s to the start of World War II, the majority of Chinese Americans in California were laundry operatives and employees, restaurant owners and workers, shopkeepers and clerks, domestic servants, farmers, and laborers in agriculture and other miscellaneous industries. Nearly all of the new immigrants began as laborers in these industries, usually getting their start through the same socioeconomic network that had helped them immigrate to America. If they saved enough money and gained enough business acumen after years of hard work, they could invest in the same or a similar type of business in which they had had their apprenticeship, becoming partners in the same or a new enterprise. Those who invested large sums of money became major partners, and those who invested smaller sums became minor partners. Major partners may or may not have engaged in hands-on work in the business, but they controlled the bookkeeping and bank accounts. During shareholders' meetings, their decisions carried greater weight than the decisions of the minor partners, who usually worked the hardest and longest day to day. The minor partners, in essence, were purchasing jobs or job security and trying to increase their earning power by collecting profits in addition to wages or salaries. As partner-employees, they were nearly always more conscientious and productive than regular employees were. Nonetheless, all of the partners wanted to make their business successful and to share in the profits according to their investments at the end of the year. How they went about realizing these goals revealed their strengths and weaknesses in business enterprises.

In family enterprises, the rooms in the back, above, or next to the business sometimes served as the family residence. In larger enterprises, it was common for owners to provide free lodging and meals for employees, especially for recent immigrants without families in America. This practice yielded reciprocal benefits for employers and employees and fostered a sense of mutual responsibility, familial obligation, and ethnic solidarity. Employees saved money on rent and meals, but stayed longer on the premises without extra pay until the job was finished for the day. From the tradition of paternalism, employers felt obligated to provide for their employees, since they were often related or from the same village, but the employees in turn had to render unquestionable loyalty and trustworthiness. Familial or social obligation was commonly the impelling reason an unemployed relative, friend, or fellow villager was hired, sometimes regardless of whether the business needed another employee. This tradition of cooperative effort and mutual responsibility, which historically helped the Chinese survive in China, also helped Chinese American businesses compete in America.

Owning and operating a business was much more desirable than being employed by others, and afforded both economic advancement and proprietary status. The types of business in which Chinese Americans engaged reflected their socioeconomic circumstances as well as the needs of their larger communities. Sojourners typically set up small enterprises that were easy to start and required low capital outlays. Laundries were the oldest and most numerous of these types of businesses; they were so numerous they became the stereotypical occupation for the Chinese. Generally, laundries catered to a non-Chinese clientele in urban areas because the economic base was broad. Operating laundries required only a limited knowledge of English and mostly manual labor rather than costly machinery. In addition, laundry operators had the flexibility to hire additional help when business demanded it and to sell their operations on short notice. The decline of the Chinese laundry was due to a combination of factors: a shortage of Chinese workers willing to do that kind of labor; competition from large companies that used efficient modern machinery; and an increased number of home washing and drying machines as well as launderettes. In any case, the laundries were products of their time, suitable for the sojourners and their clientele. This can be also said, to a large extent, for Chinese American–owned cafes and restaurants that sold only American food, and for Chinese American truck farms and produce markets that sold to an American clientele, all of which were much more numerous before than after World War II. After the war these businesses began to fade away.[8]

After laundries and restaurants, grocery stores were the most numerous of Chinese American owned enterprises. Like other Chinese American businesses, individuals and partnerships owned most of them; very few were registered as corporations. The capitalization of a business usually came from the owners' or partners' savings. Statistics on actual investment and capital of each type of business are not available, but the amount of capital required for restaurants and grocery stores was definitely greater than that for laundries, which demanded mainly "sweat equity." In addition to inventory and equipment, grocery stores required a long-term commitment to realize a return on investment. On the other hand, Chinese Americans considered grocery stores better than laundries in gaining profits. Business hours and working conditions were also deemed better than both laundries and restaurants. These factors made grocery stores suitable for families to operate, which usually relied on members for unpaid labor. In a mutually beneficial way, a grocery store enabled its proprietor to afford a family, and family members helped the proprietor to operate it.

As the number of laundries declined, the number of grocery stores rose such that by 1949 there were about two thousand in the United States, among which were a limited number of supermarkets located mainly in the smaller towns and cities in the West and Southwest. About a decade later, there were at least three thousand grocery stores and supermarkets owned and operated by Chinese Americans, the former located mostly in the metropolitan areas of Northern California. It was about this time that the number of neighborhood "mom-and pop" grocery stores began to decline because of the fierce competition from large supermarkets in nearby new neighborhoods, some of which were opened by Chinese Americans who had started out in small grocery stores.[9]

In *The Chinese Community in Sacramento,* John Fang states that about one thousand Chinese residents earned their living in supermarkets and grocery stores in the city and county of Sacramento in 1960. This figure appears to be supported by the 1960 U.S. Census, which reported that 1,033 out of 2,537 employed Chinese Americans worked in the wholesale and retail trade industry, assuming that "trade" meant primarily food. Fang also states that Chinese Americans owned about a hundred groceries and supermarkets, doing an annual business of more than $150 million, which represented about 25 percent of the area's sales volume in groceries. The number of grocery stores and supermarkets listed in *Sacramento's Chinese Directory,* circa 1960, matches closely Fang's number. But the sales figure from the 1963 U.S. Census of Business, the business census closest to 1960, does not measure up to Fang's figure. This census reported the total sales of all grocery stores, including supermarkets, at about $244 million, making Fang's figures grossly inflated. The correct amount was certainly smaller but nonetheless still impressive. Accurate sales figures tend to be difficult to ascertain because proprietors of small businesses generally do not make public this type of information. This does not, however, detract from the importance of grocery stores and supermarkets in terms of economic advancement for their owners, employment for Chinese Americans, and business for wholesalers and ancillary service providers. To underscore these points, the population of Chinese Americans in the Sacramento area in 1960 represented only 1.3 percent of the total population, but their hundred retail food stores represented about 20 percent of the total number of establishments.[10] Even more impressive was the fact that Chinese American supermarkets competed directly against national chains and large local chain supermarkets, and prospered for at least twenty-five years after World War II.

Prior to the war, Chinese Americans sought to improve their economic standing by seeking better employment, but opportunities were still very limited. There were the usual jobs in laundries, restaurants, canneries, grocery stores, meat stores, and on farms. A few found work as craftsmen in the Southern Pacific Railroad Company, as salespeople in large department stores, and as clerks in government agencies. There was a paucity of Chinese Americans in the professional fields such as education, medicine, dentistry, engineering, and scientific research. Even if they were trained in these fields, their opportunities for employment were almost nonexistent. In their ethnic communities, the population could support only so many professionals, such as those in medicine and dentistry. In the mainstream community, companies rarely employed Chinese American professionals, and Euro-American patients rarely sought the services of Chinese American doctors. At the time, this situation was typical between the dominant and the various minority populations. Segregation was the norm, and Chinese Americans generally did not expect to be employed in the mainstream economy. Hence, there was little reason for young Chinese Americans to pursue an education beyond high school.

The entry of the United States into the war quickly changed the situation. Wartime industries such as shipyards and aircraft factories, which in the past had rarely employed Chinese Americans, began hiring them as engineers, technicians, workers, and clerks. The change was based as much on political winds as on practical needs. China had become an ally of the United States against Japan, and as a result, Americans looked upon the Chinese both in the United States and China in a favorable light. Japanese Americans, on the other hand, were forced into relocation camps, which opened employment and business opportunities they had formerly held to Chinese Americans. With the acute shortage of manpower, other industries soon followed the government's example in utilizing Chinese Americans to ease the exigency.[11]

Whether immigrant or American-born, young wives worked in the family business or sought employment to supplement the family income. Few had the luxury of being just a housewife and mother. In the family business, they drew no regular wages, but received money when it was necessary to pay for household expenses or make purchases for the family. Their labor meant not having to hire and pay for outside help, and essentially they were partners in the business. They served as cashiers in restaurants and grocery stores; washed, folded, and ironed clothes in laundries; and worked alongside their husbands in agricultural enterprises. Because of their contact with the public, immigrant wives learned English on the job, which further acculturated them into the American way of life. The children of business owners were also expected to lend a hand in the family concern, helping out after school and during weekends and eating meals in the back rooms of the businesses.

Some wives secured employment outside the family business. In the Sacramento area, for example, women sewed clothes in garment factories, sorted and prepared vegetables and fruits in produce canneries, and cut fish and peeled shrimp in seafood canneries. Most of the jobs required little or no English skills and were seasonal and part-time, ideal for immigrant mothers with young children. Immigrant women commonly regarded working in the canneries as highly desirable, getting union wages and benefits and a regular work schedule from an American corporation. Working in the canneries provided not only a sense of independence and economic worth, especially coming from a culture where women were kept almost cloistered in the home and village, but also an opportunity to socialize and exchange news and gossip. This interaction helped strengthen community bonds along with the traditional family and district associations that regularly sponsored celebrations for annual festivals.

THE COMMUNITY

Social activities in Sacramento and other Northern California communities were not limited to traditional celebrations carried over from the homeland. In communities where they were not totally accepted by the greater society, Chinese Americans continued to retain a strong sense of identity and loyalty to China, especially the immigrant generation. In the early 1930s, the invasion of China by the Japanese roused the nationalistic spirit of Chinese Americans. Where their populations were large, they organized political action groups to provide financial aid to war-ravaged China. As the war progressed, various clubs with ties to the Chinese government sponsored "rice bowl" parties, shows and plays, and parades to generate funds for the war effort. Chinese Americans purchased Chinese war bonds and marched in parades while their children recited loyalty pledges to China in Chinese-language schools. These activities nurtured a sense of pride, patriotism, and unity among Chinese Americans, but these ideas that transcended their everyday concerns would be redirected toward America after its entry into the war, especially by the American-born generation.

From the 1930s to the early 1960s, the American-born generation lived a bicultural life. In urban areas like Sacramento, they learned about American ideas and values at school and absorbed popular culture through the media.

They participated in recreation, sports, clubs, and entertainment much like their Euro-American counterparts, but usually within their ethnic group in their community. In other words, they were acculturated, but not assimilated. At the same time, they learned about their heritage in Chinese-language schools and upheld the Chinese sense of mutual responsibilities at home, exemplified by helping out in the family business or getting a part-time job to supplement the family income. Less prejudice and bigotry was directed toward them than toward earlier generations, although they learned to ignore or circumvent these problems when they occurred. They lived in local neighborhoods along with other minority groups such as African Americans, Mexican Americans, and Japanese Americans. In the rural communities of Northern California, where there were fewer Chinese Americans and where they lived spread out among the dominant population, the experience of the American-born generation was mixed. Some encountered prejudice and discrimination, which caused them to keep close to their family and home or to travel to other communities with larger Chinese American populations in which to socialize. But some Chinese Americans and other minorities had little or no problems with the dominant population. A possible explanation for this can be found in the fact that in rural communities, there were no large, demarcated ethnic enclaves like Chinatowns, where Chinese Americans could lead more isolated lives, having little or no contact with the greater population. For decades extending back to the nineteenth century, Chinese Americans in rural communities were an integral part of the socioeconomic fabric. This phenomenon is revealed in Sucheng Chan's *This Bittersweet Soil,* an outstanding study about Northern California's early agricultural economy.

During the war, some of the American-born generation along with the immigrant generation joined the armed forces to serve China as well as America. Some did not volunteer, but were drafted. Others found employment in the military equipment industries. When veterans returned, they took advantage of the postwar opportunities available to them, including G.I. benefits, employment, citizenship, and immigration of foreign-born wives. Second- and third-generation Chinese Americans enrolled in colleges to major in medicine, dentistry, education, pharmacy, accounting, engineering, and other professions. They generally practiced their professional skills in or near their communities, which were rapidly growing, or found jobs in public employment, government, and military installations. Integration into the private economy of the greater community would take place gradually over the next few decades.

SOCIOECONOMIC CHANGE

In Sacramento, social breakthroughs occurred in the 1950s when Chinese Americans began to move out of the southern part of the city's central area, where most of them had lived. Since the turn of the century, Chinese American families had gradually moved south, away from the center of downtown but still within the central area. Near the center of downtown remained the old socioeconomic heart of the Chinese American community. This was the domain of the bachelor sojourners who lived in basement and second floor quarters of stores, laundries, and restaurants. A little further away, the southern central area offered inexpensive apartments and single-family houses suitable for young families starting out. The concentration of like families afforded a sense of familiarity and security for many whose language skills and understanding of American culture were still limited. But as Chinese Americans became acculturated and financially successful, they sought housing changes to reflect their entry into the middle- and upper-middle classes.

Housing segregation was gradually eroded when Euro-American friends helped Chinese Americans purchase homes in neighborhoods prohibited to them by real estate covenants and convention. Most of the wealthier Chinese Americans favored living in the affluent southern sections of Sacramento, while a few moved into the city's northern and eastern areas. The economic and educational advancement achieved by Chinese Americans after the war certainly helped to weaken the prejudices against them, especially by the acculturated American-born generation. The dominant group's acceptance of Chinese Americans moving into their neighborhoods may also be due to the fact that they were willing to tolerate one Chinese American family, or possibly two, as long as not too many families moved in and lived close to one another. This may explain why some Chinese American families were able to reside peacefully in solitude in small cities and rural areas of Northern California.

By the mid-1960s, Chinese Americans in Sacramento and other Northern California communities were well on their way toward assimilation into the greater community, or at least had greater opportunities to do so. One of the reasons for this was their prominent presence in the supermarket business. Chinese Americans opened stores in new neighborhoods and suburbs to pursue the patronage of young families who were increasing in number and size. As customers began shopping regularly in these stores, they became familiar if not friendly with the Chinese American personnel and started regarding them as members of their communities. At the same time, the civil rights movement came to fruition in the mid-1960s, making the dominant community aware that they needed to live up to the social, economic, and political ideals of America by opening the doors of opportunity.

With increased opportunities, many second- and third-generation Chinese Americans did not enter their family business after completing their formal education, although some did because the family jobs were readily available for their taking. There were fewer and fewer descendants wanting or willing to take over the helm of the family business because there were so many other choices available to them that offered better working conditions, income, and prestige. In their parents' generation, there were little or no such choices. Their parents had created their own opportunities, risking their savings and taking on long hours of hard work.

In order for most of the earlier Chinese American supermarkets to maintain their profits or expand their operations after the mid-1960s, they needed the same type of labor force that in the past was readily available, because these businesses continued to operate basically the same way. But the Chinese American population from which the businesses hired most of their labor was changing considerably. The people were more diverse and less interdependent upon each other as the influx of new immigrants from different areas of China and the Americanization of the younger generation rendered old social and family ties weaker or nonessential. The sense of obligation, belonging, and security were ideals of the past, becoming less and less relevant. Everyone was on his own to compete for increased opportunities offered by the greater society.

Business operations were also changing. They were becoming more complex, competitive, and costly. The making of allowances for hiring unemployed relatives or the retaining of employees during adverse business periods thus became unworkable.

LARGE ENTERPRISES

Before the advent of supermarkets, Chinese American enterprises were generally small. The typical owners or partners managing their businesses in neighborhood markets and competed against other local proprietors. Many small operations provided just a little more than a subsistence income. What was unique about early Chinese American supermarkets in Northern California was that they were large enterprises competing against national chains, local chains, and independent companies. They in turn expanded into chain operations and were very profitable, gaining national prominence in the industry.

Outside of agriculture, prior to the introduction of these supermarkets very few large-scale Chinese American enterprises were as successful. A few successful enterprises included the Wah Chang Trading Corporation of New York, which dealt in the trading and processing of tungsten; Joe Shoong's National Dollar Stores, clothing department stores with headquarters in San Francisco and forty outlets in the West and Hawaii; and the Bank of Canton, incorporated in California in 1937.[12] During the latter half of the nineteenth century and the early decades of the twentieth century, there were some very large Chinese American enterprises, but they eventually failed due to their inability to compete with large American corporations and to adapt to changing economic and political forces. In addition, their finances were reputed to have been mismanaged. These enterprises included import-export firms, tenant-farming and fruit-processing ventures, a shipping company, and a bank. Except for agricultural enterprises, the impact of these big enterprises was felt primarily in San Francisco's Chinatown, influencing the community's economic and political development. These enterprises and the people who ran them maintained strong links with southeast China. On the other hand, the Chinese American supermarkets and the people who ran them were integral parts of their communities from the onset.[13]

3 / Beginnings

THE BEGINNINGS OF CHINESE AMERICAN supermarkets were modest. None of the founders had specific plans, let alone grand goals, in mind. They were just trying to make as much money as possible with the opportunities and resources available to them. The early success of Chinese American grocery stores and later supermarkets had as much to do with unique circumstances, timing, and luck as it did with astute decisions and hard work. Chinese Americans took tentative steps in opening their first grocery stores, and the growth of their supermarkets followed the rapid expansion of the industry. With an increasing population, flourishing economy, and relatively manageable startup costs, it seemed that little could go wrong with operating a food store. These early entrepreneurs were provided with waves of opportunity, and they rode them toward prosperity.

The founders were immigrants with no prior experience in the grocery business, but they had acquired skills that would help them start and operate a new type of retail food store. By chance or design, their timing could not have been better. Small specialty stores and markets that sold only groceries, meat, dairy products, or fruits and vegetables were being brought together into the combination grocery store under single ownership. Self-service and cash-and-carry were replacing clerk assistance, credit, and delivery. National brands were being advertised and distributed throughout the state, standardizing the inventory of food stores. Changes in the retailing of food brought changes in the shopping habits of customers, who henceforth would consider price and selection in addition to service and convenience in choosing which stores to patronize.

The immigrants' skills as cooks, butchers, and produce growers and peddlers became useful in operating their future combination grocery stores. If they had no prior experience in these vocations, they learned on the job. Because the combination grocery store was also in its early stages of development, there was room for trial and error before mastering the ways of retailing. Social intercourse with the general public in having sold meat and produce also facilitated the immigrants' acceptance in selling groceries. Finally, their work ethic and solidarity helped them succeed, prosper, and grow.

When they arrived in America, many Chinese American immigrants were penniless, but they had youth, energy, and determination. From the beginning, their goal was to earn as much money as possible from their labor to remit to families in China and to save enough to secure a future for themselves. Deciding to settle in America was not a difficult choice because there was widespread and chronic poverty, hunger, and strife from where they emigrated. When they accumulated enough money from their labor, they opened their own businesses to earn more. A common trait among these early businessmen was their relentless drive each year to do better than the year before. The familial obligation to contribute to the collective business helped substantially to accumulate resources for growth when greater opportunities arose. If the business was a partnership, each partner worked diligently because prosperity for the group meant prosperity for the individual. Likewise, no individual wanted to be responsible for the failure of the partnership.

THE FATHER OF CHINESE AMERICAN SUPERMARKETS

Many of the large operators in Sacramento and other Northern California communities considered Lee Gim to be the father of Chinese American supermarkets. Whether or not he opened the first Chinese American–owned retail food store that sold American products to an American clientele is unclear. However, two claims are certain: his first store provided apprenticeships for many future owners, and his investments helped capitalize more than twenty grocery stores and supermarkets in Sacramento and other Northern California communities, including six of the seven Famous Food Markets, which were some of the earliest Chinese American supermarkets. His business acumen, generosity, and probity earned him genuine respect from his partners and associates and from the next generation of supermarket operators.

Lee Gim immigrated to San Francisco in about 1916, when he was sixteen or seventeen years old, and he worked in a restaurant, presumably as an all-around helper learning various skills. Soon he migrated to Northern California to work as a cook, first in a small-town restaurant and later in a ranch owned by a prominent family. For the next few years he cooked for the family and ranch workers and looked after his employer's children. Meanwhile, in the nearby town of Colusa, a friend of Lee Gim, Lee Toy, ran a successful laundry, which was so profitable that he was able to finance the construction of a two-story building on the corner of a block in 1918. Lee Toy leased the building to two Japanese brothers who operated a general store, Ono Brothers, which sold a variety of merchandise, including food products. For reasons unclear, the brothers quit the business after two years, leaving some inventory behind. Lee Toy began coaxing his good friend to take over the abandoned business and to operate it as a grocery store. Although he did not know anything about selling groceries or running a business, Lee Gim agreed, and moved to Colusa in 1921. Lee named the grocery store Chung Sun Grocery after China's nationalist hero Sun Yat-sen, whom he admired.[1]

To say that Lee's beginnings were modest would be an overstatement. His capitalization was nearly zero, but he took over a store with some merchandise to sell. He worked by himself, learning on the job and working around the clock six days, sometimes seven, a week. He did not own or know how to operate a cash register. Sales transactions were conducted on an abacus, and change was handed out from the pockets of a carpenter's apron, each holding a specific denomination of cash. The retail sales space of the store was about 800 square feet, considered very small by today's standards, but larger than the average 500 to 600 square feet of that era. Groceries were stacked in shelves that ran up the store's high walls, and produce was displayed on racks outside the store. Since there was very little refrigeration back then, only milk and cured meats, like ham and bacon, were sold. It would be safe to assume that many of the customers from the ranches slaughtered their own livestock and poultry for fresh meats. In sum, it was a typical rural grocery store.[2]

At that time, grocery stores were still providing credit and delivery; therefore, Lee purchased and learned to ride a bicycle. When a customer placed an order, he would close the store, deliver the merchandise by bicycle, collect payment, and return to the store until the next delivery. Customers with accounts would pay off their balance at the end of the week, month, or year, depending upon their credit worthiness and length of patronage. For an agricultural community where income was seasonal, this was a principal means of doing business. This credit service was extended to ranch workers as well as their employers. During the hard times of the Depression, many farmers were unable to pay their purchases or credit balances with cash. Instead, they would pay in kind with produce and other farm products, such as eggs. But some never paid their credit balances. Even to this day, there are accounts receivable that could be settled by the credit customers' descendants, who still shop at Chung Sun Market. For Lee Gim, his kindly ways built up customer loyalty and community good will that would serve him and his family well for many years.[3]

Lee Gim slept in the basement beneath the store and cooked his meals in the kitchen there. As business grew rapidly, Lee offered a partnership to a friend, who was also a former cook, to help with the increased work. Bringing in a partner was the logical choice for Lee because an associate with an interest in the business would likely be more responsible and reliable than an employee. But this would not always be the case, as circumstances later proved. Lee Gim eventually hired four or five employees, and like Lee, the partner and employees lived in the basement of the building. In traditional Chinese employer-employee relationship, the former was expected to provide room and board, while the latter was expected to render loyalty and trustworthiness. This reciprocity would help Lee Gim and other Chinese American operators maintain a high degree of competitiveness and profitability in the retail food business.

It was not difficult for employees to acquiesce to the demands and expectations of their employers. Employees were usually young, energetic men who were single or without family in America; thus, the store personnel became their surrogate family, with their employer as the head. Eating and sleeping on the premise reinforced that notion. Their industriousness and indebtedness to their employer would be further strengthened when it was their employer who sponsored their immigration to America, as was the case of Lee and some of his employees. They came from the same village as their sponsor or from a nearby village, and were related or friends. Some new immigrants would work for low or no wages for a prescribed period to pay off the cost of their immigration, which their sponsor bore. Because nearly all of the immigrant employees had limited or no occupational skills and lacked English proficiency, and because of prevalent discrimination, opportunities for other types of employment were very few. Immigrants formed a steady stream of eager employees for the next few decades. Moreover, these employees knew that they would learn skills that would prepare them to open their own businesses in an industry that was rapidly expanding and more profitable compared to other Chinese American enterprises.

Everything went well for Lee and his employees for the next five years. Some of Lee's employees saved enough money to leave Chung Sun Grocery and form partnerships to open their own grocery stores in small cities such as Marysville, Woodland, Oroville, and other Northern California locales.

Some of the new owners were still teenagers, whom Lee helped by investing as a major shareholder, although he was not involved in the stores' day-to-day operations. Lee sometimes assisted a relative or friend to become a partner by underwriting his share, which was to be paid back from future profits. The amount invested by each partner or shareholder varied; the higher the investment, the higher the share of profit at the end of the year and the greater the voice in decision-making in the partnership. The partnerships were often unequal, and there was no written contract to bind partnerships or to itemize each partner's investment, only verbal agreements or commitments. Required municipal business licenses and land deeds usually recorded only one or two names of the partners or shareholders. The partners or shareholders depended upon each other's integrity and trust to make their business a success. In their close-knit socioeconomic network, they prided themselves on these values. But this arrangement worked well only as long as the stores made good profits and all the partners and shareholders upheld their ethical bearings.[4]

The capitalization of the new stores came solely from the pooled resources of Lee and the partners. Financial institutions such as banks would not lend money to Chinese Americans, whether immigrant or American-born, for any purpose. But that did not matter, since the partners preferred to use cash to purchase store inventory, pay rent and utilities, and so forth. And they held onto their profits in cash, too, instead of depositing them in banks. Their discretion would prove judicious when many banks failed during the Depression, taking down business and personal accounts with them. It was not until the late 1940s that early immigrant Chinese Americans trusted, understood, and used financing from lending institutions.

In 1925 Lee returned to his native home to visit his family and get married. He had planned this trip for a long time and felt that his partner and employees would take care of his store in his absence. He was wrong. After a few months in China, he received an urgent message to return to Colusa as soon as possible because the business was in trouble. Leaving his pregnant wife behind, he kept close supervision of the store for the next half year to restore it to good footing. From that episode he learned what factors would cause a business to decline and what would make it successful. Foremost were the disposition of the personnel and their treatment of customers. Selling groceries was a service, requiring attentive management of personnel and customer relations. On-the-job training and trial-and-error learning could only go so far. The lesson would serve him well for the next fifty years.[5]

In 1931, Lee sent for his wife and young son to immigrate to America. The family would eventually grow to include nine children, and they would live over the grocery store in the upstairs apartments. Everyone was expected to work in the Lee family business as soon as they were able, usually at age seven or eight. There was no monetary compensation or allowance. The children worked after school, stocking shelves, filling orders (called in by telephone) for delivery, and waiting on customers. After graduating from high school, there were not many employment opportunities that provided a good income for young Chinese Americans in the small rural community. Chung Sun Grocery therefore gradually became a family-run operation as sons, daughters, and in-laws assumed key positions when partners and employees left. The profits and wages that previously had gone to partners and employees stayed in the family to be saved and invested.[6]

Because Chung Sun Grocery was a family-run operation, labor unions did not pressure the business to organize its personnel. But Lee's business did have a critical problem in its early years: finding a grocery wholesaler willing to sell products to Chung Sun Grocery. Eventually, the company that sold to the store was Arata Brothers Wholesale Grocery, renamed Valley Wholesale Grocery in 1927, located over seventy miles away in Sacramento. At the time, Arata was a small company trying to establish itself as a competitor in the wholesale business by building a clientele with its cash-and-carry trade. Owned by the Arata brothers, who operated their own food stores under the same name, the company did business with the Lees until 1957.[7]

Other grocery wholesalers were not willing to deal with Lee Gim, possibly because they had reservations about his ability to succeed and pay his bills, since he was a novice in the grocery business with no credit record. But they could have sold him products if they had demanded cash on delivery (C.O.D.), which was what Arata required when it made its early shipments to Lee. It was also possible that the other wholesalers had established business ties with Lee's competitors and did not want to strain their relationships. Similarly, Lee's competitors could have pressured their wholesalers not to sell to him. Lastly, it was possible that other wholesale grocers did not want to deal with Lee because of their racial prejudice. When other Chinese Americans opened their grocery stores in other towns and cities years later, they also had no choice but to buy from Valley Wholesale Grocery. The wholesale grocers may not have wanted to sell to Chinese Americans, but by the late 1940s, when Chinese American supermarkets became major competitors in the retail food business, they could not ignore the grocers any longer, and thus began courting their business. The wholesale purchase of meat and produce, however, was generally not a problem, since Chinese Americans were involved in those enterprises long before entering the grocery store business.

The Lees sometimes made large wholesale purchases at discounted prices and stored the surplus in a warehouse located in the back of the store for future stocking and selling. This was a common practice among grocers. The steady increase in sales volume and profit from the 1930s to 1960s allowed them to operate in this manner, which made good business sense because wholesale prices generally rose. Sometimes it was not the Lees' decision to purchase extra merchandise, however. During the early years, Valley occasionally loaded additional merchandise onto the Lees' order without their knowledge, charged them for it, and coerced them to pay for it. Tolerating such maneuvers was the cost of doing business with Valley when it was the only company willing to sell to the Lees. The cost of transporting the weekly delivery was borne by Chung Sun Grocery, so the Lees later purchased trucks to pick up groceries and other supplies, operating them themselves. Because the Lees had invested in other grocery stores and supermarkets in nearby communities, all the stores shared the use and expense of the trucks.[8]

With the profits from Chung Sun Grocery, the Lees helped finance other grocery stores and supermarkets from the late 1920s to the 1950s. Lee Gim and most of his children remained in Colusa to operate Chung Sun Grocery, while the eldest son, Leland, managed some of the other supermarkets in which the family had invested. They did not build a chain of supermarkets under one company, but became shareholders in independent operations in several communities that were interlinked by various shareholders. These shareholders created a diffusion of supermarkets, which became prominent businesses in Northern California from the postwar era to the early 1970s. They are regarded as the first generation of Chinese American supermarkets. Among this generation were chain operations whose owners began in ways that were similar to Lee Gim's experiences. As the first-generation supermarkets reached their peak, the second generation began, their owners learning the trade while working in the former.

FROM COOK TO BUTCHER TO GROCER

The following section describes the story of a Chinese American immigrant who became a cook, then a meat cutter, and ultimately a grocer. It was due to his wife's insistence that he first purchased a grocery store. In due time, this grocer opened one of the first Chinese American–owned supermarkets in Sacramento, and his family eventually operated three more stores in the area. In the mid-1970s, the family withdrew from the business; the older generation retired, and the younger generation pursued professional careers. Their success in the grocery store and supermarket business illustrates a socioeconomic advancement that was difficult to attain by most other means. The greater community as well as the Chinese American community came to regard them and others that operated similar supermarkets as models of the Horatio Alger story.

George Quan immigrated to America in 1917 or 1918 with no money. He worked in his sponsor's restaurant in Sacramento for the next several years at no wages in order to pay off his obligation. He started out washing dishes and doing other menial tasks. In due time, he learned to cook, a skill that would later help him move into a related occupation, butchering (or in today's term, meat cutting). He subsequently found employment at other restaurants, including one in a downtown upscale hotel. He earned enough money to return to China to marry his betrothed bride. He came back to Sacramento with his wife in 1926 and continued working as a cook, saving his money for the right opportunity.[9]

Quan used his savings to invest in a retail meat shop, the Liberty Meat Market, becoming one of five young partners in the operation in 1928. The meat market was located about a block from the extensive Southern Pacific Railroad yard, where hundreds of workmen were employed. They became steady customers at Liberty, buying fresh and prepared meats over the service counter. Quan remained a partner for the next ten years. In the meantime his wife had more ambitious plans for the family, which already included two sons. After arriving in Sacramento, Mrs. Quan went immediately to work at a seasonal job at the nearby Del Monte Cannery. In 1930 she persuaded her husband to purchase a small corner grocery store for her to operate. She waited on customers by herself, learning how to speak English and run a grocery store on-the-job seven days a week. The neighborhood store was named New Way Market, but regular customers called it Mary's, after its proprietor. Because both her young children and her business required full-time attention, the family moved into the rooms behind the store to reside. The next five children would be born there during the Depression, but none of the youngsters were needed to help their mother in the store. The income from the store was not sufficient to support a growing family, and Quan continued working at Liberty as well.[10]

With a larger family, Quan hatched a bigger plan that came after recognizing a great opportunity. For years the enterprising Quan sold fireworks from several stands in the old Chinese section of Sacramento in the weeks preceding the Fourth of July celebration. By the late 1930s, the city had banned the sale of fireworks, which forced Quan to find another location that did not have a similar prohibition. He found a site in Broderick, located on the other side of the Sacramento River, directly across from the railroad yard from where most of his customers would come. Down the street from Quan's new stand was a grocery store that appeared to be doing good business, also selling to the workmen who daily crossed the nearby bridge to return home. The working class neighborhood was full of houses and families, a large proportion of them Mexican American. Hence, Quan decided to "horn in" on the grocery store's business. After selling the family store and their share in the Liberty partnership, the Quans pooled their resources with capital from a partner, George's brother, to start Eye (I) Street Bridge Markets. George's brother spoke better English than the rest of the family, which rendered him indispensable in conducting business affairs.[11]

The Quans leased the dilapidated building in which they had their fireworks stand and remodeled the interior to accommodate a food store. After tearing down walls, the retail space was increased to 3,000 to 4,000 square feet, six times the size of the corner store. At the time, Eye Street Bridge Market was considered a fairly large drive-in market where customers could conveniently park their automobiles right in front of the building. The Quans set up the store without having any specific plans or knowing what was needed. With the assistance of hired help, they built wood shelving and counters for displaying merchandise. The cost of refrigeration was minimal, needed only for fresh meats and dairy products. Produce was stacked and displayed on stands, shelves, and the floors inside and outside the store. Altogether, outlay for equipment was low. The Quans opened an account with Valley Wholesale Grocery to purchase inventory, although the first few shipments required cash on delivery. As was the case with the Lees of Chung Sun Grocery in Colusa, Valley was the only wholesaler willing to deal with the Quans. At the start, store personnel consisted of the parents, children, uncle, and a few full- and part-time Chinese American employees. Later, Mexican Americans from the neighborhood were also hired. Naturally, George Quan acted as butcher, and his wife handled the over-the-counter meat sales. After school the seven Quan children stocked groceries and displayed produce under the supervision of the uncle. Work went on for hours after closing time.[12]

The early employees at Eye Street Bridge Market were inexperienced and learned on the job. Some were recent immigrants who spoke little or no

English, and others had been in America for several years and had thus acculturated to some extent. Full-time employees were paid about $60 a month for working six days a week, twelve hours a day. If an employee was exceptionally productive, he received a bonus. None received health and welfare benefits. At that time, the retail food labor unions in Northern California were still organizing, and their strength was spotty. In some areas they were strong, and in some areas they were weak, depending on the efforts of the particular union representative. Generally, they encouraged employees to voluntarily enroll in the unions. But the people the Quans hired were grateful for their jobs because of the lingering effects of the Depression. If needed, room and board was available at a house rented by the Quans located next to the market. For young Chinese immigrants without families, this arrangement was ideal. With little or no occupational skills, the employment provided them with apprenticeships that would help them operate their own stores years later.[13]

From the start, business was very good. Much of it was due to the ending of the Depression and the beginning of the war. The older, smaller grocery store down the street was virtually no competition. In the war years the Eye Street Bridge Market sold everything it could stock, yielding generous profits for the family. But the profits were reinvested back into the operation of the market, purchasing fixtures for store enhancement and building credit with the wholesalers and vendors. Ten days of credit were extended to twenty, thirty, and sometimes sixty days, enabling the Quans to eventually stock and operate the market on their suppliers' capital. However, the Quans were still novices in selling groceries efficiently, a shortcoming that was exposed when real competition came. Business was so good during and after the war that it attracted other investors to open a supermarket a block away in 1949, a supermarket with roots in Chung Sun Grocery.[14]

Quan's brother left the market for personal reasons, and the family compensated him for his partnership. Responsibility of the grocery department was given to George Quan, Jr., who was fourteen in 1941. His duties now included ordering and pricing merchandise and dealing with sales representatives, making for very long work hours, especially when he and his younger siblings were still attending school. But the family continued to manage the business in the same unstructured and unplanned manner as from the beginning: "by the seat of our pants." Pricing merchandise, for example, was done by "rule of thumb," or by marking items a cent or two below competitors' prices, and by asking sales representatives for prevailing selling prices. Then they hoped for high sales volumes to make a good profit.[15]

As a family-run operation, the Quans had the discretion to build a profitable niche market and to help customers in need. They developed a thriving business with Mexican labor contractors in several counties, for example, by selling bulk quantities of ethnic foods to them on credit to feed their hundreds of workers in labor camps. The Quans used an adjacent warehouse to store truckloads of beans, flour, lard, wine, special cuts of meats, and other products. They provided this service until the mid-1960s, when California ended its bracero (temporary Mexican laborer) program. They gave personal loans, not store credit, to individuals who were short on cash. By giving loans, the Quans fostered personal relationships and loyalties with their customers. Had they given store credit, customers may have had fewer reservations about defaulting on an impersonal matter. These particular services worked well for a one-store family operation where success was in large part the result of building "good faith" among customers as well as vendors and wholesalers.[16]

The Quans maintained few operational records and had undefined sales strategies and no long-term goals. Bookkeeping was simple. They regularly deposited revenues from sales and made payments for inventory, supplies, and expenses when due. They reasoned that as long as they had money to pay the bills and taxes, they were getting enough business. They did not know exactly how profitable the business was until after the year-end inventory, and usually they "got some big money left over." Family members received no regular wages, but each was able to draw money from the family's savings account for expenses and purchases. The Quan's simple, casual approach toward business was also exemplified in determining locations for expansion during the 1950s and 1960s. Like the Eye Street Bridge Market, the sites for the next three supermarkets were chosen because they were across the street from or very near stores that were doing considerable business. In all three cases, the other stores were part of the Lucky Stores chain, a regional company that selected locations after thorough market studies. As the Quans expanded, they combined their four supermarkets under the appellation Giant Foods. The Quans reaped "huge profits" from the rapidly growing supermarket business until pivotal changes in the economy and rapid developments in the retail food industry rendered their ways of running supermarkets unprofitable.[17]

FROM FARMER TO PEDDLER TO GROCER

Until the company was sold in 1992, the most modern and innovative supermarkets in the Sacramento area were the seventeen Bel Air supermarkets oper-

ated by the Wong family. The family was the only Chinese American operator in Northern California who departed from the industry when their
supermarkets were some of the highest grossing stores in the area. Most of
the other operators saw their sales volumes stagnate or decline and their profits
evaporate, eventually forcing them to close or sell their stores. Much of Bel
Air's success was due to the Wong family's business philosophy, which
focused on management organization, dedicated reinvestment, constant
innovation, and risk-taking, and to their sincere appreciation for their customers, employees, and vendors, which was reciprocated. Their philosophy
and orientation began with the patriarch of the Bel Air organization, Wong
Gim.

In 1916 Wong Gim came to California as a sojourner to work as a farm
laborer, following in the footsteps of his father. He had purchased "papers"
that enabled him to enter, leave, and reenter America without too much
difficulty. A year later he returned to China to marry and start a family. But
in 1922 he immigrated again to California, this time with his wife and five-
year-old son, to stay permanently. He felt that there were more opportunities in "Gold Mountain" than in his impoverished home village in China. At
the very least, America offered him a chance for a livelihood, whereas his
homeland did not. Following relatives who had immigrated there, the family settled in the rural Newcastle/Loomis area, located about thirty miles northeast of Sacramento. Wong and his wife became sharecroppers on an orchard
farm. After about five years, they saved enough money to purchase five acres
of fertile land adjacent to the Chinese settlement in the nearby town of Penryn.
The land cost about $2,000, a significant amount in those days and a good
indication of the industry and thrift of the Wongs. He cleared the land for
orchards, but on about one acre his wife planted vegetables. She harvested
so many vegetables that Wong began to peddle them door-to-door to residents in the area. As business prospered, he purchased an old pickup truck
for delivery, an expenditure that helped him expand his market further, where
he gained regular customers in communities such Auburn, located about ten
miles north. He used the truck to purchase in bulk other fruits to supplement his inventory, increasing the variety of produce for sale. Thus, Wong's
beginnings as a food retailer were fortuitous. It took more than selling products, however, to become successful. Besides his commitment to selling quality produce, his pleasant, outgoing personality and his attention to the needs
of customers helped him build and secure a loyal clientele. These attributes
carried over to his family's next enterprise.[18]

Despite that fact that there was an economic depression, the family always had plenty to eat because they were able to raise livestock and poultry as well as grow vegetables on their small farm. The farm was indispensable to the family's welfare because there would eventually be ten children to feed. The family lived fairly isolated in a rural locale; hence, they worked and played together. All of the children worked after school, each doing his or her share for the family. Their mother grew and picked the produce, while the children prepared produce for sale, loaded it on the truck, and helped their father make deliveries. Their agricultural community consisted of "humble working people" of various ethnicities, including Euro-Americans, Chinese, Japanese, and Filipino Americans. Because most of the people were in the same socioeconomic class, the family experienced no overt discrimination. They lived comfortably in a seven-room house that Wong built on a hill overlooking Sacramento in the distance. In the large basement, they prepared and stored the produce and parked their delivery truck. This period was a promising early stage in the Wong family's journey to becoming preeminent supermarket operators.[19]

The Wong family's first venture into the grocery business was undertaken by the family's eldest son, Bill, in 1937. After graduating from high school, he went out on his own to create a job for himself. He convinced a Chinese American grocer in Sacramento to hire him as a produce buyer for his three grocery stores. Wong's initial salary for working twelve to fourteen hours a day was $50 a month, which later rose to $60. Every other week he received a Sunday off. The long hours and laborious work convinced Wong to work for himself rather than for somebody else. A salesman from a produce wholesaler informed Wong about a small grocery store in Sacramento that was for sale because its owner wanted to retire. With $1,000 from his savings and $1,000 borrowed from his father, Wong pooled his money with a partner's to purchase Save More Market for $4,000 in 1938. The small store was about 700 square feet and sold some meat and produce along with groceries. But business was not good during their first year. Struggling to barely get by, Wong's partner became restless. Wong therefore purchased his partner's share of the grocery store. He then summoned two of his brothers from Penryn to assist him in running the store. Wong operated the store from 1939 to 1942, when he was drafted into the war. Upon entering the military, Wong turned the store over to his father and the rest of the family. Wong Gim gave up his produce route and moved to Sacramento to run the store, but only for a very short time.[20]

The internment of Japanese Americans left Penryn without a grocery store, which provided the Wongs an opportunity to open one there. Furthermore,

Japanese American farmers had to abandon their fields and produce markets, which created another void and opportunity. The Wongs sold Save More Market and returned to Penryn to rent a vacant building to begin operation of a grocery store. The family operated the 800-square-foot store, Penryn Market, from 1942 to 1949, and they continued selling fruit, regularly taking a truckload to Sacramento and bringing back groceries to sell in Penryn Market. Like the Lee family in Colusa, they purchased from Valley Wholesale Grocery.[21]

Recently discharged from the military, Bill Wong married a girl from San Francisco and opened a combination grocery store in Berkeley with his brothers-in-law as partner. United Food Center was about 1,000 square feet in sales space and was located in a predominantly African American working-class neighborhood. Business was very good, which allowed Wong to purchase a home in nearby upscale Piedmont, and almost the whole block of real estate on which the store and other businesses stood. With Wong's two brothers and other in-laws as additional personnel, sometimes as many as nine people worked the busy store. For working around the clock seven days a week, everyone received minimum salary, but shared in the year-end profits. Wong continued to operate the store until 1959, at which time he relinquished his partnership to his brother-in-law in order to focus on his family's Bel Air supermarket in Sacramento, in which he had a share. He had been commuting to and from Sacramento since Bel Air had opened, in 1955.[22]

Another brother, George, ventured out on his own in 1948. He and his three brothers-in-law opened a supermarket called Consumers Market in the southern part of Sacramento. At 9,000 square feet, it was considered a very large store at the time. In its new building, the supermarket was laid out according to the partners' specifications, with big grocery, meat, and produce departments. It cost approximately $10,000 to start the supermarket, a modest capitalization in that the partners were able to lease the building, finance the equipment, and purchase inventory on credit. Each of the four partners had an equal share. They hired Euro-Americans, an atypical practice at the time, as well as Chinese Americans, and paid them union wages and benefits soon after the store began operation. Unlike many other Chinese American–owned supermarkets, the partners did not offer room and board for employees. Business was very good from the onset because of the increasing population, home construction boom, and general economic prosperity in the area. These favorable trends continued for years and seemed to be unending. After some years, Wong initiated a plan to take greater advantage of these trends, and sold his share of Consumers Market to the other partners. He then ventured out again, this time with his immediate family.[23]

With opportunities abounding in Sacramento and many years of experience among them, the Wong family decided to open their own supermarket. Their approach in opening their first Bel Air supermarket established a pattern that they used in opening future stores and greatly contributed to their long-term success. After exploring various locations, George Wong found a site in the southeastern part of Sacramento that offered great potential. In addition to existing residences, new houses and families were burgeoning in the mixed working- and middle-class neighborhood. The Wong family put a deposit on the land to secure the site and then sold it to a developer, who constructed a building to fit their needs and leased it to them.[24]

Before any capital was invested, the family decided to form a partnership and to divide it into seven equal shares, including their father's, at $3,000 a share. But most important, everyone agreed, at Bill Wong's suggestion, to incorporate the partnership. Utilizing the services of an attorney, they filed for incorporation. Under the leadership of George Wong, the Bel Air Corporation financed the equipment and purchased inventory on credit to get Bel Air supermarket started. Except for Bill and another brother, the rest of the family worked in the 16,000-square-foot store, each with a clear assignment of duties and responsibilities.[25]

The Wongs initially hired just a few employees, employing more only when business increased and when particular expertise that none of the Wongs had was needed. They selected personnel by qualification regardless of the prospective employee's relationship to members of the family. From the start, the employees received union wages and benefits and worked according to established union labor practices. Finally, whereas most supermarkets, especially those owned by Chinese Americans, emphasized low prices to attract customers, the Wongs decided to emphasize superior service, selection, quality, and innovation to distinguish their operation from others. During the expansion of their company, the Wongs did not always experience a smooth ascent, and their ventures were not always profitable. But with only one store and a slow start, their approach to retailing would weather the vicissitudes of the economy and supermarket business in Sacramento for years to come.[26]

A SALESMAN AND PROGRESSIVE GROCER

Sam Wah You immigrated to the United States in 1928. He was eighteen. Or was he sixteen, or fifteen? It is difficult to determine his exact age because like most of the other young Chinese immigrants, he came over as a "paper son." For Wah You, more important than his age was the opportunity to earn money so that he could send remittances to his wife left behind in China. She eventually joined him ten years later, after Wah You had established and was operating a very successful business.[27]

Wah You did not work on a farm like his father, who was already in the country. Settling in Stockton, California, he immediately began working for a wholesale/retail meat company, A-1, selling products to an American clientele even though he had virtually no English language skills. But he was enthusiastic and persistent, often badgering potential customers until they capitulated and bought something. It is likely that some of his skills in salesmanship were learned in the old country, because he often reminisced to his children about his past experiences selling fish in China's rural towns. His sense for business also likely came from his exposure to his father's dealings in China, where he was a businessman.

Wah You brought in a good deal of business for his new employer and made friends along the way. One of his friends, a bookkeeper who also worked for A-1 and was from Portland, Oregon, urged financial backers in Portland to help Wah You purchase the meat company, which was by then renamed Daylite Store. During the next decade, Wah You opened meat stores in Oakley, Brentwood, and Tracy, rural towns located northwest and southwest of Stockton. While the Stockton store sold and delivered meat to restaurants, hotels, retail stores, and nearby ranches, the "country stores" sold some groceries as well as meat primarily to the large ranches or farms that needed provisions to feed their work crews. Establishing businesses at the rural locations was difficult because of discrimination, but Wah You was persistent, and more importantly, he made the right friends, who helped bring him trade. Unlike most immigrants at the time, Wah You had a penchant for reaching out to people who were not Chinese.[28]

Wah You's numerous contacts with people enabled him to raise enough capital to start another enterprise. In 1946, he opened his first supermarket, called Centr-O-Mart, with funds from investors. After he purchased a large building next to the first Daylite Store in Stockton, it took one year to convert the vacant automobile garage into a supermarket. His friends helped him to model the operation like the successful Fred Meyer stores in Portland, Oregon. In addition to the grocery, meat, and produce found in a typical supermarket, Centr-O-Mart also had a variety of other departments, including bakery, sundry, liquor, tobacco, hardware, stationery, and furniture, as well as a pharmacy and soda fountain/café. Centr-O-Mart was huge, measuring 20,000 square feet in floor space (100 by 200 feet). At that time, the floor space of a typical supermarket was less than 10,000 square feet. The pride of Centr-O-Mart was its hundred-foot-long meat counter. Also featured in Centr-O-Mart was air conditioning, the first supermarket in the area to have it. Soon after Centr-O-Mart opened, the wholesale business of Daylite was transferred into the building, operating under the new name Diamond D.[29]

To supply his supermarket, Wah You opened a grocery warehouse called San Joaquin Wholesale, located near the Stockton supermarket. Both were built at the same time. By operating a wholesale grocery, Wah You did what other Chinese American grocers who had storage space were doing. He bought sizable quantities of products directly from manufacturers that offered discounts for large purchases and stored them in the warehouse. The reduced cost enabled Centr-O-Mart to sell products at lower prices than its competitors and to advertise their "loss leaders" weekly in newspapers to attract shoppers, strategies also used by other Chinese American grocers. At the beginning, buying products from manufacturers was difficult because San Joaquin did not have a business record, but the line of credit and the number of manufacturers willing to sell to the warehouse soon increased. San Joaquin supplied groceries only to Centr-O-Mart, but there would be more stores before long.[30]

Like many other Chinese American supermarkets, the first Centr-O-Mart was located in a working-class and ethnically mixed neighborhood. Unlike other operations, however, Wah You employed people of various ethnicities. There were European, Mexican, African, and Japanese Americans, in addition to the immigrant and American-born Chinese. There were female grocery checkers and neighborhood boys who carried out groceries for customers. The Japanese Americans worked primarily as pharmacists, while most of the Chinese Americans worked in the grocery and meat departments. Almost all of the meat cutters were immigrants, and many lived in a nearby house provided by Wah You during their workweek, and returned home to their families in San Francisco on their days off. Centr-O-Mart paid its employees union wages after about a year into operation. To help finance the expansion of Centr-O-Mart, Wah You offered his employees the option to invest in the company, and those who chose to do so had the amount of the investment deducted from their weekly paychecks.[31]

PERSPECTIVES

The narratives above detail various approaches in food retailing by families, partnerships, and investors during the early years of their businesses. Each approach set a pattern for future expansion and was fundamental to the prominence of their supermarkets. Some of these operations began earlier and reached their height and plateau of success in the 1950s and 1960s. But most of these earlier entrepreneurs were also the first to go out of business or sell their business. Others began later, but these also succumbed to similar ends at a later time. The same factors that nurtured the success of these businesses often contributed to their decline and passing. Owners, partners, and managers were unable or unwilling to adapt to the rapid technological changes in the supermarket industry and to the socioeconomic changes in the communities in which they did business. Some went out of business not because of external forces, but because of interpersonal conflicts within the partnerships, which caused ruination. Some left the business after becoming tired of proprietorship and after accumulating considerable assets.

The early grocery store proprietors had dispositions that served them well in business. They wanted to earn as much money as possible. It was a paramount concern carried over from their personal experience of widespread destitution in the old country. Overpopulation and starvation were endemic in the Toishan and Hoiping districts, from where most of these early proprietors came. Because daily struggle for subsistence was the norm, there was no question as to why they wanted to leave China. Moreover, a political revolution with various warlords, political factions, and revolutionaries vying for national and local power had been underway since 1911, making sociopolitical life in China uncertain at best. Immigrating to America became as much a matter of survival as economic opportunity, even more so for the family members left behind in the villages who depended upon remittances. The immigrants' drive to make money sowed and nurtured an industrious entrepreneurial spirit that resulted in the competitiveness of their enterprises in America.

When retired owners of the Chinese American supermarkets returned to visit the home villages from which their fathers and they had come, they were dumbfounded by how little the countryside and life there had changed. The poverty was still overwhelming even after remittances to families to improve their living standards had occurred for decades, myriad modernization programs had been implemented by the government, and a changeover to a market economy had been implemented. But continuing conditions of poverty could be explained partly by the fact that many people, especially the young, had moved to larger cities for better opportunities, deserting the unproductive soil and austere agrarian life. In essence, the internal migration reflected the international emigration of yesteryear. Just as the flow of people supplied abundant labor for economic growth in China, it supplied low-cost labor for the competitiveness of Chinese American grocery stores and supermarkets in California.

Immigration kept the flow of labor coming, but without kinship and fraternal solidarity among employers and employees, their grocery stores and supermarkets could not have been successful during the early years. As noted earlier, immigrant employees were willing to work long hours alongside their employers for low wages or sometimes without wages. From a contemporary perspective, it appears exploitative for owners and partners to demand such conditions, but the benefits for employers and employees were mutual, and most alternatives for the latter were not better. Immigrant employees often regarded their situations as temporary, a price to pay until they started earning a good income or opened their own businesses. If employees felt exploited, they often found solace by saying to themselves, "Even if one is being cheated, it should be done by a clansman rather than an outsider." This old-world sentiment is expressed among the laundrymen in Paul Siu's *The Chinese Laundryman*.[32] Within the stores, the working conditions and compensation could not have been so disagreeable that employers could not find help. Even American-born Chinese Americans considered working in supermarkets desirable, seeking jobs in them during the 1940s, 1950s, and 1960s.

Prior to World War II, Chinese Americans operated grocery stores and supermarkets with mixed results. Timing, location, and other particular circumstances affected business and profits. As noted, the Lees did well right from the start, whereas the Quans could not support the family on the income from New Way Market. Bill Wong made good money in his second venture after the war, but barely got by with his first grocery store. Their entrepreneurship was not so much based on risk-taking as it was on seizing available opportunities. The national chain and local independent companies had already established models for food retailing. Chinese Americans basically found niches in unserved or under-served markets, or were able to become better competitors than other operators. After the war, the retail food business was rapidly changing and expanding, allowing for new grocers to enter local markets. Their grocery stores and first supermarkets were usually located in working-class communities or ethnic neighborhoods in which they were accepted. It was likely that people in these neighborhoods patronized Chinese American businesses because they identified with the grocers as working people, like themselves. More important was the fact that Chinese American grocers were selling merchandise at lower prices than their competitors, allowing their working-class clientele who were looking for bargains to get the most value for their hard-earned wages. At the beginning, the linch-pin to being able to open and operate a grocery store was Valley Wholesale Grocery, the only wholesaler willing to do business with Chinese American grocers. If not for Valley, Chinese Americans may not have been able to enter the grocery business or their start may have been delayed.

The mid-1920s to the early 1930s marked the advent of combination gro-cery stores and the initiation of Chinese Americans into the grocery busi-ness in Sacramento. Some Euro-American grocers had expertise in retailing groceries and were affiliated with grocery wholesalers, but they lacked the experience in procuring, preparing, and selling meat and produce. Because Chinese Americans had been in the meat and the produce businesses for some time, the grocers solicited them to sell their products under the same roof along with groceries. The histories of the Chinese American–owned Fulton Market and the Euro-American-owned Cardinal Grocery Stores, which were later incorporated into Lucky Stores, recount these cooperative ventures. Before long the Euro-American grocers learned the meat and produce trades, bringing the separate concessions under their management. Likewise the Chi-nese Americans learned the grocery trade, soon selling groceries, meat, and produce in their own stores. Fulton Market, for example, started out as a meat market in the late 1910s and began selling groceries in the mid-1920s.[33]

In sum, the development of Chinese American grocery stores and super-markets was neither uniform nor especially successful. Some started earlier, some later. Some small grocers never enlarged their stores into supermar-kets. A large number of first-generation supermarkets did not develop into chain operations, but remained independent operations linked by common partners. Some of the employees of those stores later formed partnerships and started their own chains of supermarkets. Whether independent or chain, some operations were profitable but did not prosper, and some simply failed soon after opening or several years later. But overall, Chinese American gro-cery stores and supermarkets did well. In 1939, the operators were proud enough of their achievements to form the Chinese Food Dealers Association, which is still existent today. The beginnings of the Lees' supermarket part-nerships, the Quans' Giant Foods, and the Wongs' Bel Air stores were very modest. With a lot of hard work, perseverance, good management, and a bit of luck, their fortunes gradually rose, but not without downturns and fail-ings. Their early experiences underscore the importance of timing. Unlike the Lees, Quans, and Wongs, Wah You entered the supermarket business at a time when the industry was beginning its long and steep ascent.

The entrepreneurship of the Lees, Quans, and Wongs appears unique in light of their humble beginnings, haphazard operations, long working hours, and struggle for profits. Their early experiences can be compared with those of the late Thomas Raley, founder of the Raley's Superstores. In 1992 Raley's had over sixty-five superstores (50,000 to 60,000 square feet each) throughout Northern California and Nevada and had purchased the seventeen supermarkets of the Bel Air chain. Raley started as a produce clerk at a Safeway store in 1931, earning $35 for working fifty-four hours a week. In 1934 he purchased property in Placerville (forty miles northeast of Sacramento) with a down payment of $500 and hired a contractor to build a 2,500-square-foot store. After building shelves and counters himself, he persuaded a wholesaler to sell groceries to him on credit, but not without help from his former employer, who wrote a letter of credit recommendation on his behalf. In February 1935, Raley opened Raley's Drive-In Market and employed six people during that year. He paid his employees $35 for working around the clock six days a week. Still, his former employees remembered the family-like togetherness among all the personnel, including the owner. At the end of the first year, Raley earned $4,500 in profit. Raley was known as a risk taker who, if he failed, tried something else. And during the early years, some of his stores did fail, but he opened more stores at other locations with reinvested profits.[34]

FURTHER INQUIRY

From 1930 to 1940 the *Sacramento City Directory* listed a few Japanese American grocers and a wholesaler in the city, although which ones sold American products are not identified. These listings should invite inquiry as to why Japanese Americans did not expand their grocery stores to supermarkets in large numbers during the later part of this period, when there was considerable development in the retail food business. It was quite possible that increasing anti-Japanese sentiment resulted in reduced or curbed patronage of Japanese American stores, enough such that owners could not undertake expansion. For similar reasons, the immigration of Japanese was severely restricted after 1924, curtailing the flow of immigrant labor of the kind that was very advantageous to Chinese American owners of grocery stores and supermarkets. Although the Japanese American population was larger than the Chinese American population, the socioeconomic composition of the former may not have been suitable for helping grocery stores achieve a higher level of competitiveness and profitability. There was a much more even ratio of males to females in the Japanese American population than in the Chinese American group, facilitating the family formation by the former. Thus, it was very likely Japanese American grocery stores were small family-run operations, dependent primarily on wives and children for labor. Such type of labor would not be conducive to rapid growth and expansion. A family-run operation would remain just that, although the Quans' experience proved that it was quite possible for a family grocery store to expand into a supermarket. In any case, even if Japanese Americans had expanded their operations into competitive supermarkets, their businesses would have had to close down or be sold because of Executive Order 9066 in February 1942, which forced Japanese Americans to evacuate their communities and relocate into internment camps.

Another inquiry should be directed into why the numerous Chinese American grocery stores in San Francisco did not develop into supermarkets, as was the case in Sacramento and other communities of Northern California. Documentary evidence to help explain this lack of development may not be readily available, but when former owners and partners of Sacramento operations were asked this question, their explanation was quite simple: high real estate cost or rent. It cost much more to start and run a supermarket in San Francisco than in Sacramento. Only large national and local chain operations, such as Safeway and Cala Foods respectively, could afford to open supermarkets in densely populated areas where real estate was at a premium. They had the financial and political clout to secure first any prime location that was available. Furthermore, countless mom-and-pop grocery stores had been serving city neighborhoods, although their number has diminished somewhat in recent years. Driving and parking in the city has always been inconvenient, and residents walk to these small stores frequently, making small purchases. This type of shopping stands in contrast to the suburban model, where residents drive to their supermarkets weekly, making large purchases. During the period under study, San Francisco also had distinct ethnic neighborhoods or enclaves, such as Chinatown or North Beach (a little Italy), where ethnic people lived and worked exclusively. People usually did not venture into a neighborhood populated by people of a different ethnicity, let alone open a business or patronize a business. But there were exceptions. Chinese Americans operated small grocery stores in the Hunter's Point section of the city, an area populated heavily by African Americans. Similar situations occurred in Los Angeles and Southern California.

It is possible that some of the Chinese American grocers in San Francisco would have expanded into supermarkets had real estate costs been more reasonable. As narrated earlier, Bill Wong operated United Food Center in a predominantly African American working-class neighborhood in Berkeley, located across the bay from San Francisco. With good sales and profits, he expanded the business into a supermarket by purchasing almost the entire block on which the grocery store was located.

4 / Golden Times

FROM THE END OF WORLD WAR II to the early 1970s, a period of proliferation and prosperity for Chinese American supermarkets took place. Business was simply great. These were the "golden times" for the operators. Their supermarkets reigned supreme in markets throughout Northern California, competing directly against national chains, local chains, and local independents in small and large communities. They led with their particular type of retailing, which combined traditional Chinese employment and management practices with standards of the supermarket industry. Taking advantage of favorable socioeconomic conditions, they made a lot of money, which was their principal goal from the outset. It was during the second half of this period that Chinese American operators built their chain operations and reputations. Their prominence was common knowledge in the industry. The operators were so acclaimed in the industry that some of them were elected presidents of trade organizations, such as the Northern California Grocers Association. Expansion for the sake of prominence, however, was not a goal for these operators when they started. The good returns of their first stores enticed the operators to open additional supermarkets to increase their profits and competitiveness. Some formed new partnerships to open single supermarkets that were linked to other supermarkets by common partners. Some opened multiple supermarkets under the same ownership or company, establishing small chains.

As noted earlier, the progress and success of grocery stores and supermarkets were not uniform and widespread. The period, level, and duration of success among single and multiple supermarket operations varied. Most Chinese American grocery stores did not expand into supermarkets, and most supermarkets did not expand into multiple or chain operations. Expansion depended as much on the ambition and ability of the operators as on the amount of business and profit of the first store to finance it.

There were two imprecise, discernible generations of Chinese American supermarkets whose business-life cycles overlapped. As the first-generation supermarkets declined and passed, the second generation rose and prospered, sometimes at the expense of the former. Most of the first-generation supermarkets began operating from the late 1930s to the mid-1950s, and most ended their operations by the mid-1970s. As outgrowths of grocery stores, most of the supermarkets were single-store operations under partnerships, whose height of success ran from the postwar period to the early 1960s. The second generation began operating in the years from the mid-1950s to 1960. Some operations grew to become multiple-store or chain operations under the ownership of private companies, which were made up of shareholders or partners who got their start in the business while employed in the first-generation supermarkets. They were very successful from the 1960s to the early 1970s, but most began to decline during the mid-1970s. In sum, the business-life cycles of the supermarkets were as varied as their generational characteristics. The reasons for their decline and passing will be analyzed in the next chapter. The following material explores their rise and growth.

LOCATION AND PRICES

The success and competitiveness of Chinese American supermarkets were basically dependent upon location and low prices. A good location for a supermarket would have a large customer base to draw upon, evident by the existing number of homes and families and the planned construction of new houses in the area. Ideally, there would be young, growing families in these homes, the kind with many mouths to feed for years to come. Novice Chinese American operators selected sites for their supermarkets by using simple, commonsensical methods. Some owners or partners literally drove around various neighborhoods to evaluate the potential for business and reported the findings to their groups to decide.[1] The locations usually proved favorable, and in selecting sites, the operators were a bit more calculating than they first appeared to be.

The operators favored locating their supermarkets in working-class communities and neighborhoods. An obvious reason was operational expense; the leases of the buildings for their stores were less costly in low-rent locations than in most other locations. But there were other intangible considerations upon which Chinese American grocers astutely capitalized. In these communities and neighborhoods, most of the residents were from an economic class comparable to that of Chinese Americans, and in some communities, most of the residents included a sizable number of minorities, such as Mexican Americans and African Americans. These socioeconomic factors created a sense of commonality between store personnel and customers, thereby facilitating patronage for the stores. Furthermore, the operators figured that because large expenditures, such as higher-class housing and real estate investments, were out of reach for most working-class people, they tended not to save their earnings for subsequent purchases, but immediately rewarded themselves for their labor with purchases of food, clothing, and automobiles. Thus, when they had money, working-class customers tended to spend it on groceries, although they keenly compared the prices of competing retailers for the best deals.[2]

Local residents were not the only ones trying to get as much value as possible for their money. In order to increase sales volume, Chinese American grocers started advertising sale items in local newspapers to draw shoppers from their competitors and from outside the neighborhoods. During the war years, China's alliance with the United States helped to largely erase lingering animosities against Chinese Americans, making shopping in their stores palatable for other classes and ethnic groups of the population. This attitude continued in the postwar period, manifesting itself mostly in retail dealings. In the grocery business, there had always been a portion of the public who shopped around weekly for the best bargains in addition to making routine purchases at their favorite or most convenient store. Grocers hoped that some of the customers who came for the advertised sale items would change their shopping habits; that is, that they would begin to shop regularly at their supermarkets, or at least make purchases of some regular-priced items to help offset the low-markup or losses of sale-priced items. Chinese American grocers called this the "hot and cold" method. With advertised sale items, the grocers drew in customers and raked in large weekly sales volumes, but the strategy was good only as long as a profit was made.[3]

Advertised sale items enabled shoppers to compare prices only on a very small number of items that competitors likewise featured, or about 1 percent of total products. Thus, shoppers could not really know if a particular store actually had the lowest prices overall. The rest of the merchandise could be comparably priced or higher priced than other supermarkets.[4] Chinese American supermarkets generally had the lowest advertised sale prices on key items which customers routinely purchased, such as mayonnaise, coffee, detergent, and so forth. To their credit, Chinese American grocers succeeded in fostering the perception that their stores had the lowest prices, making huge profits with their "hot and cold" method in tandem with their low labor costs.[5]

By the early 1960s Chinese American supermarkets had a well-established reputation among Northern California residents who readily shopped in them. Second-generation operators began locating their new supermarkets in middle-class and upper-middle-class communities and neighborhoods. Most of the new residential areas in Sacramento were built for young middle-class families. Grocers seeking a new, expanding customer base naturally would have liked to open their supermarkets in locations that either did not yet have a grocer to service them or had only one grocer, without nearby competition. Usually Chinese American grocers would just drive around new areas looking for sites, much like in the past, but occasionally developers would solicit them to occupy their shopping centers. The grocers would either purchase property on which to build shopping centers or lease buildings from landlords for their stores. Sometimes they would develop shopping centers, but sell them to investors and lease a portion of the centers for their stores.

Among the second-generation grocers there was no particular pattern or preference. Each of them did it one way or another at various points during the course of their enterprises. Obtaining financing from established lending institutions, wholesale vendors, and equipment brokers had ceased to be problematic because of the proven success and creditworthiness of Chinese Americans, although some still preferred to capitalize their new stores by using mostly their own money.[6]

CUSTOMER SERVICE

Customer service was either nonexistent or a special feature, depending upon a store's modus operandi to attract customers. Many stores neglected customer service in favor of lower operational costs, which helped them to sell at lower prices than their competitors. This method typified most of the first-generation Chinese American supermarkets that ran weekly advertisements in newspapers featuring heavily discounted items. In addition, customer service in these stores was generally inept because many of the employees, and occasionally some partners, were inadequately trained, had limited English-speaking skills, and were unfamiliar with American manners. This was especially problematic when employees were hired simply because they were family members, relatives, or friends of the owner or partners. In some instances, low-ranking management as well as customers found these employees difficult to deal with because they felt secure and privileged in their jobs. In other instances, however, they were the most productive and helpful employees because they felt that they had a remote economic stake in the store, or they felt truly indebted for being given the job. Securing employment through patronage, however, was not necessarily characteristic among all Chinese American supermarkets. Depending upon management, it occurred regularly in some supermarkets and occasionally or not at all in others. Prudent managers usually assigned gauche employees to jobs that took place away from customers, such as stocking shelves, working in the warehouse, and preparing meat and produce behind the counter. Management was quite aware of this shortcoming, but it was the trade-off for low-cost labor. Similarly, customers shopped in Chinese American supermarkets because of low prices on merchandise, not because of customer service. Because English-speaking personnel were necessary at the checkout counter, management hired Euro-American employees, generally women who worked part-time, to service the customers. This practice began in earnest after the war, and women from a store's neighborhood were frequently preferred.[7]

Stores that featured service to attract customers tended to have higher overall prices than stores that featured weekly sale items. There were fewer of the former than the latter. One company, Bel Air, acquired a reputation and identity for offering very attentive customer service. Although stores that featured service had their periods of downturns and their share of closures, they generally remained competitive and in business longer than the other type. Higher prices paid for extra service, such as more open checkout counters for faster service, grocery carryout to customers' automobiles, and special orders or preparation of meat, produce, and groceries. Accordingly, some customers liked to be pampered by familiar clerks in their local supermarket in which they shopped regularly. These stores often became social as well as economic components of their neighborhoods or communities, regularly involved in or donating to local community activities. Because of good maintenance and periodic remodeling, the stores were cleaner, better organized, and generally more up-to-date than stores that emphasized sale items. But aesthetics and service were not exclusive to certain operations or companies. Some of the first-generation supermarkets expanded, remodeled, and offered customer service to increase profits, meet new competition, or just to maintain their market share. In general, all supermarket operations had to adapt in some degree to changes in the industry and in local markets, but the ones featuring customer service tended to be much more progressive, continuously investing in the latest marketing trends.[8]

The less-than-stellar reputation for "maintenance and housekeeping" among Chinese American supermarkets, especially the older and first-generation ones, must be evaluated in the context of their local markets and competition. Considered part of customer service, maintenance and house-keeping was not much better among many stores of the national companies, such as Safeway and Lucky, from the postwar years to the mid-1960s. Until the national companies began using local surveys to determine customers' priorities in selecting which stores to patronize, supermarkets generally did not pay particular attention to good service, clean stores, and competitive prices to attract customers. When they did, the older Chinese American supermarkets were already beginning to decline fast, not wanting or doing much to maintain their competitiveness. Meanwhile, the second-generation supermarkets were implementing preferences expressed by shoppers, usually following improvements done first by the national chain companies.[9]

MORE BUSINESS BASICS

The average first-generation supermarket had about 10,000 square feet in sales floor space and was simple and relatively inexpensive to start up, generally costing about $20,000 in the mid-1930s to $30,000 in the mid-1950s. Nearly every supermarket was similar in size and modernity, and was usually the only tenant of a building, although sometimes there were a few small businesses along the front or one side. To minimize capitalization, stores were equipped with only essential equipment—refrigeration, shelving, grocery carts, and so forth—and were operated with limited maintenance. After opening, there usually would be little if any updating or remodeling of the supermarket. The Famous Food Markets—a cooperative of seven supermarkets connected by common partners or shareholders who shared the expenses of advertising and sometimes purchased merchandise in large quantities to take advantage of wholesale discounts—were typical of this first-generation type of operation. The four supermarkets of the Giant Foods chain and most of the forty supermarkets of the Farmers Market chain operated in like manner, although some later remodeled, and the ones that opened in the mid-1960s were larger, up-to-date, and better maintained.[10]

By the late 1960s, location selection became more calculated, following the trends of industry standards. The larger supermarkets, about 20,000 to 30,000 square feet, were built in medium- and large-sized shopping centers. These larger supermarkets served as anchors for numerous small businesses and sometimes for other large retailers as well.

The increasingly high costs of setting up a supermarket forced Chinese Americans to seek institutional financing. If not leased, the purchase of the land and building was the largest expenditure, accounting for more than half of the capital outlay of approximately $1.5 million. Equipment, inventory, and start-up costs made up the bulk of the other portion.[11] After commencing business, operating the supermarket was much more costly than a first-generation store. In addition, competition was more intense, profits were thinner, and trial-and-error was unfeasible.

By the mid-1970s, the national chain companies began to aggressively pursue a larger segment of the retail food business in Northern California by building more supermarkets and heavily advertising their new low prices. More supermarkets were competing for a piece of a fixed or slower-growing economic pie: the consumer's dollar. In order to remain competitive against the major national chains and a rapidly expanding local chain company, Raley's, the two remaining Chinese American supermarket chains, Jumbo and Bel Air, kept building larger stores in new neighborhoods and communities. There was an economy of scale in operating more stores: costs of advertising, administration, and transportation were spread, and the wholesale cost of merchandise was reduced through allowances and premiums that were rebated for large purchases. These stores also advertised heavily and began promoting special incentives such as discounted dishware or kitchenware, store and manufacturer coupons, and give-away prizes to maintain and expand their customer base. Expense margins grew, and profit margins shrank. Although there was little choice but to keep opening additional stores, the owners clung to management practices that had brought them success in the past.

Some of the national chain supermarkets, on the other hand, resorted to the low-overhead, warehouse-type of approach of the 1930s, offering limited selection and no-frills shopping to lower grocery prices. Other companies began building huge superstores to capture larger markets with a greater selection of products and departments.

Companies were also responding to the economic recessions and persistent inflation triggered by the Arab oil embargo of 1973–74 and the high oil prices of 1979, which drastically affected retail food prices and sales. The spiraling energy prices greatly raised the electrical costs of a supermarket's air conditioning, refrigeration, and freezers, which was usually very high under typical circumstances. Likewise, higher energy charges affected food processing and distribution costs, adding to food prices. Borrowing money to build or remodel stores was prohibitively expensive because of high interest rates. Finally, a decline in the birth rate curbed the rapid population growth, which had sustained the expansion of supermarkets after the war.[12] If any appraisal can be made about Chinese American operators during this period, it would be that they showed remarkable perseverance and optimism in a business that guaranteed high costs and risk while offering the prospect of low returns.

Profits from the grocery stores and early supermarkets enabled their owners to purchase the properties and buildings which their stores occupied. Real estate ownership saved money that would otherwise be spent on leases and provided owners with long-term tangible investments. In family operations, ownership belonged to the entire family. In partnership operations, sometimes one or two of the partners would purchase the real estate as an investment and lease it to the partnership if all did not agree to ownership. Often a new supermarket would get its facilities this way; one or a few partners would purchase the property, erect a building, and lease it to the partnership. The main purpose for acquiring additional real estate was to secure a location for a future store. During the 1970s the appreciation of real estate holdings and their sale subsequently became more profitable than selling groceries. None of the Chinese American operators initially intended to purchase real estate for the purpose of investment for profit.[13]

Capital for real estate purchases came from the cash flow of the stores as well as from personal, family, or partnership assets. The supermarket business generated a large amount of revenue every day. The receipts, whether cash or checks, were deposited in the bank daily, but payments to vendors and wholesalers were usually made every thirty, sixty, or ninety days. With accounts flushed with cash, supermarket owners made down payments on real estate. They made monthly payments on the properties with money from store receipts or rent if they were already developed and generating income. The whole scheme worked very well when the stores maintained or increased their sales volume and the real estate appreciated in value. Profits were made upon the sale, development, and lease of real estate. If a store's business declined, its real estate value nonetheless almost always appreciated in the long term.[14]

The owners of the first-generation supermarkets conducted business deals with cash. It was not necessary to rely on credit from banks because they were cash rich. For example, when plans were made for Yuba Grocery, a store in Marysville, California, opened in the 1930s by Lee Gim and his partners, each of the partners put cash into a pool with which the partnership purchased the real estate, handing over currency to the seller. Transactions were simple, direct, and expedient. This simple approach was also used in the formation of partnerships where each partner's word, backed by his reputation, consummated the union. Operations involving family members, relatives, and close friends, who were mutually trustworthy and diligent, made this type of business relationship workable. In the 1950s, owners began using the services of banks because supermarkets became more expensive to open and operate, necessitating the need for financing. They had learned to use and trust banks, and their success in business and their assets made them attractive clients. In earlier years, borrowing from banks, if possible, would have been difficult because the owners had not established a record of good credit due to their preference to use cash. Memory of the failures of the 1930s and of past discrimination against Chinese Americans by banks contributed to the owners' wariness in trusting them.[15]

By the late 1950s, Chinese American supermarket operators had no difficulty obtaining extended credit from wholesalers and vendors. By and large, they had a reputation for success, but more importantly, for paying their bills on time. They had assets accumulated in bank accounts, family homes, and commercial real estate—the properties which their stores occupied—for collateral. Grocery wholesalers were soliciting their business, offering better deals than Valley Wholesale Grocery in terms of price, transportation, and payment schedules. Vendors extended the grace period for payments due from fifteen to thirty to sixty days or more. Essentially, doing business with inventory purchased on extended credit amounted to securing an interest-free loan, or, to put it another way, doing business using somebody else's money for free. Occasionally the grocer did not pay his bill until after the due date, but the vendor or wholesaler did not dispute the late payment or complain. Suppliers needed grocers to sell their products as much as the latter needed the products purchased on credit to sell. It was a symbiotic relationship, but the more stores the owners or partnerships owned, the stronger their leverage and the better their deals with the suppliers.[16]

SPREADING SUCCESS

Flushed with profits, Lee Gim and his employees pooled their savings from Chung Sun Grocery to form partnerships to open new supermarkets. By the mid-1930s, the supermarket trend was gathering momentum throughout California, and a partnership with Lee was formed to open Yuba Grocery. The high profits from their first supermarket prompted the partners and their employees to form additional partnerships to open stores in other small communities and then in Sacramento during the 1940s and 1950s. The rapid success of each store attracted willing investors from other businesses and occupations to become partners or shareholders. Inclusion into a partnership was dictated as much by the need for a partner's ability to manage a store and to work long hours as the need for his capital. As the paternal founder of Chung Sun and the person with the most resources and experience, Lee Gim was invariably invited by prospective partners to become a partner. Their belief that Lee had a Midas touch also figured into the plans. Because some of the new owners were acquaintances, not related or longtime friends, their alliances were not as close and trusting as in the earlier stores. But the challenge of opening a new store along with cultural propriety and good profits maintained harmony in a partnership.[17]

There were primarily two types of partners: active partners and passive partners. Most partners were active and worked in the store daily, while one or a few were passive partners or shareholders who did not work in the store and occasionally showed up for inspection only. This type of ownership was found in all of the grocery stores and supermarkets in which Lee Gim was a passive partner, including the Famous Food Markets. The Farmers Market chain had a similar setup in many of its supermarkets, but one passive partner, Walter Fong, owned most of the shares in each store. At the end of the year, the partners divided the profits according to the amount of each partner's investment relative to the total capitalization. Since the active partners worked, it was expected that each received a weekly salary, but sometimes by agreement the passive partners also received regular salaries even though they did not work. Each partner also had a voice in management meetings, but often the weight of the voice was dependent upon the amount of investment. The inequality in profit distribution was understood and generally accepted. Later the unearned compensations and unequal voices often became acute points of contention when business and profits declined, views differed, and personalities conflicted. An active partner, for example, would resent the passive partner with the larger investment and voice because the latter did not perform any labor and directed the former about how to operate the store. A partner usually held on to his investment, not selling his share unless he was in financial difficulty or had other pressing reasons. If he did sell, his share was generally bought by another partner or divided equally and bought by the other partners. Very seldom did a new investor purchase the share and enter the partnership.[18]

Recognized for his unselfish disposition and good judgment, Lee Gim often served as an arbitrator for discord among partners, trying to restore harmony.

But his mediation harbored an ulterior motive. He often loaned money to a relative or close friend to help him become a partner in a new operation. This benevolence, which favored those who showed ability and promise, helped Lee to look after his investment because the novice partner would be obligated to and allied with him during management decisions. Thus, when it came to selecting a manager for a store, his choice had more sway and support than the choices of other partners.[19]

In 1927, a new partnership opened Marysville Grocery with a startup of about $10,000. The partners converted the back of the leased building into room-and-board facilities for their employees, all of whom were immigrants from China and either unmarried or without family in America. Everyone worked six days a week from six o'clock in the morning until closing time at six o'clock in the evening. As was common in all grocery stores during that time, Marysville Grocery was closed on Sundays and holidays. About eight years later the store burned to the ground. Creating opportunity from disaster, the partnership decided to purchase a warehouse located down the street and reopen as Yuba Grocery, the supermarket formed by Lee and his partners. Costing less than $20,000 to open, the sales volume, about $50,000 a week, was extremely good from the start. After World War II started, the partnership could not find enough labor to continue running the supermarket; therefore, they closed the store until the war ended two years later. When the supermarket reopened, the partnership persuaded Lee's twenty-year-old son, Leland, to drop out of school to manage Yuba Grocery. His consent to render his services for a few years stretched to over thirty years. In 1955, Leland Lee and his partnership relocated Yuba Grocery into a new building which the Lee family had built several blocks away. Lee had an architect design room-and-board facilities on the second floor in the back of the building for his employees: fifteen bedrooms, a kitchen and dining area, and a living room. Although Lee's facilities were exceptionally large, the accommodations were typical among Chinese American supermarkets that opened in the 1950s and earlier. Renamed Yuba Market, the supermarket grossed $70,000 to 75,000 a week until it closed in 1978, neither increasing nor decreasing much in sales volume in the twenty-plus years of its operation.[20]

Lee Gim's Chung Sun Grocery germinated the seeds of this kind of store dissemination. From each grocery store, new partnerships formed to open more grocery stores such that in about a decade, they were sprouting like weeds throughout Northern California. Early grocery stores included Yolo Grocery, Oroville Grocery, Willows Grocery, Auburn Grocery, Lodi Grocery, Napa Grocery, Petaluma Grocery, Fairfield Grocery, Vacaville Grocery, Stockton

Grocery, and others. It was common for stores to be named after the towns and counties in which they were located. A few of the grocery stores expanded in size to become supermarkets, and new partnerships formed to open supermarkets, some locating in the Sacramento area. One of the first Chinese American supermarkets in Northern California was Fine Food Market in north Sacramento, which opened in 1939. Wonder Food Market opened in Sacramento soon afterwards, in 1940.

During the war, the expansion of supermarkets in Northern California stopped because of the general shortage of material and labor. It resumed at a fast pace soon after the end of the war: Linda Super Market in Linda, 1948; Broderick Market in Broderick, 1949; Lee's Supermarket in Weaverville, 1949; State Fair and Freeway Markets in Sacramento, 1950; Sutter Super Market in Yuba City, 1952; Sylvan Super Market in Citrus Heights, 1952; General Food Market in Sacramento, 1953; and El Camino Market in Carmichael, 1955. Like most of the supermarkets in the 1950s, each had about 10,000 square feet in retail sales space and accommodations in the back of the building for employees, for whom a cook was usually hired. Napa Grocery expanded into a supermarket within a shopping center in 1956. Wonder Food Market relocated down the street into a larger building in 1957, enlarging from 9,000 to 14,000 square feet. Throughout this "store crazy" period of openings and expansions, including a new Chung Sun Market in 1956, the Lee family had shares in various amounts in all of them.[21] A few shareholders also had investments in more than one supermarket. In 1958, Fine Food, Wonder Food, Broderick, General Food, State Fair, and El Camino joined with Freeway Market to form the Famous Food Markets. Their weekly advertisements featuring low sale prices ran in the *Sacramento Bee* for almost ten years.[22]

The booming neighborhoods in Sacramento and its suburbs provided larger markets with higher sales volumes than in the small communities, but they also attracted more competition from national and local chain companies. It was a trade-off. Nevertheless, Chinese American operators felt that they had their competition beat with their lower prices via cheaper labor. They found out their competitors' prices simply by making regular visits to their supermarkets. New or better operating and merchandising methods were observed and sometimes adopted for use. This practice still goes on today among all supermarket operators. On the whole, the Chinese American supermarkets had sales volumes ranging from $70,000 to $85,000 a week, and profit margins ranging from 5 to 10 percent of sales. Because the supermarkets were private enterprises, the owners kept their exact sales volumes, profit margins, and accounting methods confidential. And because most owners did not incorporate their operations, they did not pay corporate taxes, which would have reduced their gross profits.[23]

The sales volumes and profit margins of Chinese American supermarkets were very impressive when compared to national standards. The national chain companies, for example, had net (after-tax) profit margins ranging from 1.1 to 1.5 percent for the years 1948 to 1958 and from 0.99 to 1.4 percent for the years 1962 to 1969. Profit margins of single- and multiple-supermarkets of local companies were usually a little higher, as were some individual supermarkets of national companies, depending upon local markets, operating policies, and management skills. In comparison, the profit margins of non-food retailing operations—for example, Sears, J. C. Penney, and Woolworth—ranged from 3.4 to 5.1 percent in 1965. Generally the sales volumes for supermarkets that opened in the 1960s were higher than for those that opened in the 1950s. The retail sales space of supermarkets was likewise larger as the industry became more competitive. Although varying greatly, the national average for the 1967 sales volume of a local independent or chain supermarket was about $1.46 million, and about $1.57 million for a national chain supermarket, or about $30,000 a week.[24]

The good profits mitigated the unwanted terms of the labor contracts coerced upon the Chinese American supermarkets by the labor unions. Beginning with Yuba Market, nearly all of the supermarkets eventually operated under union labor agreements. But this did not prevent the management from requesting payment for the cost of room and board from the employees who resided on the premises. There was also the tacit understanding between employers and employees to work extra hours without compensation. Eventually this arrangement ran into difficulty when some employees informed the Retail Clerks Union about it. In 1955 the union sued Leland Lee and his partners in Marysville and Yuba City for about five million dollars for noncompliance of labor agreements and for employees' back wages. The union solicited the help of the federal government to look into any matter related to immigration and the use of immigrant workers. At that time, the federal government was investigating the possibility that the "paper son" scheme was being used to infiltrate Chinese Communist agents into the country. Chinese American owners of other supermarkets watched the litigation carefully because they had been engaging in the same labor practices. The lawsuit was eventually settled, but Lee as well as the managers of other first-generation supermarkets became more careful with their labor practices and sharply curtailed their sponsorship of immigrants.[25] By the early 1960s, such activities either ceased or tapered off among first-generation supermarkets.

The second-generation supermarkets did not rely on unpaid labor, although work performed voluntarily by ambitious employees was not unheard of. Furthermore, the type of employee that Lee and other employers depended upon to help them maintain low labor costs and high profit margins was already diminishing in number and changing in his outlook. At the same time, many employers had changed feelings toward their employees, which consequently adversely affected the competitiveness of their supermarkets.

DICK'S MARKET

One of Lee Gim's partners in the early grocery stores and supermarkets was Dick Yee. Yee subsequently branched out with his own group of partners, consisting of family members and relatives, and opened supermarkets in the San Jose area. In 1948, Yee opened the first Dick's Market. Like Lee's supermarkets, Yee relied on high sales volume achieved by low prices to make a profit. Within a few years, Yee began expanding Dick's Market by acquiring established stores and building new ones while selling his stake in the old partnerships. Using their real estate assets for leverage, the Yee partnership decided to lease their future stores rather than to purchase property and construct buildings, thereby avoiding tying up large amounts of capital. In addition, wholesalers readily co-signed leases to help the partnership expand. By the late 1960s the partnership had invested in eleven Dick's Markets in the San Jose area.[26]

One of the primary reasons for Yee's success was economy of scale. Advertising costs were spread out over numerous stores, and the wholesale costs of groceries were reduced by volume purchases. Direct purchases from food manufacturers and drop shipments from wholesalers were stored in large warehouses in the back of the supermarkets. The savings were passed on to customers or retained as extra profits for the stores. During the high inflationary period from the mid-1970s to early 1980s, the value of the inventory increased greatly, which consequently raised the price of products and profits for the stores.[27] But storing products was financially risky if they were purchased on credit and did not sell before their invoices came due, which could put a squeeze on the stores' cash flow.

From the start, the employees were enrolled in the Retail Clerks Union Local 428. The local was very strong in the area, forcing all stores to consent to the union labor contract. At Dick's Market all personnel, except for one manager, had to join the union, including Dick Yee's children, who served as department managers. The strength of the local was such that in the early

1950s, Dick's Market had to follow the rates set by the union when charging employees for room and board in the stores.[28]

Most of the employees were immigrants who had families in China and were related to Dick Yee, such as cousins or distant relatives from the same village. Some of them became minor partners in the stores in which they worked. When Dick's Market began rapid expansion in the early 1960s, the management began employing Euro-Americans who did not need living quarters. At that time, the immigrant employees began bringing their families over to America, where they lived in homes or apartments. Hence, there was a decreasing need for room-and-board facilities in the stores, the last of which was built in 1959.[29]

Since the Yee family had majority interest in all of the stores, Dick Yee's eldest son, Gene, eventually took over the helm of the family's businesses, Dick Yee Incorporated, which controlled Dick's Market. Dick's Market became a prominent competitor in the San Jose area in the 1960s, surpassing most of its competitors in the number of stores and in sales volume per store. Chinese Americans operated only one other supermarket in the San Jose area, but it never expanded into a chain. Chinese Americans also operated small grocery stores in the area, but they never became supermarkets. Gene Yee increased his control over the corporation by purchasing shares from relatives to consolidate his family's holdings. In the early 1970s, a tidal wave of supermarket expansion led by national companies seriously challenged Dick's Market in the San Jose area, which itself was undergoing rapid population growth and transformation invigorated by an emerging personal computer industry.[30]

GIANT FOODS

In 1949 the Quan family, which had its roots in the grocery business in the late 1930s with the Eye Street Bridge Market, began advertising in the *Sacramento Bee* after being persuaded by a salesman from the newspaper. The advertising was also undertaken in response to the opening of Broderick Market one block away from the Eye Street Bridge Market. The Broderick Market was operated by a partnership that included Lee Gim. The weekly advertisements increased the Quans' sales volume tremendously as shoppers from outside the neighborhood traveled to Broderick to purchase sale items at Eye Street Bridge Market. For the next twenty-plus years, the Quans depended on advertised low prices to draw customers and to attain high sales volumes. The increased revenues permitted the Quans to expand their operation.[31]

1. Eye (I) Street Bridge Market, Broderick, c. 1939. This was a typical drive-up market, in front of which customers would conveniently park their automobiles. Courtesy of George Quan Jr.

2. Interior of the Liberty Meat Market, Sacramento, c. 1930. Many Chinese Americans got their start in the retail food business as butchers in meat markets. Courtesy of the Anna W. Lee Collection, Sacramento Archives and Museum Collection Center.

3. Chung Sun Grocery, Colusa, c. 1949. Many Chinese Americans apprenticed in the grocery business at Chung Sun, which opened in 1921. From Ling Lew, *The Chinese in North America* (Los Angeles: East-West Culture Publishing Association, 1949), p. 22.

4. Wonder Food Market, Sacramento, c. 1949. Fountain service was a feature that became popular in supermarkets earlier in the decade. From Lew 1949:23.

5. Stockton Grocery, Stockton, c. 1949. Some early supermarkets occupied the lower floors of buildings located in downtown areas. From Lew 1949:22.

6. New Vallejo Grocery, Vallejo, c. 1949. The opening of a new Chinese American supermarket regularly drew hordes of shoppers who were enticed by low sale prices. From Lew 1949:22.

7. Dick's Market, San Jose, c. 1949. The real estate that this supermarket occupied eventually became more valuable than the business itself. From Lew 1949:27.

8. Centr-O-Mart, Stockton, c. 1949. Unlike typical supermarkets, Centr-O-Mart had many departments, including bakery, sundry, liquor, tobacco, hardware, stationery, furniture, a pharmacy, and a coffee shop/soda fountain. From Lew 1949:24.

9. Coffee shop/soda fountain of Centr-O-Mart, Stockton, c. 1949. Amenities such as this began disappearing from supermarkets in the 1960s, only to reappear and gain popularity in the 1990s. From Lew 1949:25.

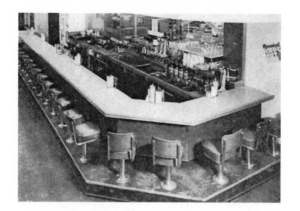

10. Liquor Department of Centr-O-Mart, Stockton, c. 1949. Although a license to sell was expensive, liquor sales provided high profits for stores. From Lew 1949:25.

11. Meat Department of Centr-O-Mart, Stockton, c. 1949. Almost 100 feet long, the full-service meat counter was the pride of the supermarket. From Lew 1949:25.

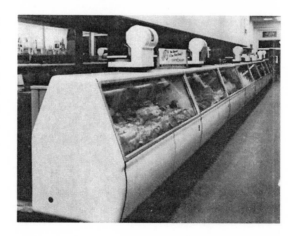

12. Wonder Food Market, November 1949. Its anniversary sale drew shoppers with a raffle that awarded food baskets, small and large appliances, and even a bicycle. Courtesy of the Boyd Jensen Collection, Sacramento Archives and Museum Collection Center.

13. *(facing page)* Anniversary celebration sales, such as that of Stop-N-Shop's 31st anniversary, sometimes featured the prize of an automobile as well as other awards, such as a trip to Hollywood, televisions, radios, and appliances. Of course, there were super saver specials as well. From *Sacramento Guide,* April 7, 1959.

14. Stop-N-Shop, Sacramento, c. 1929. A.G. Kassis (proprietor) and sons Walter, Frank, and John in front of their small market. Courtesy of Greg Kassis.

15. Stop-N-Shop, Sacramento, c. 1949. For customer convenience, this supermarket on Riverside Boulevard included a U.S. Post Office, a pharmacy, and a bakery. Stop-N-Shop featured S&H Green Stamps, which were given with purchases to customers, who saved and exchanged them for gifts. Courtesy of Greg Kassis.

In 1951 the Quans opened a supermarket in North Highlands, a community that had its economic foundation in the McClellan Air Force Base. The origin of McClellan Market had begun about six years earlier, when a product salesman invited an uninterested George Quan, Jr., to join him to look at a potential location for a supermarket. They drove out to an area north of Sacramento where there were many single-family houses and where more were planned. There was already a Cardinal Grocery Store in the area—an operation that was later purchased by the Lucky Stores—which was, as Quan discovered by talking to the local bread vendor, the leading store in sales volume in the Sacramento area. The family immediately secured a small parcel near the base and within five years purchased the parcel and its adjacent property for about $50,000. In order to finance the construction of a building on the ten-acre parcel, they went to their bank, which required from them a financial statement. Such a statement was something that the Quans knew nothing about, let alone had in possession. But with substantial cash balances in their bank accounts, they had no problem obtaining a five-year loan, which they were able to pay off in three years.[32]

With money in hand, the Quans wanted to make plans for the store, instead of doing things the old haphazard way. But their approach was not much different from that in the past. George Quan, Jr., and a brother drove down to Los Angeles to inspect the successful operation of a well-known supermarket, Panorama Market. They studied the layout and equipment of the store and made sketches of what they saw. Back home, an architect finalized the design, from which a contractor constructed the building. McClellan Market opened for business with prices lower than any of its competitors. During the opening week it drew in shoppers so numerous that automobile traffic was backed up on the street and highway leading to the store. The supermarket had one of the highest weekly sales volumes in Northern California in that year, but its profit margin of 1 to 2 percent was lower than that of other Chinese American–owned supermarkets. Accordingly, the Quans had to generate high sales volume to make a profit.[33]

For years George Quan, Jr., had been eyeing a location in the eastern part of Sacramento where a Lucky supermarket was doing good business. In 1961 the Quans purchased a building near this location that was occupied by Grand View Market, a supermarket operated by a Chinese American whose business appeared to be on the decline. The Quans enlarged the floor space by tearing down the walls and commenced business as Giant Foods, a name to which their other stores would change over. Nine months later the Quans purchased another supermarket in the same way in northeast Sacramento.

It became the fourth Giant Foods Market, but the last supermarket the Quans would open.[34]

Like other Chinese American supermarket owners, the Quans eventually had to deal with the labor unions. With a one-store family operation, Eye Street Bridge Market, labor union representatives did not doggedly pursue the Quans to accede to their demands. But soon after the Quans opened their second supermarket, an operation whose personnel did not consist mostly of family members, union representatives applied heavy pressure on the Quans to agree to labor contracts. The Quans thereafter paid union rate wages and agreed to abide by contract provisions; for example, they no longer paid their employees once a month, but weekly.[35] The operational expenses of the Quans' supermarkets quickly rose to a level similar to their non–Chinese American competitors. The Quans continued to turn good profits, but other pressures during the early 1970s would be more difficult to overcome.

GOING UPSCALE

The Wong family first ventured into the grocery business in the late 1930s with Save More Market. The first year of business was not prosperous for its Bel Air supermarket, which opened in 1955. With almost the whole family working the supermarket, the Wongs were able to endure this period by drawing nominal wages for themselves and working long hours. They advertised their grand opening in the newspaper, but business was slow in coming. In hindsight, this was not surprising, since the primary reason the public shopped in Chinese American supermarkets was for their reputed low prices. Bel Air's prices, on the other hand, were higher overall than those of other stores, including those of national chain companies, because of higher labor expenses, which were necessary to provide customer service. From the beginning to the end of the Wongs' ownership, Bel Air supermarkets were known to have higher prices than nearly all of their competitors, but they also had the best service and selection and were the most innovative.[36]

The Wongs' attempts to be innovative were not always successful. Bel Air started offering pre-packaged, plastic-wrapped products soon after opening, and it was one of the first stores in the Sacramento area to do so. But customers were not receptive to this new type of merchandising, and the store was forced to return to the conventional method. This experience taught the Wongs to first sell an idea to the public through advertising so that a product or service had a chance to succeed. Even that did not guarantee success. During the 1970s the family opened a small chain of Chinese fast food outlets and several discount, warehouse-type liquor stores. Assigning the next generation of Wongs to manage them, the first venture was truly an innovative enterprise, whereas the second followed a retailing trend. They advertised heavily and gave time for their new enterprises to build up business. Unfortunately, both ventures failed due to unforeseen and unsolvable problems in operations and miscalculations in public preferences. The Wongs also invested in a centralized bakery to produce products for their supermarkets, but it turned out to be inefficient even though it looked promising on paper.[37]

Failures were not limited to new types of enterprises. During the 1960s the Wongs operated two Bel Air supermarkets that were marginally profitable, and subsequently closed them because they had low sales volumes. An inherent problem for one of the supermarkets was that the building and layout were smaller than their newer stores, which made it unsuitable for enlarging or remodeling to bring it up to the company's newer standards. In addition, both stores were located in neighborhoods where customers favored lower prices over better service. These missteps impacted the family's bottom line, but the Wongs cut their losses and moved on.[38]

Regarding its successful innovations, Bel Air supermarkets were among the first stores in the Sacramento area to offer pharmacies, postal service stations, full-service bank branches, and utility bill payment stations in their stores, conveniences that drew in customers who may not have otherwise shopped in a Bel Air. These services also pleased their regular customers and strengthened their loyalty. Some stores even provided play-care centers for children. Taking advantage of the Sacramento region's ethnic diversity and the cuisine's popularity, they opened Chinese hot food take-out departments in their stores, which immediately became enormously profitable. It became a trend that competitors soon followed.[39]

The Wongs were also willing to commit resources to adopt general trends of the industry. They started a trucking company to transport merchandise from warehouses to stores and a wholesale florist for processing flowers and plants, which reduced product costs. Along with other local chain supermarket companies, one of which was also a major competitor, Bel Air invested in a wholesale grocery company and a dairy processing plant. While these investments reduced expenses, they also provided additional revenue from the contracting of services and products to other food retailers. These ventures and investments occurred during the 1970s and 1980s, when many other supermarket operations were cautious about committing capital for expansion because of the vicissitudes of the business. In essence, the Wongs' risk-taking spirit exemplified the true meaning of the word entrepreneur and challenged the popular notion of the conservative Chinese American businessmen, a description more fitting for most of their peers. Their willingness to take risks and commit resources yielded strong gains in both profits and market share.[40]

About two years after opening the first Bel Air store, the Wongs opened a second supermarket in a middle-class neighborhood. More supermarkets opened as they built new stores and purchased stores from other operators. The Wongs continually enlarged and remodeled the older stores to reflect Bel Air's emphasis on superior service and selection, both of which served as its identity. After the closure of two stores in the 1960s, nearly every subsequent supermarket was larger and more modern than the previous one, reaching about 50,000 square feet in sales-floor space. Their constant vigilance toward quality merchandising and service was measured not only within their stores but also against their competitors, whose stores they continued to scrutinize through regular visits. Altogether the Wongs operated seventeen supermarkets in the Sacramento area by 1992.[41]

Bel Air's expansion began in the mid-1970s. Business cycle uncertainties and industry trend misfires created opportunities for Bel Air. The economic recessions of the 1970s caused the national chain companies to delay opening new supermarkets. In addition, the new concept of total discount shopping and the reintroduction of warehouse-type shopping in response to the recessions were not completely successful. Hence, the expansion of national chain supermarkets in Sacramento appeared stalled, and their marketing strategies seemed aimless, if not confused. Real estate developers thus began courting the Wongs when national companies backed out of their agreements to become tenants of upscale shopping centers located in prime locations. They desperately needed occupants for their nearly finished buildings. The Wongs seized the opportunities, calculating that the customer base to which Bel Air catered was less affected by recessions than other segments of the population. Nevertheless, the Wongs had to endure periods of low sales volume in their new stores before turning good profits. In the early 1990s the Wongs themselves became primary investors for the development of shopping centers in which they opened their supermarkets.[42]

When the Wongs began Bel Air, they hired the most qualified people, whether they were relatives, friends, or ordinary applicants, giving them a probationary period to determine whether they would work out. This was a distinct departure from the practices of the early Chinese American supermarkets, whose operators felt obligated to employ relatives or friends, especially those from the same villages in China, and to retain them whether they were productive or not. As Bel Air expanded, the hiring and training of new personnel became the responsibility of a human resource director. This was in line with the Wongs' employment of company-wide supervisors and directors, acknowledging that they themselves could not micromanage everything. Although they delegated authority to department managers, the Wongs did not totally distance themselves from the day-to-day operation of their supermarkets. They were in the stores daily, working in the same capacity as before, acting like the parents of a growing family of employees. Certainly there were some interfamilial disagreements regarding management, but they were not insurmountable, a fact confirmed by their long history as an effective working family. Regarding the Wongs' children, some of them also worked in the supermarkets in various capacities because the jobs were readily available. Others sought occupations and careers outside the retail food business, but all had greater opportunities for more kinds of livelihood than their parents did.[43]

The Wongs bestowed concern and commitment to their employees, who reciprocated with dedication and hard work. Their reputation for personnel management was so highly regarded in the local industry that clerks of other supermarkets coveted employment in a Bel Air supermarket. Similarly, the Wongs treated with respect and courtesy the vendors and salespersons who called on their stores. They held annual parties for everybody associated with the operation of their supermarkets to show their appreciation. But simple success could not be consummated without the patronage of loyal customers. To express appreciation towards them, the Wongs gave each female customer a rose during Christmas. This was in addition to the loaning of appliances such as large coolers and coffee urns at no cost to community, family, business, and other types of gatherings. Finally, the Wongs regularly provided tours of their supermarkets to neighborhood schoolchildren, the next generation of shoppers.[44]

JUMBO MARKET

Jumbo Market was one of the two most prominent Chinese American supermarket companies in the Sacramento area during the 1960s and 1970s. The other was Farmers Market, a chain that opened forty supermarkets and then declined rapidly, selling closing stores during the later half of the 1970s. Jumbo Market grew to eleven stores before it gradually faded out of business. The first Jumbo Market opened in 1961 and was owned by nine partners, a majority of which received their training while employed in first-generation super-markets. The success of the first and subsequent stores was based primarily on high sales volumes. This was achieved by drawing in shoppers through the use of weekly newspaper advertisements featuring sale items, the same strategy the first-generation supermarkets used.[45]

Business was phenomenal the first year, with weekly sales of about $100,000. Jumbo Market advertised "loss leaders" to bring in customers, but made its profits from the sale of other items marked at average prices. The partners made regular trips to their competitor across the street, a local chain called Mayfair Market, to check its prices. Jumbo Market would then under-cut Mayfair's prices by one or a few cents on each item. Years later, business at the location was good enough to attract a national chain company, Safeway, which opened a large supermarket diagonally across the street. Both com-petitors eventually succumbed to the economic recessions of the 1970s and the changing demography of the neighborhood.[46]

The partners earned huge profits because they were the core personnel. Each held a key position in the operation and willingly worked long hours to ensure productivity and profits. At first they needed to hire only a few employees, but as business increased more employees were hired, including several Euro-American women checkers who worked part-time, and a few Chinese Americans, some of whom were relatives and close friends. Because old practices do not cease overnight, Chinese American employees were expected to work extra hours without compensation. This practice, in addi-tion to the partners working long hours, kept labor costs very low. Except for the designated manager who was not allowed to join, the partners, along with the employees, were labor union members, receiving health and wel-fare benefits. Years later when the partnership incorporated, the partners were forced to leave the unions, whereupon they became shareholders of the corporation.[47]

The partnership was not conceived with the goal of building a supermar-ket chain. But profits were so great at Jumbo Market that the partnership decided to open another supermarket. In 1963, their second Jumbo Market opened in a developing area of southeast Sacramento that was void of a super-market. The rapidly growing middle-class neighborhood provided Jumbo Market with even greater sales volume than the first store. Flushed with suc-cess, the partners opened a third Jumbo Market in 1965 in Sacramento's north area. The location proved much less successful than the first two because the neighborhood, although still growing, was already established with homes and was served by other supermarkets. The fourth Jumbo Market opened in a middle- and upper-middle-class neighborhood in the southwest area of Sacramento in 1966, encroaching on the market of a smaller Safeway store in an adjacent shopping center. It did great business because of its lower prices and newer, bigger facilities than Safeway's, both of which attracted hordes of customers from the burgeoning neighborhood. The fifth Jumbo Market formed from a merger during the late 1960s with an existing Chinese American supermarket located twenty-five miles west of Sacramento, in the rural community of Dixon. It was not until late 1974 that the company opened its sixth supermarket at the eastern edge of Sacramento. The seventh supermarket formed in the following year from a merger with a Giant Foods Market. The opening of the next four supermarkets continued into the early 1980s, three in the suburbs of Sacramento and one in the foothill town of Jackson, an hour's drive away. Although the neighborhoods that the stores served were still growing, all four stores had to compete with nearby established supermarkets immediately upon opening.[48]

CENTR-O-MART AND DIAMOND PROPERTIES

Within a few years after opening his first Centr-O-Mart supermarket in Stockton in 1946, Sam Wah You also enlarged his three "country stores" into Centr-O-Marts, which sold basic products such as groceries, meat, and produce. Later, he opened another Centr-O-Mart in Brentwood. In these country stores, there were no cafés or household and pharmacy departments, as in the larger Stockton store. In the early 1950s, Sam Wah You began opening more supermarkets in Stockton, building a few in new middle-class neighborhoods and others in working-class neighborhoods. When he finished, there were six stores in Stockton competing against national chain and local chain companies as well as independents.

Unlike the first Centr-O-Mart, the newer Stockton stores were typical supermarkets in size and merchandise. They received fresh bakery items from the main store and groceries from San Joaquin. During the decade, business was very good. One year, the ten supermarkets were totaling $1,000,000 in sales a week.[49]

The first Centr-O-Mart was unique among Chinese American supermarkets, like Sam Wah You was among Chinese American entrepreneurs. Wah You was not active in the day-to-day operation of the supermarkets, like other owners. Running the Centr-O-Mart supermarkets was the responsibility of a Chinese American supervisor who was also a major investor. Wah You's forte was salesmanship. He invited others to invest in the development of his enterprises, although what they invested in, whether shares or partnerships, and what the investments were worth, were never clearly defined. Those omissions would eventually come back to trouble the investors, but during the rapid expansion of Centr-O-Mart, along with its good profits, few if any questioned the soundness of their investments and Wah You's direction. As the number of supermarkets and ventures grew, Wah You became more dependent on others to manage his businesses and give him advice.[50]

Wah You increased the number of supermarkets under his corporation with the acquisition of a small chain of supermarkets in the San Jose area. In the late 1950s, Diamond Properties Corporation bought eight Hob Nob stores, but left the supermarkets' former management in place to operate them. The details as to why the management was left intact are not clear. Diamond Properties was incorporated some time before the transaction to minimize Wah You's tax and personal liabilities. Soon after the Hob Nob deal, the corporation purchased ten Farmers Market stores (not affiliated with Farmers Market of Sacramento) located in towns throughout the northern part of the Sacramento Valley. Their management was left intact, too. Furthermore, there was little or no remodeling done to the Hob Nob and Farmers supermarkets. The Farmers deal was considered better than the Hob Nob transaction because the purchase came with wholesale grocery, drug, and liquor warehouses.[51]

Diamond Properties was like a corporate train, with Sam Wah You, the president, as the head engineer in the lead locomotive. With supermarket and wholesale meat companies in tow, Diamond Properties acquired a 550–acre cattle ranch on Bethel Island, located in the San Joaquin Delta northwest of Stockton. The ranch supplied cattle to the corporation's wholesale and retail meat operations, Diamond D and Centr-O-Mart respectively. During the operation of Daylite Store, Wah You had ties to a slaughterhouse called Brannon Meat Company. The company was an important link to the cattle ranch business. Diamond Properties later extended its cattle business by purchasing another ranch near Winnemucca, Nevada. In the mid-1960s, Diamond Properties diversified its holdings by investing in the Bank of Trade of San Francisco, a sum large enough to make Wah You an executive officer of the bank. At about the same time, Diamond Properties moved its headquarters from Stockton to San Francisco. The old office was too small, and the San Francisco Chinatown office was closer to the Hob Nob supermarkets and the bank. Moreover, Diamond Properties could just as well oversee the Farmers Markets up north from San Francisco as from Stockton. The new office also oversaw the cattle ranches, while the supervision of Centr-O-Mart remained the responsibility of the head of operations, who worked out of the main Stockton store. The San Francisco office was equipped with computers to help handle the bookkeeping tasks of each store in Diamond Properties. Wah You retained Euro-American accountants and lawyers to advise him on managing and proffering investments. All the while, Wah You continued to invite others to invest in Diamond Properties to help finance his acquisitions.

Soon after the move, Wah You launched his most ambitious venture, opening a slaughterhouse called United Meat Company in Taipei, Taiwan.[52] But before long it became apparent that this new venture required more money, time, and effort than anticipated to keep it viable, factors that would push the rest of the corporate train off its track.

COMPETITION

A glance at the development of Chinese American supermarkets would convey the notion that operators achieved success and prosperity by maintaining ethnic solidarity and deference, collaborating with one another to avoid interfering with each other's local markets because they were brethren. The history of the Chinese Americans' struggle against Euro-American institutions in which cooperation was vital, and the founding of their own trade organization, the Chinese Food Dealers Association, reinforces that assumption. In reality, competition among Chinese American grocers was intense. They competed directly against each other without reservation because, as one operator put it, "Competition was competition." They tried to "steal customers from one another," opening supermarkets nearby or across the street from supermarkets that were doing excellent business. They made regular visits to each other's stores to scrutinize prices and merchandising. Every operator tried to gain as much business and profit as possible, even to the point of forcing his competition out of business.[53] Historically, such maneuvers were not unusual among Chinese American enterprises. In *The Chinese Laundryman,* Paul Siu noted that competition occurred regularly among the laundrymen of Chicago during the late nineteenth and early twentieth centuries, resulting in many failures.[54]

Merciless competition among themselves was one of the reasons for the decline and passing of the first-generation supermarkets in the Sacramento area. Several of the Famous Food Markets, for example, were overwhelmed by the competition of Farmers Market supermarkets that opened nearby. The latter drew customers away from Famous Food Markets with lower prices and newer facilities.

As a specific example, Broderick Market succumbed to a new Farmers

Market in its neighborhood in the early 1960s. And yet it was Broderick Market that opened one block from Eye Street Bridge Market in 1949 to take away Eye Street's flourishing business. Farmers Market opened a supermarket across the street from a Bel Air and another across the street from a Jumbo Market in the early 1970s, but the two Farmers could not compete and closed not long afterwards. In the mid-1960s, Bel Air opened a larger supermarket less than a mile from a Jumbo Market that had been operating for only a few years. The two supermarkets, however, withstood each other's competitive pressures because it turned out the area could support both operations.

The smaller Chinese American supermarkets were not affected very much by the fierce competition because they tended to be located in older neighborhoods or markets that yielded smaller trade and profits, which larger companies considered not worth pursuing. According to one large operator, in terms of easy profitability the smaller supermarkets "have seen better days."[55] Finally, it is worth noting that because the Chinese American community was not very large and diverse until after the late 1960s, some of the competing operators were distant cousins or related by marriage.

ECONOMIC REWARD AND SOCIAL ASSIMILATION

The success of the grocery stores and supermarkets brought tangible rewards for employers and employees and helped pave the way for social assimilation. As noted earlier, owners and partners used their profits to purchase the property which their stores occupied and to invest in real estate for future expansion. They then purchased homes, automobiles, and other personal property, enjoying the fruits of proprietorship. Those who were single had the resources to afford to get married and raise a family. Years later they gave their children the financial support necessary to pursue higher education or engage in other endeavors.

The union rate wages enabled employees to also afford to have families and homes and to send their children to college. Employees who were married but without families in America could now manage to bring them into the country. Because of employers' contributions to union benefit plans, employees were able to retire with pension plans and supplemental health insurance. To some extent, the labor unions facilitated the assimilation of employees into the American way of life. They weakened mutual responsibility and ethnic solidarity by establishing job security, wages, and welfare benefits, subrogating the traditional role of Chinese employers.

Low prices in the Chinese American grocery stores and supermarkets helped breach racial barriers, enticing shoppers who would otherwise not shop in a Chinese American–owned business. The alliance of China and America during World War II resulted in a more favorable public opinion of Chinese Americans and also helped to break down racial prejudices. But the breaching of racial barriers in terms of employment began in the Chinese American supermarkets. Notwithstanding the rare exception of Sam Wah You and his Centr-O-Mart in 1946, Chinese American employers began hiring Euro-American women to work part-time as cashiers during the 1950s. Before then, a few grocers occasionally hired neighborhood schoolboys to work part-time. By the 1960s, it was not unusual to find Euro-American men or people of other ethnicities working in Chinese American supermarkets as clerks, meat cutters, and in other positions. Bel Air, for example, was noted for hiring many people who were not Chinese Americans. At the same time, Chinese American clerks who received their training in Chinese American stores began getting jobs in national and local chain supermarkets, although the number who did was not very large.

Although the 1950s marked the entry of Chinese Americans into the economic mainstream, their acceptance into the social mainstream was not unruffled. In Sacramento, many residents still tried to keep Chinese Americans out of their neighborhoods. There was outright racial discrimination in which real estate agents in collusion with home sellers refused to sell to Chinese Americans. Some deeds even contained covenants prohibiting owners from selling their homes to people of racial minorities. Chinese American supermarket owners, who were determined to move into middle- and upper-middle-class neighborhoods to declare their success, circumvented obstacles and restrictions by getting their Euro-American friends to purchase the homes and then to immediately sell the homes to them. Once they moved in, their relations with their neighbors were basically congenial. Some Chinese Americans purchased undeveloped parcels of land and built custom homes in budding neighborhoods, a maneuver that evoked less discord among residents.[56] Since Chinese Americans had been accepted as grocers throughout Northern California for quite some time, it appears that stubborn resistance to change was the primary reason for the opposition, rather than strong prejudice against Chinese Americans.

5 / Decline and Passing

THE DECLINE AND PASSING of Chinese American supermarkets did not come without foreboding signs. Some operators were astute, saw the portentous "handwriting on the wall," and got out of the business while they could still profit favorably from selling their supermarkets. Some were blinded by past success and ignored the need to adapt to the rapid changes around them to remain competitive. Quite possibly, they thought that they did not need to adapt. Then there were those in between who were aware of new developments, but were unable or unwilling to do anything about them. They fathomed that the end was coming and milked the business for all the profits they could before facing an undetermined departure.

The passing started in the early 1960s with the gradual decline in business of many first-generation supermarkets. Competition from new Chinese American supermarkets encroaching on their markets was a major agent, but disintegration of harmony among partners and between employers and employees was also a principal factor. These rupturing forces came at a time when owners were becoming increasingly weary and indifferent about operating a demanding business after years of hard work. Amid external challenges and internal conflicts, many simply closed their doors.

The competitiveness of second-generation supermarkets started declining in the mid-1970s. National companies began making inroads into local markets, supermarkets became increasingly expensive and complex to operate, and labor unions were determined to exercise their strength. Some operators were fortunate enough to sell their supermarkets, usually one by one at distressed prices to enterprising buyers who thought that with plenty of hard work and perseverance they could squeeze a profit or build up the business. Others, not able to find buyers, ceased business, sold their inventories and equipment, and leased their buildings to tenants who used them for purposes other than selling groceries. A few operators barely kept up with the trends but weathered the vicissitudes of the market. Ultimately, a small number of single-store operators were able to carve out niche businesses. The owners of the last supermarket chain, however, sold all their stores to a competitor. By the end of the century, all the prominent Chinese American supermarkets were no longer in business, but their passing did not occur before their owners attained financial security for themselves.

FAMOUS FOOD MARKETS

The decline of the first-generation supermarkets was rooted in large part in the owners' business strategy, which turned out to be inherently weak and fleeting. As discussed earlier, they drew shoppers into their stores with advertised sale prices that were lower than those of their competitors. These "loss leaders" were sold at cost or at a small loss, but they attracted large numbers of shoppers. The strategy was profitable as long as shoppers purchased non-sale merchandise in addition to the sale merchandise, rendering a profit for the stores. Also, this strategy worked only in conjunction with low-cost labor, which enabled operators to minimize losses and make a profit. In the long run, the strategy could not be sustained because shoppers patronized the stores primarily for the low sale prices. Shoppers became conditioned to look for advertised sale items, went to stores that offered them, and bought only sale items. Some shoppers stocked up on them. It was not unusual to see housewives who weekly went from one store to the next to stock up on sale items. These "cherry pickers" did not buy anything else, let alone become regular customers.[1] Regular customers usually patronized those stores that were conveniently located. That same reason was why shoppers from outside the neighborhood generally did not switch from shopping regularly at their own local stores.

Until the early 1960s, the Famous Food Markets dominated their local markets because there was little if any competition nearby. Their good sales volumes and the potential for more, however, attracted other supermarkets to open in the same neighborhoods. The most formidable competitors were larger Chinese American supermarkets, like the rapidly expanding Farmers Markets. Like Famous Food Markets, the new competition advertised weekly "loss leaders" to draw in customers. The new supermarkets were outfitted with up-to-date equipment and amenities, much like the older supermarkets had been when they opened a decade or more earlier. Because many of the shoppers who were drawn to the new supermarkets or to Famous Food Markets did not have any loyalty to either group, the former, with their newer facilities, garnered the bulk of their patronage. Since the beginning of the modern supermarket era, the shopping public had been enthralled with modernity, pursuing almost anything newer, bigger, and more convenient. To minimize operational costs and to maximize profits, the owners of the Famous Food Markets had been operating with minimum maintenance and with little if any updating or remodeling since opening. This was due in part to their success, which nurtured their complacency and dulled their vigilance towards potential competition. It was also due in large part to interpersonal problems among partners, which arrested any initiative to improve or remodel the stores. Everything was fine as long as business and profits were good, which should have been a caveat.[2]

When national chains and local companies opened supermarkets in the same markets that Chinese Americans did business, they yielded the "loss leaders" niche to the Chinese American supermarkets. Their supermarkets instead offered service and convenience, which attracted and held regular customers. Some of them turned a profit and became competitive, while others never became profitable and soon closed their doors. In both cases, they drew customers away from the older, smaller Chinese American supermarkets already reeling from other competitors challenging their niche, pushing them closer to the edge of insolvency.[3]

Partnership Problems

New competition triggered the decline of the Famous Food Markets, but the ingredients for their rapid descent had been brewing within them for a long time. One ingredient was the disintegration of harmony among the partners and between employers and employees. There were many facets to this predicament. In the beginning, cultural propriety, challenges of a new operation, and sanguine expectations had forged harmony among the personnel. But as daily work became routine and as each person became familiar with their coworkers' tasks and personal habits, perceived differences in productivity and minor idiosyncrasies became major chasms, regardless of the fact that business was very profitable. The bonds of mutual responsibility and reward that were indispensable to the success of the operations were also dissolving because some partners developed a sense of self-importance and selfishness that was fed by success.[4]

The most self-destructive forces occurred among the partners of these early Chinese American supermarkets. The partnerships were generally harmonious, but there was always "one sour grape in the bunch." Such a predicament was not uncommon because, as noted earlier, often one or more of the partners were less familiar and affiliated than the others were to each other. After an operation was well under way, for example, a partner might feel that he was working more than the others were. Feeling that they were not doing their fair share of work, he built up resentment towards them. The resentment intensified when he received his share of the profits, an amount that he felt was unfair, especially when there was one or more partners who were passive investors not involved in the daily operation of the store. In retaliation, he produced less work than before. Sensing the partner's discontent and seeing him do less work, the other partners either maintained their dispositions or adopted the same attitude. It took a partner with a strong, unselfish character to exercise the former response, but usually the latter predominated. Productivity decreased, necessitating the manager to hire extra help to compensate for the shortfall in work output. Without an increase in sales volume to offset it, the additional employee or employees increased the labor costs, thereby reducing the net profits. This in itself would not have caused the demise of an operation, but it was a symptom of decline. Another symptom was evident at the daily closing of the supermarkets. Mistrust and jealousy had grown to the point where each of the partners cleared and tallied the receipts of one cash register. The manager then recorded the total receipts of the day.[5]

If problems did not arise soon after an operation was under way, five or ten years later there would be at least one partner who felt that his contribution was greater than that of the others and that he was the primary reason for the store's success. He believed that he should be striking out on his own to make more money, even though he was getting good income. He would propose to the rest of the partners that they purchase his share for what he considered market value. Unfortunately, his valuation was often too high, and not what the other partners figured. They therefore refused to purchase his share. Likewise, an outside investor would be unlikely to purchase his share at the asking price even if the rest of the partners agreed to let him into the partnership. Thus, there would be an impasse, and the partnership and supermarket would "hang in limbo" while feelings of resentment emerged and intensified and productivity declined. Some partners did not want to work as diligently as they did in the earlier years or any more than the least productive partner did. Meanwhile, all the partners still retained their positions and salaries.[6]

Ill feelings among the partners impeded any plans and expenditures that required consensus. The partnerships, therefore, very seldom invested even a minimal amount of capital for purchasing new equipment or remodeling their supermarkets. With little or no response to new competition, the future of the old supermarkets was fated. When equipment needed extensive maintenance, or broke down and needed repair, it usually was not done. If repair work was authorized, management often used repairmen who were less competent, but who charged less than repairmen from reputable companies did. Management got what it paid for. But no partner wanted to spend money on something with an uncertain future, let alone something that was causing aggravation. The downward spiral accelerated. Fine Food Market, for example, closed in the mid-1960s, pushed to insolvency in part by a new Farmers Market nearby. By the end of the 1960s, most of the Famous Food Markets closed, and the rest continued to operate under different partnerships.

A perceptive manager could have recognized potential problems at the onset and stopped them before they developed into detrimental proportions. But one of the critical weaknesses among first-generation supermarkets was the lack of strong management and leadership. Because the stores were owned by partnerships, management was generally by consensus, and work was strictly by division of labor. There was a titular manager to fulfill bookkeeping duties, oversee meetings, and represent store interests. Resolute decision-making was not a strong point. The supermarkets, therefore, generally lacked the direction and coordination a strong manager might have provided, but they made up for shortcomings with high sales volume attained by "loss leaders." Long hours of low-cost labor got things done, but masked inefficiencies. And good profits ameliorated pent-up resentment, delaying the onslaught of destructive forces.[7]

Lee Gim of Colusa's Chung Sun Market was a partner in six of the seven Famous Food Markets. Although not a working partner, his opinion was respected in store meetings because of his age and experience and his reputation for fairness and unselfishness. Thus, he often served as mediator in disputes or discords, persuading contentious factions to come to terms or a self-centered partner to relinquish his share. But he was not always successful in helping to maintain harmony or in getting partners to agree on a response to new competition. Lingering discords and new challenges taxed Lee's capacity; consequently, he sold his shares in the Famous Food Markets when he saw the end coming.[8]

Even if the partnerships had the unanimity and resources, most partners did not have the aptitude to compete against new competition. In other words, they personally did not have, let alone know, what was necessary to be competitive. Resourcefulness and resolve were not major characteristics of their faculties. After years of operating the same way, the typical response to new competition was to continue on the same path with more effort, which in the past was very successful. After visiting their competitors' new stores to assess the operations, they could have adopted some of the new or different ways of retailing, but the partners remained indecisive about what to do. Again the dilemma was rooted in their lack of strong leadership. The partners could have hired people with expertise to help with management and direction, but that meant employing outsiders to take over some control of their stores, a situation to which the partners were not disposed. They seemed to want to exercise authority, but not to assume the responsibility that goes with it. Time wasted because of inability, indecisiveness, and ineradicable bickering led to lost competitiveness that became impossible to regain.[9]

There were personal reasons that caused partners to lose interest in maintaining their stores' competitiveness. As their material comfort became satiated and their financial future secured, the partners' attitudes began changing. Feelings of mutual responsibility and welfare decreased as personal wealth increased, and concern for store matters yielded to concern for family matters. Ownership of a store had always been just a means to achieve a comfortable life at home. There was never any grand intention to continue operating and expanding supermarkets. As the partners got older, they wanted to retire. This inclination came at a time when competition was increasing. As for passing the partnership to their heirs, most of their children did not want to work in the retail food business because they had better options, more enterprise, and more resources than their parents did. The partners likewise did not want their children to work long hours with the likelihood of undergoing stress and aggravation, as they did. Given these personal reasons, it is no wonder that many of the partners did not want to invest money to remodel their stores. They just wanted to get out.[10]

The partners had a difficult time getting out of the business. Not well maintained or remodeled, their stores were worn and outdated. Old equipment frequently needed repair. The size of the stores was very small compared to the new competition, and modern amenities were lacking. Even if the partnerships sold their stores at low prices, the new owners needed a large infusion of capital to bring the facilities up to current industry standards. Most of the stores were in neighborhoods that had passed their prime in providing high sales volume or in supporting more than one store. In sum, the stores had been doing business for fifteen years or more in neighborhoods with families that had matured. When families got older, the children moved out of the households, often out of the neighborhoods, consequently decreasing the number of consumers for groceries. Thus, the supermarkets had captured the patronage of a generation, but unless the old neighborhoods rejuvenated extensively, the prime locations for doing business were in new neighborhoods with young families.[11]

Before the situation became very unfavorable, some partners were fortunate enough to sell their shares to their other partners or outside buyers who thereupon entered the partnerships. The stores then continued to operate until the partners agreed that it was time to quit business because sales were so low that there were very little or no profits, or because most of the partners wanted to retire, whereupon the stores were either sold or closed. Some partnerships accepted offers from remaining partners and employees who wanted to continue. Such was the case of Wonder Food Market, Broderick Market, and El Camino Market. The reorganized partnerships built up the business and squeezed out a profit with minor improvements on the facilities and equipment and with low-cost labor. The partnerships that closed their stores sold whatever inventory and equipment they could, divided the proceeds, and locked the doors. As discussed earlier, there were some stores in which the partners could not agree on anything. Their stores just faded out of business. After the stores closed, individual partners either retired or took employment in other stores or jobs, and the partners who owned the real estate leased the buildings to other types of businesses to draw rental income.[12]

Employer-Employee Relationships

If the bonds of mutual responsibility and reward among partners had weakened, so too had those between employers and employees. Employees also became more focused on their own welfare as they entered the middle class and gained job security, albeit with the help of labor unions. Most of the employees married after a few years of employment, and their wages afforded them the opportunity to purchase homes and raise families. Naturally, they ceased rooming and boarding at the store and began directing more time and concern to their families at home. They came to resent the long hours of work and sought remedy with the help of the labor unions. With the cooperation of employees, the unions strengthened their position against employers, enabling the former to force the latter into complying with union labor rules regarding hours worked. Hiring unmarried younger workers did not help the stores recapture their low-cost labor because the new employees did not have the disposition to work long hours without compensation, as their predecessors did. This different attitude was due in part to the influence of stronger labor unions, increased opportunities for other types of employment, and changing socioeconomic norms in the Chinese American community. Thus, the low-cost labor that had enabled the owners of the supermarkets to profit in spite of "loss leaders" began shrinking as longtime employees were working fewer and fewer hours without compensation and new, younger employees refused to do so.[13]

Low-cost labor must be placed in perspective. Chinese American employees were never reputed to be efficient workers, only diligent workers putting in long hours. When store management expected employees to work long hours, the goal was to get the job done regardless of the employees' efficiency. In other words, employees set their own work pace without management closely supervising them, but their tasks were expected to be completed before the employee ended work for the day. On the other hand, management never trained its employees when the latter began employment. New employees were just handed an apron to wear, and they simply followed the work of experienced employees. Work was routine. Just like their employers who were unwilling to change their ways of management in the face of new challenges, employees were resistant to change their ways of working. At the same time, the cost of compensation was rising, and sales volume was stagnant if not declining. The union wages and the health and welfare benefits which employers had to pay did not appear merited for the level of productivity from employees. But management could not afford additional help without firing current employees, something they were very hesitant to do because often the employees were relatives or friends of employers and other employees.[14]

The low labor cost resulting from employees working extra hours without compensation was thus unsustainable, causing Chinese American supermarkets to lose much of their competitiveness. The labor system of the 1940s and 1950s ceased to exist partly because of the success of the supermarkets, which provided an opportunity to lead a middle-class life to their employees. The same success attracted the attention of the labor unions, which sought to enforce labor rules uniformly on all competitors. Finally, the success of the supermarkets drew the attention of new competitors, who sought to take away as much business as possible.

FARMERS MARKET

On the surface, the Farmers Market chain of supermarkets, the largest locally owned company during its peak period, looked very impressive, but strong undercurrents were pulling it down. Many of the stores closed in rapid succession during the late 1970s. Under the proprietorship of Walter Fong, the origin of Farmers Market had been a small grocery store, the North 12th Street Market in Sacramento. Fong opened it in 1935, and then started a few combination grocery stores under different names before the war. In 1949 he opened his first Farmers Market supermarket and began expanding it into a chain operation over the next three decades. By the mid-1970s, Fong and his partners had opened a total of forty supermarkets, a number that is somewhat misleading in that in certain years they had closed unprofitable stores while opening new ones. As noted earlier, the Farmers Market supermarkets were the chief competitors of the Famous Food Markets, relying on advertised sale items to draw in customers. The strategy worked fairly well for the company, but it could not support Farmers Market for the long duration. Increased competition from national chain supermarkets took its toll. Some of these national chain supermarkets offered better service and facilities, and others offered storewide discount pricing. Furthermore, the economic recessions greatly strained the Farmers Markets' financial soundness because many of the stores were capitalized with minimum outlays.[15]

During their rapid expansion from the late 1960s to early 1970s, the purpose of the stores appeared to be not so much to generate profits, but to create cash flow for their primary partner, Walter Fong, and jobs for the multitude of minor partners who invested a few thousand dollars each. These minor partners included former employees of the Famous Food Markets and other supermarkets, and novices in the grocery business, some of whom were recent immigrants. Basically, each store was owned and operated like a partnership, with Fong as the primary partner, similar to the setup of the Famous Food Markets. But whereas each Famous Food supermarket had only a few partners, it was not unusual to find a Farmers Market supermarket with numerous partners. The company expanded too fast during a period in which there was no latitude for mistakes. Furthermore, Farmers did not have a strong, central management in place, which was necessary to coordinate operations for the stores. In each supermarket the numerous partners became a quandary, a situation similar to what happened in the Famous Food supermarkets, but at a larger scale. Recognizing the need for a company-wide supervisor, Fong hired one. But Fong and his partners were unwilling to commit resources and to relinquish some of their control. The few people responsible for company-wide managerial duties lacked expertise and experience. Subsequently, Fong lost control of the company, and his ineffectual supervisors, managers, and partners were unable to run the extensive operation, which included supermarkets near the Bay Area. Sometimes merchandise that was advertised, for example, was not in stock for sale, causing customer inconvenience and displeasure. Because only a few of the stores had high sales volume, a downturn in business caused critical shortages of cash. The recessions of the mid- to late 1970s also halted the expansion of the supermarkets, which had formerly fed the growth of credit. Wholesalers, vendors, and suppliers became increasingly impatient with overdue payments on the products they sold to Farmers. Many of the stores soon became insolvent, and their dissolution resembled that of the Famous Food Markets. By the mid-1980s the last of the Farmers Market stores were sold.[16]

In addition to the fact that many of the Farmers Market stores were not as large, up-to-date, and well maintained as those of their competition, the employees were not adequately trained. Like the employees of the Famous Food Markets, a new employee was given an apron to wear and immediately started working by following the example of an experienced employee. Many immigrant employees did not have a working knowledge of English; consequently, customer service was often lacking. This shortcoming, while prevalent in Chinese American supermarkets of the past and tolerated by their customers, was detrimental in the highly competitive markets of the 1970s. It was no surprise that supervision was virtually nonexistent. Few managers and their assistants wanted to take responsibility for decisions, and many lacked the necessary skills for their duties.[17]

YUBA MARKET AND CHUNG SUN MARKET

Leland Lee operated Yuba Market in Marysville until 1978, at which time he sold the supermarket to another grocer. During twenty-two years of operation, its sales volume remained fairly constant at $70,000 to 75,000 a week. In the 1950s and 1960s this amount was relatively high compared to Yuba's competitors, and with low-cost labor, the net profits were substantial. Upon further analysis, however, the steady weekly sales volumes over the years revealed a gradual decline in business when accounting for inflation. The decline was due primarily to competition from other locally owned supermarkets, most of which opened and closed depending on conditions of the local markets. In addition, the operating expenses—including labor, equipment, utilities, insurance, and supplies—increased steadily over the years. The escalating expenses were absorbed somewhat by the profit margins, which thereby maintained a satisfactory level of competitiveness. Eventually the profit margins became close to nil due to rapidly rising labor costs beginning in the early 1970s. The labor unions were demanding higher wages and more benefits for their members. Lee was "running harder to stay in place." The vicissitudes of the economy did not bode well for Yuba Market or for the prospects of the local markets, which at best had been stagnant for years. By the middle of the decade, Lee, the controlling partner, decided to get out while he could still ask for a favorable selling price. The new owner operated the supermarket until he went out of business a short time later, whereupon Lee rented the building to another retailer, who sold general merchandise.[18]

At this writing, Chung Sun Market continues to operate, but barely at a profit. Since opening in 1956, the store has realized a weekly sales volume of $60,000 to 70,000, depending upon economic conditions and competition. Like Yuba Market, this amount was relatively high for the 1950s and 1960s. With family members holding key positions and working long hours and with the personnel not in the unions, labor costs were minimized, and profits were very respectable. The Lees remodeled the store and continued to offer customer service to maintain their competitiveness while other locally and nationally owned supermarkets opened and closed. But again, like Yuba Market, the steady weekly sales volumes over the years reveal an actual decline in business when accounting for inflation. Profits decreased as they absorbed the rising expenses. The most difficult years were during the recessions of the 1970s and during the entry of large supermarkets owned by national chain companies in the 1980s. But Chung Sun has remained resilient, primarily because it has a loyal customer base in Colusa, a small community where everybody knows each other.[19]

There are, nevertheless, some ominous signs for Chung Sun Market. In the past the smallness of Colusa was the safeguard that kept Chung Sun's business secured from national competitors, which did not make inroads into the market because it was not worthwhile. But recent population growth in the region and changes in shoppers' preferences have altered the situation. Huge supermarkets and discount mass merchandisers have opened in shopping centers located twenty minutes away from Colusa, drawing many local residents with their low prices and vast selection of merchandise. Although the community is growing, new residents do not have the loyalty and habits of the long-time natives, who still shop at Chung Sun Market. Many familiar customers are making regular trips to the shopping centers for large purchases and making convenient trips to Chung Sun Market for smaller ones.[20] Changes in community, food retailing, and shopping patterns are forcing the Lees to soon make important decisions about maintaining their supermarket's solvency with no thought about regaining their former competitiveness and profitability.

GIANT FOODS

Giant Foods benefited from the growth of the economy, population, and supermarket industry during the 1950s and 1960s. As a family operation, Giant Foods did not undergo detrimental internal conflicts, as in the partnerships of the Famous Food Markets. A combination of external forces overwhelmed Giant Foods. Rising labor costs due to demands by the labor unions greatly impacted the bottom line of the stores, but George Quan, Jr., attributed their decline largely to increased competition from large national companies such as Lucky and Safeway. In previous decades, the national companies did not make determined attempts to gain and hold a respectable portion of the Sacramento and Northern California markets, which were well known in the retail food industry as areas dominated by independent and local chain operators. After the recession of the early 1970s, which weakened the hold of independent and local chain operators, rapid changes in the retail food industry and a surge in housing in new neighborhoods for baby-boomer families provided opportunities for the national companies to expand their supermarkets into the Sacramento metropolitan area.

The national companies had the resources to open bigger and more modern supermarkets in ever-larger shopping centers than the independent and local chain companies had. The national companies opened their supermarkets near Giant Foods, drawing away some customers, but what was even more detrimental to the competitiveness of Giant Foods was the fact that the national companies could afford new computer systems, which they used effectively. Only two Chinese American supermarket chains in Sacramento had the resources to do the same—Jumbo Market and Bel Air—but older, smaller chains like Giant Foods did not. The computer systems stored and analyzed information regarding the inventory, cost, selling price, sale, and profit of merchandise as well as costs in labor and other expenses. Important data on customer transactions and traffic were also produced. With copious information, store management could effectively manage variables such as inventory, profit margins, and labor costs, and do it immediately. The instant information gave national companies the edge over Giant Foods stores, which had to rely on periodic and year-end statements. Computer systems helped reduce expenses and excesses, the savings of which were reinvested into the operation and passed on to customers.[21]

The company that was most effective in using computer systems to help compete against Giant Foods was Lucky. Able to fix the gross profit margin by adjusting the per-item markup, the national company offered everyday low prices on all the merchandise in its stores. There were no more weekly sale prices. Customers thus had the reassurance of knowing that the items they purchased were marked at a relatively low and constant price, even if they were perhaps not the lowest priced. This compared to the sale and regular pricing of merchandise in Chinese American supermarkets in which shoppers were not certain that they were getting a good deal when purchasing non-sale items. All too often for supermarkets like Giant Foods and Farmers, shoppers from near and far would purchase the featured sale items only and do their regular shopping at Lucky or other national and local operations, such as Albertson's, Safeway, and Raley's. The local operations did not offer low prices like Lucky, but they had up-to-date equipment and facilities and the service and selection that appealed to customers. Because sale items were usually "loss leaders," they became a financial drain for supermarkets that continued to rely on them. Thus, Giant Foods could not afford to compete, and Farmers Market could not commit to compete.[22]

The Quans eventually sold or closed each of their Giant Foods Stores by the end of the 1970s. Before the last Giant Foods store went out of business, it merged with the Jumbo Market chain. A slight majority in ownership was given to the latter, and the former was saved from total insolvency. The store changed its name to Jumbo Market, received an infusion of cash for minor remodeling, and made some personnel changes. It benefited from the advantages of a multi-store operation such as name recognition, shared expenses, extended credit, and increased wholesale buying power. The attempt to increase the stores' sales volumes to restore their profitability was not successful because the timing was inauspicious. Soon after the merger, another recession struck, and business was unfavorable everywhere.[23]

JUMBO MARKET

The Jumbo Market chain reached it zenith in the early 1980s in terms of the number of its stores. The high profit years, however, were in the 1960s, when the partners worked long hours in the stores. From the 1960s to the early 1970s, Jumbo Market was at the forefront among Chinese American grocers in the Sacramento area. In terms of sales volumes and profits, Jumbo Market had some of the highest per store.[24] Flushed with success and sanguine expectations, the shareholders began their expansion. But the 1970s turned out to be much less propitious. The same factors that had affected other supermarkets also worked against Jumbo Market: two recessions, rapid developments in the industry, rising expenses, increased competition, and changing neigh-borhoods. Within the first year, each store reached an average weekly sales volume that did not vary much thereafter. Hence, while the sales volumes remained relatively the same, expenses such as wages, rent, utilities, and insur-ance kept rising, chiseling away at the already narrow profit margin and tax-ing the management's ability to counteract its predicament. In other words, the Jumbo Market stores—like Yuba Market, Giant Foods, and Farmers Market—had steady sales volumes but declining profits. The shareholders persevered, hoping for things to turn around.

Jumbo Market weathered the first recession of the 1970s, but rapid devel-opments in the retail food industry challenged the shareholders' resolve to maintain competitiveness. Their competitors' new supermarkets were increas-ingly bigger, with more departments and services. To meet this challenge required that the shareholders invest large amounts of capital, a demand that not all of them were totally committed to. The older Jumbo Markets were enlarged and brought up-to-date, while the new ones were built bigger and were outfitted with the latest equipment. The company put in new depart-ments and expanded old ones. But their efforts were a step behind their com-petitors, who seemed to have more resources and better strategies and management. Basically, it came back to the attitudes of Jumbo Market's share-holders, who were by then responding to, not leading, the trends of the local market.

When Jumbo Market consisted of a few supermarkets, the shareholders gave managerial responsibilities to employees based on their abilities and pro-ductivity. As the company expanded in the 1970s, the shareholders, rather than promoting from within the company, brought in supervisors to handle company-wide management and to help develop long-term plans. The super-visors in turn hired people from other supermarkets to become managers and assistant managers in the new stores. This action caused resentment among some longtime employees who were passed over. They were further aggra-vated when they saw that the primary qualification that the new managers and assistant managers sought was being socially skilled. Because a great deal of supermarket work was routine and did not require much supervision, get-ting the maximum productivity from employees had in the past been achieved largely by managers themselves working diligently and setting an example for employees, much like the shareholders did in the early years of Jumbo Market. Most of the new managers and assistant managers, however, did not demonstrate this type of work ethic. In addition, many of the employees that the new managers hired tended to be like the managers. As a result, many longtime employees were less inclined to work as hard as before, and in due course, the company's productivity declined.[25]

Much of the responsibility for lapses in management at the store level precipitated from the top. The shareholders were trying to build a management organization for their growing company, but did not know how to go about it. Some of the shareholders were not willing to relinquish their control and delegate authority because in the past they were entirely responsible for the success of their departments. They protected their domain at the expense of the welfare of the whole company and often did not completely support their managers and supervisors. They also became distant from their old employees, who had helped them reap good profits in the early years.[26]

The shareholders also lacked long-term plans and goals. The growth of the company, for example, started somewhat haphazardly. Additional stores were opened to make as much money as possible with the smallest capitalization possible. The shareholders did not envision building a supermarket chain or increasing their competitiveness. Thus, it was not surprising that the shareholders did not have definitive strategies and were unwilling to expend the resources to carry out and complete even short-term objectives. No longer able to generate customer traffic solely by using featured sales items, they followed whatever trends other companies initiated, hoping to profit by them as well. They supported a policy to offer better customer service, for example, only to withdraw it soon afterwards. They opened new departments after their competitors did, but always too late to capitalize on them. Many other agendas faltered, leading to plummeting confidence towards shareholders and management among the employees.[27]

The period following the mid-1970s was very taxing for Jumbo Market. As mentioned earlier, the weekly sales volumes of each of the Jumbo Markets in subsequent years seldom exceeded the levels reached during the first year. If a competitor went out of business, a burst of new business materialized for the nearby Jumbo Market. But such business was usually insubstantial or brief. The stores had a difficult time gaining and retaining new customers, a problem which was attributed to the ineffectual management discussed above. But much of the problem was also rooted in the neighborhoods being already saturated with other supermarkets. In other words, there was a fixed economic pie for the competing stores to make their cuts or shares. When Jumbo Market number six opened, for example, there were already three supermarkets within a mile radius of its location, and another one was planned to open within two years. And most of the houses and apartments that were planned for the community were already built. In sum, Jumbo Market could not compete against the large national companies that had ample resources for expansion in the same markets. The large companies remodeled old stores to make them competitive and supported unprofitable stores until they became profitable. They could afford the retraining of managers and the hiring of professionals, such as marketing and accounting experts. Moreover, they could afford to close unprofitable new stores.

A supermarket needs to attain a specific sales volume to break even, beyond which it makes a profit. With sales volumes remaining stagnant amid rising expenses and competition, it was difficult for Jumbo Market to maintain solvency, let alone profitability. Something had to yield. Subsequently, the labor unions and employees granted wage and benefit concessions, which enabled the company to remain profitable. But cutting expenses and forgoing improvements only forestalled insolvency. An outright sale of the company was an option, but an unprofitable company with modest, outdated stores was difficult to sell. It appeared that the shareholders did not know what to do or how to find any good way out. Like the other Chinese American supermarkets before them, each store was sold or closed one by one from the mid-1980s to the mid-1990s. Some of the stores continued to operate under new ownership, retaining some of the Jumbo Market employees. The closed stores were leased out to other types of enterprises, yielding income for the shareholders who still owned the real estate.[28]

DICK'S MARKET

By the late 1990s there remained only one Dick's Market, located in a large shopping center in Sunnyvale, California. Business has been very meager for quite some time. Dick Yee Incorporated had been selling the other stores since the early 1970s. Most of Dick Yee's children have retired from the supermarket business, while others work in the remaining store and other retail businesses. One of the reasons for the stores' decline was that national companies began opening bigger supermarkets at a rapid pace in the San Jose area. They had the resources to locate their up-to-date stores in enormous shopping centers in burgeoning new communities, which drew customers away from the smaller, older supermarkets. In addition to the Safeway and Lucky stores that were already in the area, Mayfair, Ralph's, Alpha-Beta, and Albertson's stores entered the market, putting more competitive pressure on older operations. In addition, the discount trend led by Lucky captured more customers during the latter half of the 1970s. Dick's Market tried to follow the trend but could not generate enough sales volume to offset low gross profit margins, causing the stores to lose money. Thus, Dick Yee Incorporated sold its stores while it could.[29]

As Dick Yee Incorporated has divested, it has directed its resources to the management of its numerous real estate holdings, acquired during its years of supermarket expansion. The acquisition of real estate in the 1950s and 1960s turned out to be a fortuitous move in light of the skyrocketing value of real estate in the Santa Clara Valley, a result of high demand by the booming computer technology industry in the 1980s and 1990s. Rental and development of commercial and residential real estate thus became the primary business enterprise for members of the second and third generation of the Dick Yee family.[30]

BEL AIR

While Jumbo Market declined, Bel Air ascended. The Wongs of Bel Air continually upgraded their equipment, enlarged floor space, and set up new departments and services, reinvesting profits back into their stores. They opened new shopping centers, with their stores serving as mainstays. This reinvestment was expensive and required commitment, but the Wongs were willing to postpone their financial dividend to remain competitive and build sales volume. During the late 1980s and early 1990s, for example, sales volumes for Bel Air supermarkets ranged from $350,000 to $450,000 a week, whereas Jumbo supermarkets would be fortunate to achieve half the smaller figure.[31]

By the early 1990s, the Wongs felt that it was time to get out of the supermarket business. Since the mid-1980s, they had been the preeminent supermarket operators in Northern California, highly regarded among their competitors for their business acumen. Bel Air had a very loyal clientele and was highly profitable. As the six original shareholders were getting old, they could "see the handwriting on the wall." They felt that "there was a time to be in and a time to be out." The time to sell was when "there is a profit, not when you are going downhill." In regards to passing the business to their heirs, they felt that the business "can never go back" to like it was in the past. There were also "too many nieces and nephews to get involved." Dividing the assets to continue the operation would have been too complicated. Word about the Wongs' desire to sell their supermarkets quietly circulated in the supermarket industry. Soon the Wongs had numerous prospective buyers soliciting them, including national companies and a company from the Netherlands.

In 1992, they sold all their supermarkets and much of their ancillary operations to Raley's, a large, locally owned chain company which was Bel Air's partner in wholesale ventures as well as its chief competitor. The Wong family retained much of its real estate and investments holdings, living comfortably from the revenues.[32]

CENTR-O-MART

During the 1970s the Centr-O-Mart supermarkets in Stockton continued to turn a profit, albeit not like in the earlier years. Unlike many of the first-generation supermarkets that opened at about the same time, the stores were upgraded with equipment to keep up with industry trends. The "country stores" outside of Stockton were a different matter. Their profitability needed to be reevaluated due to the changing demography and economy of their markets. Furthermore, the future of the two Stockton Centr-O-Mart stores appeared uncertain because of changing neighborhoods and the city's plans for their redevelopment.[33] After about a generation of doing business at one location, it was not surprising that a supermarket's sales volume and profits were not what they used to be.

The United Meat Company in Taiwan, which had already consumed quite a bit of time and capital before commencing production, was demanding constant attention from Diamond Properties. Sam Wah You had taken up residence in Taiwan to oversee its development and operation. Business at the pork slaughterhouse was very good. The slaughterhouse processed up to five thousand heads of pigs daily, which were supplied by the government. During the Chinese Lunar New Year, the company processed as many as ten thousand heads. But there was no profit. The persistent problem was the "squeeze," commonly known in the West as extortion, payoff, tribute, and so forth. In order to keep the slaughterhouse operating smoothly, exaction had to be paid regularly to the many Taiwanese who had some involvement in the operation, from government officials to truck drivers.[34] The squeeze has always been a common practice in Chinese society; therefore, it was very likely that Wah You anticipated it, but probably not to the extent at which it played out.

Diamond Properties was drawing funds from its other enterprises to keep United Meat operating. The constant outflow of capital was draining Diamond Properties, but Wah You was determined to make the Taiwan venture successful. In need of more money, Wah You and his advisors in San Francisco decided to liquidate some of Diamond Properties' investments and assets.

The Hob Nob stores had already been sold in the early 1960s because they turned little or no profit. The distant Farmers Markets and the "country stores" would be put up for sale. Wanting to focus his energy on United Meat, and because the Stockton Centr-O-Marts were going to require more resources to stay competitive, Wah You decided to quit the supermarket business altogether.[35] At the time these matters were being deliberated, a serious health problem was threatening Wah You.

While residing in Taiwan, Wah You had contracted an ailment that doctors were unable to diagnose, causing chronic illness that got progressively worse. Not only was Wah You making regular trips to San Francisco to confer with his advisors, he went there to obtain medical treatment. In 1976, after years of illness, Wah You passed away in Taiwan. When Wah You was with his family in Stockton during his return trips, they sensed his great bitterness in not being able to resolve his affairs in Taiwan. The family rarely saw Wah You even before he moved to Taiwan, and his son was too young to learn the business to be able to take over the family's interests in Diamond Properties.[36]

By default, the advisors in the San Francisco office took over the complete management of Diamond Properties. The corporation maintained stewardship of the Farmers and Centr-O-Marts while the stores were offered for sale to the employees who worked for them. It was during this time that the worth of the Centr-O-Mart stores as expressed in shares of Diamond Properties was determined. Eight of the Centr-O-Marts were sold to six partnerships. While all the stores retained the name Centr-O-Mart, the partnerships operated them independently. They did, however, form a cooperative for purchasing, advertising, and budgeting. In late 1985, the partnerships incorporated under a familiar name, Centro Mart. Seven of the original Centr-O-Marts are still in business today. The advisors of Diamond Properties, who already owned shares in the corporation, purchased the remaining shares, including those of the Wah You family, to acquire ownership of the other assets. Wah You's death at a pivotal time in the history of Chinese American supermarkets cannot help but give rise to many "what ifs" about his corporation.[37]

FINAL PERSPECTIVES

The early Chinese American operators implemented changes in their supermarkets to make more money, not to enhance their reputation in the industry. They could not care less how their competitors thought of them as long as they made as much money as possible as soon as possible, typically doing it in ways to avoid expenditures. After World War II, for example, they were among the first to open their stores on Sundays, and they extended their daily store hours to 8:00, then 9:00, and then 10:00 P.M. to increase sales volume. Their competition followed suit. But the Chinese American operators had the advantage because extending business hours required only additional utility costs, since they were operating with low-cost labor.[38] Whereas their competitors reinvested profits to upgrade equipment or remodel stores, most owners or partners of Chinese American supermarkets did not. It was not uncommon to see a store unchanged many years after its opening, even if it meant losing business to a new or remodeled competitor.[39]

By the early 1960s, the better enforcement of union labor rules and the changing disposition of employees were chiseling away at low-cost labor. The number of immigrants who were sponsored by their employers and were a source of low-cost labor had been greatly reduced since 1955. A solution to restoring low-cost labor might have been to employ new immigrants, who had begun arriving in the United States in large numbers after 1965. But there were some fundamental difficulties. At a time when customers were demanding better service, nearly all of the immigrants lacked proficient English language skills. In an increasingly competitive industry, there was little room for mistakes or time for learning. Unlike earlier immigrants, recent ones came with their families; hence, they were not amenable to living on store premises and working long hours. In regard to solidarity, new arrivals tended not to be from the same village or lineage as the old immigrants; therefore, they were much less likely to feel akin and obligated to their employers to work long hours. Over the decades the old immigrants had already sponsored most of their family and relatives' immigration to America, so there was not much of a pool of kindred kinsmen from which to offer employment. In addition, as economic opportunities increased, the traditional mindset that had sustained the "us against them" struggle, which for over a hundred years was necessary for survival, began eroding, along with competitive spirit. Finally, the employers would have had to pay union wages and benefits, which they felt were not cost-effective with new immigrant employees at a time of rising expenses.[40]

In the 1970s, the national chain companies expanded rapidly in Northern California. They did not become more adept in competing against local independent and chain operations, but they had more resources available to open stores, which allowed some critical advantages. Developers of shopping centers offered them choice locations because national companies tended to be long-term, solvent tenants. With many supermarkets in many different locations, large companies could better weather the vicissitudes of the economy, absorbing the losses of unprofitable operations until they become profitable or closed. The same resources enabled their supermarkets to be updated with the latest equipment and to reflect the latest trends.[41]

The national chain companies, however, did not have uncontested superiority in all aspects of retailing. Their stores usually had to follow centralized management and standardized practices that often led to less efficiency, even though most had the advantage of vertical integration of food processing, purchasing, wholesaling, and distribution. Even if approved by the main office, implementation of changes regarding personnel, equipment, and inventory at the neighborhood level came slowly, although store managers did have the authority to act on specific minor requests, such as ordering special merchandise for customers or making donations for community activities.[42] Chinese American supermarkets, on the other hand, had an advantage over national chain operations in autonomy and efficiency in that they could respond to the particular needs of their local markets.

But this advantage has been eroding as the industry and society changes. In large prime markets, shoppers have come to expect uniformity in products and service, reflecting the ongoing standardization of the consumer culture. At the same time, the trends of the supermarket industry require a constant, large infusion of capital, something to which most Chinese American operators have never been able or willing to commit. Thus, they have been effectively shut out, by circumstance or by choice, as competitors in prime markets. Their prominence as supermarket operators can only be assigned to the past.

6 / Employees and Salesmen

EMPLOYEES WERE THE SUSTENANCE and scorn of employers in Chinese American supermarkets. Employers needed and used the low-cost labor of Chinese American employees to make good profits, but they later regarded the rising cost of employee labor as one of the chief causes of their decline. In retrospect, it was not so much that Chinese American employees' labor cost was too high as it was that their compensation rose and workload declined in parity with their non-Chinese counterparts. There may have been some legitimate arguments from employers that Chinese American employees were not as efficient and productive as their counterparts, but that assertion can be traced back basically to inadequate training and management of Chinese American employees.

The experiences of Chinese American employees—their employment, compensation, union membership, and so forth—help complete the history of Chinese American supermarkets. Providing balance to proprietors' views, employees expressed their opinions as to why the supermarkets rose, prospered, and declined. Criticism against their employers can be expected because employees were less concerned about competitive pressures from outside the stores than about management practices that affected them daily inside the stores. This interesting collage of experiences and perspectives gives expression to voices that are seldom heard or recorded.

Included in this chapter are the observations and opinions of grocery product salesmen who, although not involved integrally in daily operations, saw and knew of the workings of countless Chinese American supermarkets as well as their supermarkets' competitors. Their work usually required them to be attentive to the thoughts and gripes of both employers and employees with whom they had business and, sometimes, social intercourse. From their regular contacts with store managers, they learned about the soundness of various operations. Although in competition among themselves, salesmen usually discussed with each other what all the competing supermarkets were doing. They gathered information about supermarkets and compared and analyzed the supermarkets' actions and results. Accordingly, all managers regularly tried to pry information about their competitors from the salesmen.

GETTING HIRED

Most of the personnel in early grocery stores and supermarkets were partners. The few employees they hired were either related to them or were close friends of the same village from which they immigrated. As the grocery stores expanded into supermarkets and new supermarkets opened, more labor was needed. In addition to immigrant employees, employers began hiring young American-born Chinese, whose population was rising. For them, getting hired was simply a matter of going to the business and asking for employment, but usually there was someone working at the store to whom the job seeker was related or acquainted. In the close-knit Chinese American community, a strong network for job referral helped the unemployed find work. This network also helped maintain a sense of solidarity against the larger economic community that was by and large not receptive towards employing minorities.[1]

In the 1940s and 1950s, young American-born Chinese men sought work in grocery stores and supermarkets because there were not many other types of jobs available to them. As discussed earlier, the work was better than toiling in restaurants, laundries, canneries, and on farms. Coming from large families with parents who were working people, only a few had the financial resources to continue their education beyond high school if they wanted to do so. Even if they attained vocational schooling or a college degree, there was very little chance that they would be hired at a job commensurable with their training or education in the private sector. Because they spoke English, an asset for customer service, they were readily hired in grocery stores and supermarkets. And because they were single, energetic, and living at home, it did not matter too much to them if their employers paid them minimum wages for their first job. A job was something to do, and they did not think too much about their future.[2]

WORKING AND MANAGEMENT

Once hired, a new employee with prior experience went to work at assigned tasks. Those who were inexperienced learned skills while on the job by simply following an experienced employee at his duties and emulating his labor.

In the 1940s and 1950s, when store operations were simple, learning on the job was not difficult, just a matter of using "common sense." Except for Bel Air, the lack of methodical employee training typified nearly all Chinese American grocery stores and supermarkets, even that at Jumbo Market, Bel Air's contemporary.[3] But Bel Air started its employee-training program in the early 1970s, when most of the other Chinese American supermarkets were no longer in business or in decline; therefore, it is difficult to make a fair comparison.

In the grocery stores or supermarkets, daily work was basically routine and seldom needed close supervision. In general, a sense of mutual responsibility among employees kept them productive. At Yolo Grocery in Woodland, for example, partners came and went, leaving the employees to fulfill their duties without oversight.[4] But employees also wanted leadership and direction from management. In stores without strong management, some employees would habitually complain about their work and circumstances and try to do as little as possible. When employees felt that their employers were not showing concern and responsibility toward the operations of the store, they adopted the same attitude.[5]

Before the mid-1960s, Chinese American employers and employees considered all work the same. There was no such thing as overtime work and pay. When employers needed employees to work beyond twelve hours, the latter acquiesced with the knowledge that they would not be monetarily compensated for the extra hours. Employees knew that they would frequently work long hours because it was a common practice in Chinese American enterprises. Immigrant employees regularly worked long hours without compensation because they agreed to do so as a condition of employment and immigration, which their employers sponsored.[6] Employees worked six days because the stores were opened six days a week. Because employees had very little or no contact with their non-Chinese-American counterparts in other stores, they had very little information about the type of work and number of hours worked by them with which to compare their own situation. By the late 1950s the labor unions demanded and obtained a five-workday week for unionized employees, but that did not mean that old labor practices ceased immediately.[7]

After the mid-1960s, an employee working long hours without compensation became an increasingly unlikely occurrence. In older operations, some managers still expected unpaid work from their longtime immigrant employees. But in newer operations, managers did not figure in unpaid work to reduce labor costs because of the disposition of younger employees and the vigilance of strong labor unions. Although a manager did not expect unpaid labor from American-born employees, it was not rare to find one doing it on his own initiative.

WAGES

Until the early 1950s, employee wages varied depending upon the store and terms of employment. The labor unions were not entirely influential in determining wages because they had yet to enroll most Chinese American employees and were not strong enough to demand uniform compensation. If an employee were a member of a labor union, he would have received only a modest measure of health and welfare benefits because they were still in development. Chinese American employees, therefore, did not see any advantage in joining the unions. At the Eye Street Bridge Market in West Sacramento, for example, the Quans paid their Chinese American employees about $60 a month for working six days a week, twelve hours a day. If the employee was productive, he was paid a little more. In addition, the Quans provided three meals a day and rooms for lodging if needed, but there were no health and welfare benefits. The employees received their earnings once a month until the Retail Clerks Union, after successfully enrolling the employees, forced the Quans to pay their clerks twice a month in accordance with the terms of the contract.[8]

After the war, Leland Lee paid his employees of Yuba Market in Marysville union rate wages, including health and welfare benefits for working six days a week. But not all the Chinese American supermarkets paid union wages and benefits. In the early 1950s, employees at Yolo Grocery received about $125 a month, but no benefits for working six days a week, twelve hours a day. Getting paid for work done beyond twelve hours a day did not occur. During this period, the enrollment of employees of a particular store or area into the Retail Clerks Union depended mostly on the efforts of the field representative. Until employees were enrolled into the union, they usually did not receive regular pay increases, let alone benefits.[9]

JOINING THE UNIONS

When the Retail Clerks Union began increasing its efforts to organize Chinese American employees after the war, field representatives entered the stores to identify the employees who were working and to check them against a list of unionized employees. They came about once a week at an unscheduled time to check their lists against the employees and to encourage nonmembers to join. Although employers agreed to let labor unions enroll employees, it was not unusual to find some store employees who were union members and others who were not. Of course, employers did not encourage their employees to join. The situation was quite the opposite. When a union representative was seen entering the store, word would quickly spread to warn of his arrival. Often there were secret code words or phrases announced over the store intercom by the clerks working at the front checkout counters. Upon hearing them, nonunion members in the aisles would immediately stop what they were doing and hasten to the back of the store to conceal themselves in the warehouse or to leave through the back door. They waited until the union representative left, and then resumed work. Employees who were union members did not volunteer information or answered evasively about their nonunion coworkers to the representative.[10]

For Chinese American employees, there were good reasons for not joining the labor unions. During the 1940s and early 1950s, employees were wary of their intentions and purpose. Other than their association with customers and female Euro-American cashiers, many Chinese American employees had little contact with people who were outside their ethnic group. History and life experiences taught them to be suspicious and cautious with Euro-Americans. The employees did not see how joining the unions and paying dues would benefit them. Wages were a little higher for union members, but union members had to pay about six dollars a month in dues, which were collected by the union representative when he made his visits. Some employees wondered if the representative was pocketing the dues. The health and welfare benefits for being a union member amounted only to medical care with an assigned doctor. There was no pension plan, which was only later implemented. Thus, it was difficult to enroll employees into the Retail Clerks Union, especially young men without families. Moreover, there was a lack of communication between union representatives and employees. On the one hand, the representatives did not provide much information about the union and the few advantages of joining; on the other hand, many Chinese Americans were not proficient in English, and union representatives did not speak Chinese. The fact that none of the union representatives were Chinese Americans did not avail the labor unions to Chinese American workers either. Before World War II, Chinese American employees were not encouraged to join or were ignored altogether by the labor unions. After the war, Chinese American employees saw the labor unions as only wanting monthly dues from them and the union representatives as collectors. Essentially, Chinese American employees did not trust labor unions.[11]

The employees' attitude towards the labor unions, however, began changing during the mid-1950s. Before then employees were less concerned about wage differential than about job security and solidarity with their employer against their competitors.[12] But as more and more employees joined the unions, information spread about the better wages and benefits that membership provided. There were also employees who wanted the help of labor unions to get better work conditions and their due pay. This was exemplified by litigation against Yuba Market in 1955, in which employees asked the Retail Clerks Union to sue for noncompliance of labor agreements and for back wages because they had been working long hours without compensation.

Generally, employees struck a balance with their employers and labor unions to get job security and good wages and benefits. They grudgingly acquiesced to working extra hours without compensation as long as they were paid the union scale and received benefits. But the number of unpaid hours that employees were willing to work began decreasing gradually. Younger American-born employees who were not bound by old-world traditions were taking the place of older immigrant employees. With a middle-class income, unmarried employees got married and purchased homes. Married employees started families. Those who had families in the old country brought them to America and settled. Hence, employees with families and resources wanted to spend more time at home than at the store. With wages, benefits, and rights derived from being members of labor unions, they weaned away from their employers. But they always kept in mind that if they quit or were fired from their place of employment, it was still very difficult to get jobs in stores that were not owned by Chinese Americans. It was rather ironic that the success of the supermarkets, which enabled better incomes and welfare for their employees, eventually led in part to the decline of their competitiveness.

LIVING QUARTERS

The first-generation supermarkets had quarters on the premises available for employees who needed room and board. It was common practice among Chinese enterprises in America and China for employers to provide facilities for their employees. By agreement, sometimes a charge for accommodations was deducted from the paychecks of employees. Various types of employees used the facilities. There were young immigrants without families, either unmarried or with their families back in the homeland. There were those who lived a long distance from the store and returned to their hometowns on their days off. They included immigrants and American-born employees who may have had families. There were some employees for whom the store was their only home.[13]

The accommodations usually consisted of bedrooms with communal bathrooms and a kitchen and dining area. There may have been a sitting or living room for watching television, reading, or other recreational activities. Depending upon the size of the operation, there could be as few as three bedrooms or as many as fifteen. Stores employed cooks to provide three meals a day for employees who lived on the premises. All employees who worked a full day were provided at least one meal a day during an hour break. The accommodations were usually located upstairs on the backside of the store. Although connected to the store area by a stairway or hallway, there was a door that was locked by the night manager to separate the work area from the living quarters. This ensured security for the store and safety for the residents. Of course, the residents could always leave and enter the premises by another door opening to the outside.[14]

SALESMEN'S PERSPECTIVES

In the mid-1950s, food product companies began hiring Chinese Americans to represent their merchandise because Chinese American grocers were gaining prominence in the industry. Before that time there were very few Chinese American salesmen working for food product or food brokerage companies. Companies realized that in order to gain access to the growing number of Chinese American food retailers, they needed Chinese American salesmen because Euro-American salesmen were having difficulty trying to meet owners or managers. When Euro-American salesmen sought managers to persuade them to stock their company's products or to expand their products' display space on the store shelves, Chinese American employees often said to the salesmen, "The boss not here." This response helped employers avoid contact with persons who could be immigration or internal revenue officials investigating them. Even if an employee knew for certain that the person was a salesman, he was wary that a Euro-American might divulge, unwittingly or deliberately, damaging information to the authorities. As noted earlier, it was not uncommon for employers to sponsor immigrants who entered under questionable status. Employers dodged internal revenue officials because they often used cash in their business dealings to avoid leaving records that might result in paying income tax. Thus, it was only fellow Chinese Americans whom employers trusted to speak because they understood their situations, experiences, and needs. After representing a single product or company, Chinese

American salesmen began to operate their own food brokerage companies, contracting their services to various food companies.[15]

As callers to countless supermarkets, the salesmen were cognizant of the differences between the operations of Chinese American stores and their competitors. The first-generation supermarkets especially stood out. A salesman noted, "The real old timers were not progressive. They don't remodel and keep up with the times." When the owners did equip their stores, they did it with "whatever was necessary to start" and operated by doing "whatever they can to get by." Until Jumbo and Bel Air opened, the "laofan stores" (Euro-American stores) had the "advantage of service and cleaner stores."[16]

A demand that Chinese American owners or managers regularly made of product salesmen was that the latter must stock the shelves with the merchandise they represented. This practice occurred as frequently as every week, and the salesmen complied because it assured them that their products would retain display position and space on the shelves. It also gave the salesmen an opportunity to encroach on their competitors' shelf space if the latter did not diligently do the same. In essence, the store manager was playing one competitor against another to save on the cost of labor for stocking merchandise. Sometimes a manager would not let his employees stock certain merchandise because he knew that a salesman would call on the store shortly. This practice was widespread among Chinese American grocers and violated union contracts that stipulated that only employees were permitted to stock shelves.[17]

Although they provided low-cost labor, store personnel also formed a weak link in the earlier Chinese American operations. Immigrant employees usually lacked English-language skills and American manners, which facilitated customer service. When a customer asked where a product was located, they either ignored the customer or just pointed, not understanding what was said. The employees figured that customers shopped in their stores for the low prices, not for the service, and that they were very unlikely to get fired because their employers wanted low-cost labor. Because they worked long hours and extra days without compensation, one salesman said, "They always gripe. They try to do as little as they can. You notice that in their attitude." This demeanor towards their work was often directed at salespeople, who were at the receiving end of jealous innuendoes. They did "not want you to get ahead" because they felt that salespeople "have such easy jobs making so much money." Sometimes when a salesman asked to see the manager, for example, an employee would not offer any help at all.[18]

Some owners were not much better. After years of success, some owners became haughty with "their heads up in the air." They were less courteous and respectful to those salesmen who in the past they had depended on to help develop merchandising strategies. And this demeanor carried over to others. Partners became less accommodating towards each other, which often times led to outright enmity. Without trust and cooperation, management itself became an intractable problem for the store.[19]

WHY STORES DECLINED

Employees' opinions as to why Chinese American supermarkets declined converge on management. It is natural that they focused on management, because management affected them directly and tangibly. They pointed out that one of management's principal shortcomings was the lack of employee training to teach employees how to work efficiently and provide customer service. Bel Air was the noted exception.[20] Naturally, this criticism was presented in hindsight, measured in contemporary standards. But it is important to bear in mind that employee training was not as essential during the early years of the supermarket business as it was from the mid-1970s onward, at which time competition became very intense, and various strategies for retailing were being tried. Hence, management felt that employee training was not absolutely necessary and was an added expense.

In one particular situation, criticism was directed towards the supervisors and managers whom the shareholders of Jumbo Market had hired. During the early years, the shareholders worked alongside their employees, showing concern for their welfare. As their operations expanded, the shareholders became increasingly distant from their employees, using their supervisors and managers to maintain the employer-employee relationship that was nurtured in the past. It did not work out. According to one former employee, the shareholders were "listening to the wrong people, only the ones they liked." The old bonds of communication and concern between employers and employees deteriorated. Because the supervisors and managers came from outside the company, longtime employees felt alienated towards them, which inevitably extended to the shareholders. As a result, the morale and productivity of employees declined. They felt that their employers were not taking care of them and were only "for themselves." As one longtime employee put it, "All they were looking for was the old mighty buck." He said that on one Christmas holiday in the late 1970s, Jumbo Market gave each employee only ten dollars. Feeling insulted by his employers' lack of appreciation, he handed the miserly gift back to the manager and said sarcastically, "Give it back to whoever gave it. I think they need it more than we do."[21]

Generally, nearly all the Chinese American operators were trying to make quick profits by relying on low-cost labor rather than by building sales volume and earning thin but steady profits from it. Running their stores on the cheap, they did not want "to pay good money to get good people" to manage and work their stores. As one observer said, the operators of the older supermarkets ran their stores like "sweat shops," akin to the infamous immigrant enterprises of the past. The operators of the newer supermarkets were not much better. They did not invest capital to keep up with the trends that shoppers preferred: bigger stores, checkout scanners, and new product and service departments. When national companies started opening larger stores, for example, an employee noted that his former employers built their new Jumbo Market stores "the same size like what [they] have."[22] In sum, the steadfast effort among most of the operators of older and newer supermarkets was to cut labor costs and minimize outlay, a persistence which proved unsound when more and more customers wanted and expected better service and facilities.

A UNIQUE PERSPECTIVE

A unique perspective comes from the comments of George Chan, who worked for several supermarket companies for about thirty years starting in the late 1950s. He was born in Folsom, California, where his immigrant father operated a family grocery store. For five years, Chan was employed at Palm Market in Auburn, California, a supermarket operated by a partnership whose origin can be traced back to Lee Gim of Colusa. Afterwards, he worked four years at an Albertson's, and two years at a Giant Foods store. Lastly, he spent fourteen years working at Corti Brothers, a company of four upscale supermarkets operated by the local Corti family. Chan's outspoken, colorful observations and opinions would be illuminating even to experienced and knowledgeable people in the business.

Opened in the mid-1950s, Palm Market was a large supermarket that employed immigrants, American-born Chinese, and Euro-Americans. For immigrant employees, their terms and conditions of employment were similar to those of Yuba Grocery in Marysville: they received five days of union wages, but worked six days. Some of the American-born Chinese had to do the same. Each workday they put in more hours than other employees did. Conscious about annoying customers with non-English-speaking personnel, the management assigned immigrant employees to work in the warehouse and aisles, which kept them away from customers. (Located about fifty miles northeast of Sacramento, Auburn was a town in which very few ethnic minorities resided and in which there was a history of anti-Chinese violence.) But there were offsetting considerations to the immigrant employees' apparent plight. Their productivity, according to Chan, was much less than his and other American-born employees. "They dragged their butts" and were in "no big hurry" to do their work, possibly because they had to put in longer hours. And "nothing was said to them." Room and board was provided to them ("a pretty nice place to stay"), and "food was furnished." These immigrant employees could thus save their money and use it for other things if they so wanted.[23]

Management at Palm Market tended to be inattentive, but there was tacit expectation to get the work done. For most employees, they assumed their duties and responsibilities without hesitation. Chan remarked that:

> The only thing good about it was that they let you sort of work at your own pace. If you didn't get it done, you had to keep working at it. There was no time clock or nothing . . . but our work ethic was work on it until you get it done. And if you stayed over, you didn't feel [abused] because most of the time the bosses were doing the same thing. You know the bosses actually worked. They put [in] a hell of a lot more hours than you did. But of course they were all part owners.

Management tried to ameliorate the extra time at work by providing drinks and snacks to employees at no cost during rest breaks. But there were employees who took advantage of the situation, consuming much more than a fair amount of food and drink and doing very little work when the management was not watching. Chan observed, "You got some there, boy, they wouldn't do anything but they lived good." Although both American-born and immigrant Chinese American employees regularly worked beyond their scheduled time, the Euro-American employees rarely did. "The white guys got away with murder," Chan exclaimed.

Chan worked in an Albertson's store during the mid-1960s. At the time, a Chinese American employee working in a national chain company was uncommon, and Chan was the only ethnic minority employed in the store. Chan described the work as "very regimented; that's because [I was] coming from a Chinese store [which was run much more loosely]. Everything had to be done [in] certain ways and like that." Supervision was strict. "Just like any big company. I was told what to do there [more] than at the Chinese store." At the Chinese-owned store, "They assume you knew what you were doing.

Then you just did it." At Albertson's, "You built the display a certain way and things like that. There wasn't much give to it."

When he arrived at and departed from work, Chan punched a time clock. Because Albertson's was a unionized store, an employee was not to do any work "off the clock." It was the official rule. "You couldn't punch in five minutes before or five minutes after." Unofficially, something else occurred.

> Oh, they wanted that [putting in extra time]. Definitely, you know. [If it] didn't get done, something was going to happen, so you stayed until it finished. But they wanted you to be punched out. The supervisor would say, "Don't work off the clock." But then the store manager would look the other way because he wanted to make sure it was done. Actually, it was a lot more work there than at the Chinese store.
>
> Albertson's [was] funny. Each store manager would have his own little empire. When he took over a store, the first thing he wanted to do was to get rid of anybody who wasn't his. He wanted to bring [in] his own [department] managers. That way he can do these things. He says [that] we got to cut labor [costs] down this week for the labor report. So he would see if he could get the guys to do this. If he's got a good produce manager, he would buy him lunch or maybe give him a six-pack of beer out of his pocket because he's worried. He's worried because he can't get it done by himself. [Acting on his own initiative, the produce manager] would put in an hour or an hour and a half [off the clock, to get the work done].
>
> Basically, that's what he did. And the store manager didn't want to hear anything about it. That's why he wanted to bring [in] his own meat manager, produce manager, grocery manager. Then they're part of the group. Naturally, he promised these guys there's something upstairs [a promotion]. So these guys would fall for it and tow the line with him. The store manager never wanted you if you weren't part of the team because of the fact that these kinds of things might get them into trouble.

The labor unions were very strong. If an employee reported this kind of activity, the union would immediately follow up on it. A store manager and his cohorts caught working off the clock by a union representative would be fined fifty or seventy-five dollars.

Working off the clock went beyond the department manager level. The store's general manager was responsible for keeping total labor costs of the store within a limit dictated by the administrative office. Department managers had to stay within the limits of the employee-labor hours set by the general manager. The former, therefore, depended on a few of his trusted, complicit employees to also work off the clock when the need arose; for example, when there were not enough hours allotted for meat cutters to prepare for a sale. "It went on through the industry," Chan observed.

> But it was really stupid for guys to do that because if they got hurt off the clock, they wouldn't be covered by workmen's comp. But they're not thinking about that. All they're thinking about is getting promoted. I know some guys that did get promoted, but there's a lot more that didn't.

Store labor costs were based on projected sales for the store, which was determined by the administrative office. The office was not concerned with how the general manager met the sales projections or stayed within the labor costs' limits. He just had to do it. The general manager, in turn, put pressure on his immediate subordinates, and they did the same to their subordinates, all the way down to the ordinary employees. "That's how they made the money, off the labor." Hence, at Albertson's, the work may have been recorded on paper as taking eight or ten hours to complete, but in reality, it took employees fourteen hours. They labored off the clock to cover it. As for Chan, he was a strong supporter of the labor union. "So if I clocked off, I'm going home."

If the actual labor cost differential was not very great, how did national chain supermarkets like Albertson's overtake Chinese American supermarkets like Palm Market in the 1970s? According to Chan, the latter was not able to secure the type of labor it had in the past. Furthermore, the store was forced to keep employment records, pay full union wages, and so forth, raising the cost of labor. In the late 1970s, Albertson's prevailed upon the Retail Clerks Union to reorganize employee rankings and grant wage concessions, thereby reducing its labor costs. The reduced labor costs were passed on to shoppers in the form of lower prices for merchandise and better service to increase competitiveness. Better service came in the form of additional lower-paid employees. Palm Market, on the other hand, had the advantage of being a local independent operation. Its management was able to react more quickly to changes in the local market and to give special service and attention to its customers. But Albertson's sold its name and size. "The fact that they were big, people would see that and go there." Because Albertson's was big, "they can just outlast you." Furthermore, the company made profits not necessarily at the store, but at its wholesale and transportation operations, which were part of the vertical integration of its business.

Palm Market had great business, but nonetheless collapsed. And its downfall came from within. The supermarket did so much business that the partners recouped their capitalization in two years. "That's when the trouble started, because the partners became so rich." They "got greedy" and started fighting among themselves. The minor partners who invested small sums and were doing the daily work became jealous of the major partners who invested large sums and did no work in the store. The investing partners, or "silent shareholders," came only for visits and collected the lion's share of the yearly profits, causing resentment among the working partners. To aggravate the situation, one of the primary "silent shareholders" installed his son to manage the store. Soon the partners went their own ways, and one opened a competing supermarket, Alpine Market, in the area. Not long afterwards, Palm Market lost its business and went bankrupt. Alpine Market, on the other hand, became very profitable, but its success attracted large independent and national supermarkets, including Albertson's, which outlasted Alpine Market and "beat it to the ground."

Chan worked in a Giant Foods store before it was sold to Corti Brothers. He was retained by the new owners and subsequently worked in all of the Corti Brothers stores. Like Giant Foods, Corti Brothers expanded to four stores and then plunged. In Chan's opinion, it appeared that having four stores was the point at which companies were "either going to make it big or not going to make it." At four stores, a company became big enough to be out of control, whereas a company with one or two stores did not have to deal carefully with control. If a small company made mistakes, its losses were not so great that they could not be recovered by increased sales volumes. With more stores, mistakes and losses were multiplied, making it very difficult and costly to recover. It was therefore imperative that expanding companies had in place a strong management organization to maintain control. Corti Brothers, Giant Foods, and Farmers Market did not. An administrative setup like that of Albertson's and other large national companies may not have worked efficiently, but it "worked better than no control at all."

Corti Brothers was a family operation. When it expanded, the owners put their adult children in charge of the stores or departments, but they appeared to have had little or no experience working in a supermarket, let alone managing one. As a result, employees with many years of grocery experience had to follow directions that sometimes ended with bad results. In addition, they were reprimanded for not using their own judgment to countermand the orders. Naturally, resentment toward the young managers grew, and employee productivity declined. "If the crew's unhappy, it [the store] will go down the tube." In addition, daily supervision of employees was lax, resulting in "a lot of things never getting done." Because they were inefficient, the owners were "having to pour money" into the stores to keep them operating. Eventually, Corti Brothers had to close three stores. One is still in operation today as an upscale supermarket.

7 / Chinese Management
and Labor Unions

THE OPERATION OF CHINESE AMERICAN grocery stores and supermarkets was in many ways different from and yet similar to that of their competitors. Management of personnel was definitely different, which often invoked reproaches from competitors and labor unions. But to the employers, their management was nothing out of the ordinary, but a standard modus operandi that came from the old country. Because entrepreneurship in America, like in China, was highly competitive, utilizing traditional Chinese management practices made sense to them. Earlier Chinese American entrepreneurs used these practices for decades with successful results. It is worthwhile, therefore, to examine the method of management, and to also examine the organizations that were determined to restrain it, the labor unions.

The bane of Chinese American employers and management was the labor unions. Labor unions began in earnest to sign up Chinese American employees after the war because of the increasing prominence of their employers' supermarkets. The unions' demands for higher wages and benefits cut into the high profit margins of the supermarkets, but more aggravating to the employers was the enforcement of labor rules that curtailed their control. Before the imposition of union labor rules, employers basically ran their stores in a paternalistic manner. But as the labor unions began enrolling more employees and supplanting the role of employers to provide for them, employees began to become less compliant with traditional Chinese management. Likewise, the labor unions helped erode the solidarity between employers and employees. They vigilantly made sure management complied with the labor rules and wages stipulated in the contracts. Consequently, there was always tension between the management and labor unions.

CHINESE MANAGEMENT

Very few studies have been completed about Chinese American enterprises; therefore, information about their management practices is sparse. Apart from Paul Siu's *The Chinese Laundryman,* treatment of the subject has tended to be cursory, general, or celebratory. However, there have been some studies on various types and sizes of enterprises in China and Asia that described the characteristics of traditional Chinese management. From the findings in those studies, it becomes apparent that early Chinese American employers closely followed these traditional methods in management. Basically, they practiced paternalism, the fundamental system that permeates the traditional Chinese way of life. It was natural that early grocery store and supermarket employers, who were not far removed from the old country, used the paternalistic method. Combined with ethnic solidarity and good timing, it helped produce good profits. But its practice became less and less efficacious for employers as the standards of operating supermarkets, which their competitors implemented, rapidly advanced and as the character of their core personnel, Chinese Americans, changed. Employers who did not modify old ways or adopt new ways of management lost their competitiveness. It is worth noting that most studies pointed to traditional institutions and practices as factors that contributed largely to the success and failure of the enterprises.

In "The Institutional Foundations of Chinese Business: The Family Firm in Taiwan," Gary Hamilton and Kao Cheng-shu make four points. First, personal relationships and social rules were at the heart of Chinese business activity, just as Westerners regarded laws as appropriate in their business environments. But not everyone adhered strictly to rules. Just like many Westerners who broke, circumvented, or ignored laws, many Chinese did the same with relationships and rules. The most important point was that this institutional framework existed, forming the basis for activity and evaluation. Second, businesses of all sizes operated in the same institutional environment and were subject to the same framework of rules and relationships. The ubiquitous family firm, for example, was based on organizing principles that owners regarded as legitimate. These principles could not be ignored if owners wanted to succeed in business or any other activity. Not all Chinese businesses, however, were organized exactly the same way because principles only provided a base from which variations could be used. Third, "the family firm is not a type of organization doomed to be replaced by more modern organizational types. Instead, in the Chinese context, participants use close relational bonds as organizational principles to create and manage large, modern firms." Thus, the archetypal family firm was highly adaptable and flexible in all levels of business activity. Fourth, Hamilton and Kao found that the personal relationships and the ensuing networks that they describe in the making of modern Chinese businesses were close "replications of relationships found in traditional China." Of course, what is "traditional" needs a common definition and understanding for those who prescribe using it. Nonetheless, Hamilton and Kao state that "this 'tradition' is not merely adaptable to a modern way of life, but may actually remake it, may recreate in its own image what it means to be modern in Asia, and maybe in the rest of the world as well."[1]

Hamilton and Kao's findings reflected some of the points uncovered in this study of Chinese American grocery stores and supermarkets. Relationships were the foundation in starting, capitalizing, and operating these enterprises. Similar to the firms that Hamilton and Kao surveyed, ownership of stores was by family members, close relatives, or partners. Starting a business always revolved around a personal decision and an invitation to others to invest in the enterprise. The core enterprise was then followed by opportunistic expansion in the same line of business. The strategy was to start new stores rather than to enlarge the size of the original company.[2] This was a model for business expansion in modern Taiwan, which resembled that of conglomerates.

The stores, like those in Taiwan until recently, had no formal, unified management organization to closely supervise and coordinate their operations. Day to day management was in the hands of the owner or partners in each store. In Hamilton and Kao's study, the lack of a formal structure that characterized Western companies was compensated by a highly flexible system that rested on networks generated by personal relationships. "In the Chinese context, personal relationships identify role sets that link individuals together and that consist of generally fixed and reciprocal obligations. The important quality of these relationships . . . is the fact that they are based on reciprocal trust, loyalty, and predictability." It follows that relationships constituted an owner's or partner's personal network, which allowed him to secure resources and manpower for the company. In general, the larger and more cohesive the person's network, the more effective was the person.[3] In their expansion and operation of grocery stores and supermarkets, Lee Gim and his partners exemplified this interpretation. The same was true for Walter Fong and his partners in Farmers Market, and for Sam Wah You and his investors in Diamond Properties.

Hamilton and Kao confirmed that not only were networks crucial in getting business done, they also overlapped around a handful of key persons in the businesses who shared the greatest degree of trust and confidence towards each other. This inner circle consisted of owners, a few close family members, and longtime business associates. The closeness of the group members and the separation of businesses and managerial positions strengthened the control of the core owners and their associates and lessened the possibility of a challenge to their dominant position. This exclusiveness and concern for control also rendered practical consequences. In business groups, for example, each firm kept a separate account book. These accounts were not integrated into the business's official accounting system, but remained separate, their contents known only to members of the inner circle. Another consequence was that owners were very reluctant to register their firms for public stock offering for fear of losing control and of having to divulge financial information about the business group.[4]

As noted above, the workings in the partnerships of Chinese American grocery stores and supermarkets in Northern California closely resembled those of the business groups in Taiwan. As in Taiwan, only a few core partners had control of the partnerships and were privy to information kept in separate account books. That sometimes led to resentment, jealousy, and mistrust towards them by the lesser partners. Soon the Chinese American stores' productivity declined, operations stagnated, sales volumes fell, and profits shrunk, and eventually the partnerships disintegrated along with the businesses.

In "The Chinese Family Firm: A Model," Siu-lun Wong exposes the shortcomings of Chinese family firms and Chinese partnerships in Hong Kong and the Philippines in the 1960s and 1970s. Wong first establishes that the family firm is a major form of Chinese business organization and is not restricted to a particular locale or a specific economic enterprise. He then points out that when the family as a unit controlled the capital, the growth of the enterprise would be hindered. In other words, there seemed to be a limit to the growth of the family business "beyond a certain point." Two explanations are given for this restraint. First, there were only so many competent family members to occupy managerial positions to preserve familial trust, loyalty, and control. Second, the family was intrinsically conservative in its financial policies because it was especially wary of external interference or takeover. Consequently, ambition for growth was "diluted or absent." The objectives of the family business were to avoid the use of credit, to make the highest profit possible on a given turnover, to amortize capitalization debt as rapidly as possible, to build up sizable reserves, and to finance any expansion from the reserves.[5]

Despite the apparent concern with "conservation and consolidation," Chinese family enterprises in this form were short-lived. Conventional wisdom alleges that family firms seldom last three generations because of the practice of equal distribution of assets to male heirs and the nearly certain appearance of the proverbial prodigal son, both of which arrest resource growth and entrepreneurial ambition. But there were exceptions to this generalization that family firms tended to be limited in development and permanence. Some family firms in China, Hong Kong, Southeast Asia, and elsewhere, for example, have been engaged in manufacturing, banking, retailing, mining, and so forth for decades and are still in business. And some family firms also took advantage of external financing when conditions were favorable; for instance, Hong Kong family firms in textile manufacturing had a high portion of their capital in the form of bank loans.[6]

To support his argument that family firms in general were short-lived, Wong details the four phases of evolution of the Chinese family firm: emergence, centralization, segmentation, and disintegration. In sum, new businesses often emerged by the way of partnerships, but mistrust and factions offered opportunities to partners with strong positions to increase their control and interests, and this resulted in family firms. Decision-making in the family firm soon became centralized in the hands of the family's head entrepreneur, who delegated a low degree of responsibility to subordinates. After the family grew in size through marriage and family formation, subsequent distribution to heirs caused segmentation of resources and responsibilities. If a strong leader did not rise to take central control again, the family firm became enervated as individual shareholders pursued divergent interests. Emotional and economic ties became increasingly distant and diminished, causing shareholders to seek the disintegration of the family firm for immediate, tangible gains.[7] The narratives of some Chinese American family-owned grocery stores and supermarkets bear striking parallels with Wong's description of the evolution of the Chinese family firm. The period immediately before the passing of the founding entrepreneur usually marked the pinnacle of the company's success, followed by a decline in vigor and prosperity unless a strong leader and organization were in place to ensure continuity.

Based on the studies above and the history of Chinese American grocery stores and supermarkets, it is safe to assume that the organization and management of earlier enterprises by their immigrant owners were grounded on the traditional model, with some adaptations to fit within the American socioeconomic structure. As such, salient features of the traditional model deserve a final review. In "The Organizational Structure of the Traditional Chinese

Firm and Its Modern Form," Wellington Chan identifies the ownership of the traditional firm as either a proprietorship or partnership. If an individual owned the firm, the proprietor would manage it himself or hire an experienced manager to run it. If a partnership owned the firm, the number of partners and the size of the capital contribution of each varied widely. One or more of the partners who contributed smaller amounts would usually serve as manager; otherwise, a manager would be hired. The manager had complete authority over the business. He hired assistants and selected and supervised apprentices. Minority partners might recommend their friends or kinsmen for employment, but did so only with the manager's consent.[8]

In operation, the business was opened for long hours, fourteen hours or more each day. There were few holidays, only for major Chinese festivals. There was only one work shift, and all clerks worked demanding, long hours. Partly because of these long hours, but more because the managers expected total loyalty and dedication from the staff, practically everyone except the senior personnel roomed and boarded in the stores. This practice was facilitated by the custom of hiring only those who came from the same county or village as the owners and managers. New apprentices or employees had no formal training. They learned by observation and by task assignments.[9]

Chan argues that the traditional Chinese firm remained fairly constant in its organizational layout in the early to mid-twentieth century in China and Hong Kong. Innovations tended to be within the area of strategy, which allowed firms to achieve considerable growth. The structure, however, stayed within the confines of tradition. Ownership and management, for example, continued to be highly personalized, which exposed a firm to vulnerability when the firm's patriarch passed away or was no longer in command. The few firms that adopted Western organizational models, such as professional managers, an administrative structure, employee training, public stock offering for capital, and so forth, continued to grow and prosper.[10]

LABOR UNIONS AND LABOR COST

Former Chinese American employers or operators often cited onerous labor costs demanded by labor unions as a principal factor in the decline of their competitiveness and profitability. Labor costs in wages and benefits formed the most sizable operating expense, and keeping it under control largely helped make or break an operation. The employers' assertion can be substantiated, but the unionization of supermarkets also benefited employers. Unionization meant that wage rates and labor rules were set in contracts between employers and labor unions, which represented the interests of employees. From the early 1950s onwards, most supermarkets in Northern California were unionized soon after they opened, their operators reluctantly agreeing to contracts proffered by the Retail Clerks and Amalgamated Meat Cutters Unions. Although employers did not want any kind of restraint in their management capacity, unionization was tolerable if every competing supermarket operated within the same labor rules. This was not the case. Unionization brought parity to wage rates, which the unions could easily audit, but not every unionized store complied strictly to the labor rules, which the unions had difficulty enforcing. Although they were far from being the only operations that did it, all early Chinese American supermarkets circumvented labor rules, which worked to their advantage against their unionized competitors. It was no secret in the supermarket industry.

Early Chinese American supermarkets were able to circumvent labor rules because nearly all of their personnel were also partner-employers. Allowed to join the unions as store personnel, the partners readily enrolled when they realized the value of membership. As personnel they earned regular wages and received union health and welfare benefits, while as partners they shared in store profits. Of course, as employers they had to pay the premiums for the benefits, but they happily did so in order to participate in the generous plans. More important, as employers they had the prerogative to circumvent the unions' labor and work-hour rules. Union field representatives could not force employers to follow the rules, although they could do so for the few regular employees that were hired. The unions had to be content with unionized partners paying their monthly dues and benefit premiums. The Retail Clerks Union, however, did not allow a partner who was also the general manager to enroll, but eventually he was permitted to participate in the health insurance plan.[11] Naturally, the partners saw to it that labor was utilized in ways to maximize store profit, usually by working long hours themselves over six or seven days a week. By setting an example of diligence, they tacitly pressured their Chinese American employees to do the same. Chinese American supermarkets, therefore, had a distinct advantage over their competitors not in wage rate differential, but in their work-hour scheduling and the number of hours their personnel worked.

Although Chinese American employees were being solicited by labor unions after the war, they were reluctant to voluntarily sign up because of their sense of loyalty, solidarity, and indebtedness towards their employers. They were also suspicious, if not ignorant, of the unions' motives, especially in regard to paying union dues. Memories of past discrimination and exclusion helped maintain their suspicion. When they did become members, they often continued working in ways that violated labor rules, hoping not to get caught in the act because they and their employers could be subject to fines imposed by the unions.[12]

As the labor unions became more effective in enforcing labor rules, the Chinese American supermarkets' advantage in labor costs decreased. At the same time, the success of the operators prompted them to open more stores, which required hiring additional employees, many of whom were Euro-Americans and American-born Chinese not amenable to working extra hours without compensation. Long-time employees were less willing to work long hours when they saw their employers distancing themselves from daily operations and from them. Nevertheless, employers or management often reminded their employees of the obligation to finish their assigned responsibilities regardless of the work-hour schedule permitted by the unions. It was not uncommon for management to assign tasks that would require more time than an employee was scheduled to work. But nearly all supermarkets in Sacramento and in other Northern California markets—national as well as local companies, chains as well as independent operations—did this to maintain competitiveness or just to survive. The Retail Clerks Union Local 588 knew about the practice and consistently tried to end it. But it was difficult for the union because some employees would cooperate with their employers, even though ending it was in their welfare. Over time, labor transgressions became less common as supermarkets became larger and more complex. This required more personnel and division of labor administered by teams of supervisors and managers who worked less closely with employees than in the past.

UNIONIZATION OF SUPERMARKETS

Whether labor unions tried to enroll the employees of a single-store operation depended upon the amount of business, makeup of the personnel, and effort of the individual union field representative. But it was on multiple-store operations that labor unions focused their efforts. Some single-store supermarkets were barely profitable, and any increase in expenses due to paying higher union rate wages and benefits could very likely push them toward insolvency, causing them to dismiss employees, which essentially would undermine the foundation of the unions. In addition, labor unions often considered it not worthwhile to expend resources to pursue individual operations to enroll a small number of personnel, which often were mostly family members and relatives not amenable to joining. If a single-store supermarket, however, was doing exceptionally well and many of its personnel were not family members or relatives, then the labor unions might try to enroll the employees. This happened to the George Quan's Eye Street Bridge Market after the war. In any event, the aggregate number of personnel of individual supermarkets was insignificant to that of chain supermarkets, where the enrollment of their personnel yielded extensive power and substantial dues for the labor unions.

The unionization of supermarkets developed with the industry, advancing rapidly in the years immediately preceding and following World War II. The largest unions are the Retail Clerks Union and the Amalgamated Meat Cutters Union. The unions' strength varied according to the type (chain or independent) and size of a supermarket and its region. Large supermarkets of national chain companies that had high sales volumes were much more likely to be unionized than small independent supermarkets. Unionization by region was based on local market conditions, but settlements in one region often put pressure on another. More important was the unionization by department, which spread to the rest of the store. With the exception of some meat departments, store employees have been organized by the strength of the Teamsters Union, which used its power to help the Retail Clerks Union organize store employees. The key element was the drivers, who delivered products to the stores. If the drivers stopped delivery, the supermarkets had no choice but to close. Getting products to the stores on a regular schedule, especially fast-selling items and perishable produce and meats, was of the utmost importance to supermarkets. In addition, drivers who daily or weekly delivered "vendor products," high profit items such as snack foods, soft drinks, and alcoholic beverages, would not cross picket lines. In this highly competitive business, it was necessary for supermarkets to come to an agreement with unionized drivers without any disruption as soon as possible.[13]

Over time, the Retail Clerks Union found that it was most successful in organizing stores by using coercion, pressure, and dealings with employers rather than by enrolling individual or group employees who may or may not be willing to join. The union used three basic techniques: the strategic alliance, accretion clause, and direct approach. The strategic alliance relied on the cooperation of the Teamsters truck drivers, who refused to cross picket lines set up by the union, the effects of which were noted above. In some instances, supermarket employees were part of the unionizing effort, but often they were not. The union hired people to walk the picket lines so that the strike would not cause estrangement among employees, employers, and customers during and after the action. It was not the strike by the union which employers feared, but rather the presence of picket lines, the mere threat of which was usually enough to prompt their recognition of the union.[14]

The labor unions tended to unionize first the stores of large chain companies, next the local chain companies, and finally the independent companies. Their organization tactics fostered this trend, which resulted in a concentration on the chains, where the number of members and sum of dues were large. As a result, smaller independent stores particularly and stores located outside of large metropolitan areas were largely able to resist unionization.[15] As mentioned above, stores whose personnel consisted mostly of family members opposed unionization, and unions very rarely attempted to organize them. This was evident in Chung Sun Market in Colusa.

This pattern of unionization occurred throughout Northern California, where the local chains always acceded to nearly the same terms reached between the national chains and labor unions after negotiations. Chinese American employers and employees resisted unionization after the war, but almost all of them ultimately acquiesced. For example, the Famous Food Markets that opened in the 1950s were under union contract within a month after opening because of the threat of picket lines. Chinese American operators sincerely believed that their competitors pressured the labor unions to vigorously organize their supermarkets to reduce their labor cost advantage when they became leading competitors after the war.[16]

The Retail Clerks Union did not always coerce and pressure employers. During World War II, the union tried to persuade store employees to join by delineating the benefits of membership and by comparing organized labor with patriotism and democracy. The 1945 booklet "Thousands of People Like You" summarized the improved working conditions and wages which the forty-two affiliated local unions gained for their members, and encouraged employees to fill out and send an enclosed card to the local union's office for more information. The union hoped to build support and consensus at the rank-and-file level and then help the employees organize.[17] This approach achieved mixed results. It was not uncommon in Chinese American supermarkets, for example, for some employees to sign up with the union while others did not. In the 1940s and early 1950s, employees were paid approximately the same wages whether they were union members or not. From the Chinese American employees' point of view, joining the labor unions meant paying monthly dues—an added expense—to something they did not fully comprehend or were suspicious towards. At the same time, the Retail Clerks Union itself was still organizing. As it gathered memberships and alliances, the union's increasing solidarity and strength forced employers to deal directly with it. The union was then able to negotiate wage rates, labor rules, and benefits for its members. These gains included a guaranteed work week, reduction of working hours, guaranteed overtime pay, sick leave pay, seniority provisions, holidays off with pay or premium pay for holiday work, guaranteed vacations with pay, pro rata vacation pay, choice of vacation period, and wage increases. The more wage and benefit gains the union was able to successfully negotiate, the more support it got from employees, much to the perturbation of employers.[18]

All supermarkets in Northern California under union contract had the same provisions until the late 1970s. Because of the recessions that caused serious downturns in the supermarket business, small local chain and independent operators appealed to the Retail Clerks Union to modify some employee classifications, wage rates, and labor rules. It basically involved an additional classification of employee doing similar work at reduced wages and a small reduction in wage rates compared to the rates for larger companies. The national companies and robust local chain companies were not parties to these special agreements. The union concessions were meant to provide a little competitiveness for struggling companies, including Jumbo Market. From 1980 onwards, there continued to be many different contracts between the various supermarkets and the union, making for minor disparities in job classifications, wage rates, and labor rules among union members in the region. The concessions were not a victory for small local chain and independent operators, but a sign of their decline.[19]

WAGES AND LABOR RULES

Labor costs have always been a significant expense in supermarkets. Total wage and benefit compensation represented about 11 percent of expense as a percentage of sales, depending on the sales volume and number of man-hours worked. The novelty and scale of non-wage compensation, commonly known as benefits, provided in contracts with California's Retail Clerks Union and Amalgamated Meat Cutters Union were well known in the retail food industry. An agreement included a health care package with comprehensive hospital and medical care, prescribed drugs, preventive medical diagnosis, dental care, free eyeglasses, and psychiatric treatment. These benefits were provided not only to employees, but also covered their spouses and children. The costs of these benefits were completely paid for by the employers. Employees, however, might have to pay up to one quarter of the cost of their drug and dental benefits. It was not so much the rising wages that store management resented, but the expanding coverage and rising costs of the benefits demanded by the labor unions. In the early 1950s, for example, benefits cost fifty to sixty cents an hour. By the end of the decade, the cost rose to a dollar an hour. Finally, there was the pension fund for the employee, which was also completely paid for by the employer.[20]

It is little wonder that Chinese American employees were shifting their allegiance from their employers to the labor unions. Most employees did not rise to management positions, and the unions' mission was to protect and provide for them in addition to negotiating higher wages. As Chinese American employees became more financially secure and more Americanized, they felt less obligated towards their employers and came to regard the unions as providers of social welfare, guardians of job security, and protectors against job abuse. They became less tolerant of working long hours uncompensated and of violations in paycheck kickbacks.

A supermarket's high wages could be overcome by increased productivity. However, union rules and regulations tended to inhibit productivity by restricting the most efficient and economic utilization of labor, innovations, and technology. Labor rules limited the ability of management to set work-hours in accordance with the demands of the business and customer. It forced the use of personnel when not needed and prevented their use when needed; required the employment of skilled workers to do unskilled work; and prohibited the use of vendors to stock the shelves.[21]

It was not uncommon to find a labor rule enforced in one store and not in another, despite the rule's existence in both operations. This situation depended upon the union's local field agent or representative, district manager, and other personnel, or possibly furtive relationships between store management and union officials. The Retail Clerks Union definitely tended to more rigidly enforce rules in the larger, more established supermarkets and tended to overlook violations on the part of smaller stores or chains. A strong relationship between an agent and store management made contract enforcement difficult, which may have helped the operation stay in business, but put competitors at a labor cost disadvantage.[22] This disparity in enforcement was especially pronounced during the early years of the labor unions and supermarkets, especially among Chinese American operations, whose success depended in large part on their operators' skills in "cultivating relationships" with union agents as well as employees, wholesalers, and customers.

LOW-COST LABOR AND EMPLOYEES

As discussed earlier, Chinese American operators were able to sell their merchandise at lower prices than their competitors and still make good profits because they had low-cost labor. Initially, low-cost labor was achieved because nearly all of the personnel were working partners. But as operations expanded and employees were hired, low-cost labor depended on the employees' acquiescence to their employers' expectations to work extra hours or days without pay. Not all employees participated in this practice, which was determined by particular employer-employee relationships and mutually agreed-upon conditions for employment. Basically, it affected immigrant employees, especially recent arrivals who were related to their employers, to whom they were beholden for their immigration and employment. On the other hand, non-Chinese-American employees and usually American-born Chinese were not expected to work without pay, "off the clock," or during "free time."[23]

Other practices to reduce labor costs involved forms of payments and kickbacks. Some of these methods were borderline legitimate, and others were outright unscrupulous. After cashing their weekly paychecks in the store, some employees returned a portion of their union scale earnings to their employers as compensation for room and board. The amount varied from store to store and from employee to employee, depending on the agreement between employer and employee.[24] In a more sophisticated form of kickback, some employers handed out two paychecks to their employees, one in accordance with union wage compensation, the other a lower amount. The employee immediately signed both checks and turned them over to management, but received cash only for the lower amount. The other check remained in the possession of management, who would produce evidence of proper compensation to union representatives conducting inquiries.[25] Other kickbacks were much simpler. While in the store, an employee cashed his paycheck and then handed back a portion of the cash to the employer, who would summarily fire them if they did not do so. This tacit threat was underscored by the fact that the employees, especially immigrants or teenagers, would very unlikely find as good or better employment elsewhere.

There were some longtime employees who did not mind too much having to return a portion of the wages to their employers as long as they and their families were covered by the union's health and welfare benefit plans, for which their employers paid the premiums. Like the teenage and immigrant employees, they were concerned that they would not be able to find employment elsewhere, but moreover, they had the welfare of their families to consider. With few alternatives, they were bound to their situation. In fact, they considered themselves fortunate because there were many other Chinese Americans who worked in stores that were not unionized and who were more than happy to take their place. These nonunion employees generally worked just as hard and long but received lower wages and no benefits.

Another way in which employers reduced labor costs was uncovered only many years after the practice occurred. This practice involved underpaying the amount a store was required to contribute to an employee's retirement trust fund. Basically, for every hour an employee worked, a fixed amount was paid into a fund. But an employer sometimes reported fewer hours than were actually worked, thereby reducing the store's contribution and the accumulated amount of the employee's trust fund. It was only when employees retired that they discovered that they had been shortchanged during their years of employment. This underhanded activity continued until the labor unions tightened up their auditing practices, matching the hours worked annually with amounts deposited and then reporting the results to employees.[26]

These labor and compensation practices project an ignominious side of Chinese American solidarity, which is usually renowned for its benevolence, benefits, and economic success. It could be argued that what was celebrated was incongruent with what occurred in reality. And from a contemporary perspective, what happened was exploitative. But in a larger context, which takes into account available opportunities, suitable qualifications, and comparative compensations for other types of employment at the time, supermarket employment was acceptable, if not desirable, especially for immigrants. It was very unlikely that new employees, immigrant or American-born, took a job without knowing what was expected from them and what were the conditions for employment. They usually gained employment by referral from someone they knew working in the same supermarket. Furthermore, work conditions were steadily improving because of developments in the supermarket business and demands by the labor unions. With regard to the employees' day-to-day work, supervision and tasks seemed to be less exacting than in non-Chinese-American supermarkets. But it was a trade-off. Chinese American employees worked under less supervision, but their productivity was higher because of longer work hours.[27]

Labor union officials knew about these surreptitious activities, but generally did not earnestly try to put an end to them. These activities, however, were not exclusive to Chinese American supermarkets, and it was common knowledge that other operations did the same. To what degree the various supermarkets violated union labor rules has never been documented, let alone determined precisely. Single-store operations were less worthwhile targets than national chain-store operations for union officials enforcing contract labor rules. Union officials tended to look the other way when it came to the first-generation of Chinese American supermarkets, which consequently helped them to achieve their high profitability. But that did not mean that there were no legal actions brought against the supermarkets for violating labor rules. The 1955 litigation against Yuba Market was a prime example. By 1970, gross infractions of union labor rules were rare among second-generation Chinese American supermarkets, and their low-cost labor advantage over competitors had been largely erased.[28]

8 / Stop-N-Shop

LOCAL CHAINS AND INDEPENDENT COMPANIES dominated the supermarket business in Sacramento and other Northern California communities until the mid-1970s. National chain supermarkets like Safeway and Lucky had difficulty securing a strong presence in Sacramento, which yielded the metropolitan market to Chinese American stores and other local companies, such as Vans, Holiday, Mayfair, Bi-Rite, Raley's, Compton's, and Stop-N-Shop. Each competed fiercely in neighborhood markets, often doing business across the street from or near each other. It was not unusual, for example, to see three supermarkets located near a street intersection, each occupying the corner section of a block. If there was not enough business for all three, as was usually the case, in due time the national chain or local supermarket would go under. All of these local companies, except for Raley's, are no longer major competitors or are out of business, like their Chinese American counterparts. How these local companies started, operated, and ended business provides a good opportunity to compare them with Chinese American operations. A narrative of the local supermarket chain Stop-N-Shop affords such an opportunity. Founded by an immigrant from the Middle East, the family-owned company operated from 1928 to the early 1970s, the same period that Chinese American supermarkets thrived. At its height, the company included thirteen grocery stores and supermarkets, a wholesale grocery warehouse, and shopping centers in Sacramento and nearby communities. In sum, good timing and hard work yielded success for the company, but overwhelming financial pressures, mostly unrelated to the supermarket operation, forced its demise.

At one time, the Stop-N-Shop supermarkets were the most popular and successful stores in Sacramento. There is not a resident who lived in the 1950s and 1960s who does not remember the Stop-N-Shop jingle on radio and television:

Let's go down to Stop-N-Shop
And push the cart around-n-around.
You'll get a lot more for your dollar there
Than anywhere else in town.

By the mid-1970s, the supermarkets were still profitable, but they, too, were being left behind by the rapid changes in the industry that had affected the Chinese American supermarkets. In addition, the stores' revenues were used to plug up the financial drain that the owners' real estate developments were causing. Together, these challenges quickly overcame Stop-N-Shop.[1]

Among the thirteen stores in the company, eight Stop-N-Shop supermarkets competed against Chinese American operations that were located about a mile or less away. According to eighty-eight-year-old Lewis Kassis, one of the sons of the family-owned company, "It was hell to pay if you had Chinese grocery stores as competition. They were always selling cheaper than you were." It was no secret to Kassis that low labor costs enabled Chinese American supermarkets to compete. But the Chinese American supermarkets' advantage gradually came to an end due to the persistent efforts of the labor unions to enroll the employees. Although the Chinese American employees played key roles in the "problem," Kassis sympathized with their predicament.

> They [the Chinese stores] had an advantage from a salary structure. They could work their people around the clock when necessary and still pay the minimum wages. And this went on for a good twenty years. Naturally we had a really tough time competing with those prices. . . . It was there. It was a problem. Even the unions couldn't do [much] about it. What the unions did, they went out and signed up each individual. Took them into the union, made them swear to the regulations and so forth. Over a period of time, we overcame that. . . . Another thing too, Chinese boys grew up and wanted to be like the rest of us. They didn't feel that it was fair that they would work longer hours [and] get less pay. Once they got over their obligations to whoever brought them over here, then they were free to do what they wanted to do. That period is all gone, and thank God it's over with.[2]

Although the labor practices in Chinese American supermarkets drew disapproval from Kassis, his opinion on the facilities was rather favorable.

> I think they weren't bad. They were pretty nice. They had the labor to do it and they kept them up pretty good. I can't fault them very much on that. I didn't

appreciate the fact that they [employees] were living in the back room and upstairs. I didn't think that was good. I didn't think it was healthy. Again, that's something that's past now.[3]

Stop-N-Shop's rise, prominence, and passing bear remarkable similarities to the narratives of Chinese American supermarkets, including the immigration of the founder, the checkered business fortunes early on, and the humble beginnings in the grocery business. In 1890, Abe (A. G.) Kassis and his wife, Freda, emigrated from Lebanon to North Dakota, where his brother and other Christian Lebanese families had settled earlier. On property that he purchased, Kassis engaged in grain farming, like most of the other immigrants, but was unsuccessful. Consequently, Kassis moved to a nearby city to operate a small grocery store with his five brothers. The income from the business was not enough to support everyone; therefore, they branched out into other businesses. They opened a successful billiard parlor, where Kassis managed to save a substantial sum. But Abe Kassis and his family had to leave North Dakota because the cold climate was adversely affecting the health of one of his young sons. Selling all their possessions and business interests, the Kassis family moved in 1920 to Rio Linda, a small rural town located just north of Sacramento, California. Kassis tried his hand at farming again, this time growing vegetables and fruit and raising livestock, including goats and chickens. The chickens and eggs that Kassis sold generated a good income, but a fatal disease struck the chickens one winter, devastating the business. Meanwhile, Mrs. Kassis worked in a local produce cannery to help support the family. Two of the sons also worked in the cannery while attending high school and helping out in their father's business ventures, which included a livestock feed store and a miniature golf course. Those ventures also ended in failure.[4]

In 1928, Kassis opened his first store, called Stop-N-Shop, on the corner of 28th and Y Street (now Broadway) in Sacramento. It was by happenstance that Kassis opened the store. He noticed an ice retailing business in disuse, and decided to lease the dilapidated wooden building in which the business was housed and give the business a try. In the beginning the store, with its dirt floor, sold only a few items: watermelons and ice during the warm season, wood blocks and coal for heating during the cold season, plus vegetables and fruit from the family farm and other growers. The sales for the first day totaled $7. Kassis gradually stocked more and more grocery items for sale as his customers began requesting them. Because Stop-N-Shop was not yet a regular grocery store with a wholesale supplier, Kassis and his wife purchased products from Black's Food Store, located in downtown Sacramento. They repriced and resold the items for two or three cents higher. As the grocery business grew, Kassis joined United Grocers, a wholesale grocery cooperative.[5]

Not long after starting the business, the family moved from the farm in Rio Linda to a house a few doors down from the store. By then the family had grown to include five sons: Frank, Lewis, Edward, John, and Walter. Everybody in the family worked in the store during those early years, which was remembered as very laborious. On busy weekends, the work went on for twenty-four hours, the sons taking turns working the shifts. For their work the sons received a salary, which they assiduously saved. The store was often opened from morning to midnight, depending on the amount of business. Fortune then struck Stop-N-Shop. Its sales volume rose sharply after an ice cream store opened next door, which resulted in increased customer traffic.[6]

During the 1930s, Abe Kassis formed partnerships to open additional grocery stores throughout the Sacramento area. These early partnerships were financed by Kassis himself, who gave part ownership of the stores to his sons after each graduated from high school. His two oldest sons, Frank and Lewis, received them first. The second Stop-N-Shop was opened with the aid of United Grocers, which helped secure a failed grocery store for Kassis. Profits from the second store were reinvested to open a third store, and Kassis gave a partnership to his third son, Edward. A fourth Stop-N-Shop opened just prior to World War II in a building that formerly housed an automobile garage. The Kassis family hired a cousin to manage the new store while two of the sons enlisted and served in the United States armed forces for the next few years. During the war years, obtaining supplies to operate and products to stock the stores was difficult, but the stores remained opened and did brisk business.[7]

After the war, the Kassis family opened a fifth Stop-N-Shop. Again, the capitalization of the newest Stop-N-Shop came from the profits of the other stores, and another son, Walter, received his partnership. The family agreed to divide the supervision of the stores according to departments with a son heading each. Walter undertook the position of grocery and advertising manager, Frank was general manager, Lewis was meat and delicatessen supervisor, and Edward became produce and flower manager. John did not enter the grocery business like his siblings, but became a medical doctor instead. The partnership was not bound by legal contract, but was just a family affair based on mutual trust.[8]

Stop-N-Shop expanded rapidly, becoming twelve supermarkets by the mid-1960s. Most of the stores were small compared to the new supermarkets of the mid-1970s and later, making them relatively easy to run with only about a dozen employees needed. Labor union representatives vigilantly watched the supermarkets to ensure that labor rules were not violated, but management did not have a vexing time with them like Chinese American management did. Good employees would leave and find work elsewhere if they were not treated fairly or paid union rate wages because the supermarket business was expanding and in need of employees. After the war, Stop-N-Shop hired Japanese Americans to work in the produce departments because of their experience in farming and in the grocery business prior to the war. But very few Chinese Americans were employed.[9]

The first grocery store closed in 1950. About two years later, the brothers opened a warehouse to supply their supermarkets with groceries, fresh meats, delicatessen products, produce, frozen foods, and sundry items. The Kassis Brothers Wholesale Grocery also sold products to other retail outlets and restaurants. Their entry into the warehouse business followed a trend that involved single-store operators joining wholesale cooperatives or multiple-store operators starting their own warehouses to maintain their competitiveness. It was at this time that the Kassis family incorporated their business, but they still ran it like a family concern, with decision-making based on consensus.[10]

Banks financed this phase of rapid growth, which formed a departure from relying solely on the operating revenue and profits from the stores. During the 1930s the Kassis family quit doing business with banks because of the many failures in the banking industry, one of which resulted in a substantial loss for the family. But from the 1950s onward, borrowing was the primary method for financing the expansion of stores and real estate investments. Hence, the Kassis family was always in debt, and they became deeper in debt as they developed larger shopping centers in which their Stop-N-Shop supermarkets were located. Securing loans, however, was not without difficulty, even though the Kassis family had a very successful record in the supermarket business. It appeared that Stop-N-Shop was not large enough to interest lending institutions to underwrite its ventures. In order to acquire enough capital for their later developments, the family sold shares to investors to supplement the loans. On the other hand, large supermarket operations such as the national chain companies had virtually no problem obtaining credit to secure prime locations to build their stores. Although short-term loans were approved for initial construction, long-term loans needed for completion, operation, or expansion of large shopping centers were not forthcoming from the same lenders. This created a predicament for the Kassis family, who had only the operating revenue and profits from their supermarkets to keep their developments from defaulting. A large part of the Kassis family's financial problems was due to the fact that their major developments occurred during the recession of the early 1970s. In addition to tight credit, the recession brought about a slowdown in the supermarket business, reducing the revenue that the Kassis family needed to keep their shopping centers going. The shopping centers themselves had difficulty securing and holding onto retail tenants, who also had to deal with the recession.[11]

Caught in a credit squeeze, the Kassis family could only sell their supermarkets to generate cash. The stores were still profitable, but at ten or more years old, they were very small compared to their competitors' latest offerings. And the equipment needed updating. Hence, the Kassis family had a difficult time selling their stores. Most of the other local operators were no better off than the Kassis family and did not want to purchase the stores. Large corporations did not want the stores because of their size. To remodel them would have required not only a substantial expenditure, but also more space than the stores had. Because many of the stores occupied prime locations, they were purchased for their locale. The buildings were then razed, and the properties developed for other uses. Only a few Stop-N-Shop stores were sold and operated as supermarkets. One store was given to Walter Kassis, who with his immediate family ran it for ten years. Lewis Kassis's son purchased the wholesale grocery operation, which is still in business today.[12]

In the final analysis, Stop-N-Shop ceased operating because of a convergence of unfavorable circumstances that was all too familiar to the Chinese American supermarkets. They included rising operating expenses; increased competition from newer, larger supermarkets; stores in matured neighborhoods that yielded diminishing sales; and outdated stores that were too costly to remodel. The economic recession that occurred at a time when the Kassis family was trying to complete their shopping centers precipitated disagreements over the future of their stores. It was likely that most of the Stop-N-Shop stores could have continued operating profitably, but not for very long. Moreover, the Kassis brothers were ready to retire from the business and concentrate on managing their investments, like their Chinese American counterparts. Their adult children wanted to run their own businesses and pursue other careers.

The Kassis family gave back to the community that had supported them for decades. A portion of the proceeds from the subsequent sales of the shopping centers was used to establish charitable foundations: the A. G. Kassis Memorial and the Lewis Kassis Family Foundation.[13]

Conclusion

BY THE EARLY 1980S, the prominence of Chinese American super-markets and supermarket chains in Northern California had effectively ended. The national chain companies and a large local chain company, Raley's, garnered the largest share of the market and continued to expand with their superstores, not supermarkets. The early, small supermarkets, Famous Food Markets, Farmers Market, and Giant Foods, went out of business. Their passing was humbling to say the least. With sales volumes and profits stagnant or on the decline, the shareholders of Jumbo Market also closed and sold their stores. The last sold in 1996. In 1992 the Wongs sold their Bel Air supermarkets and most of their ancillary operations. The only supermarkets noted in this study that remain in business today and are still operated by the descendants of their founders are Chung Sun Market in Colusa and a Dick's Market in Sunnyvale. The first is doing adequate business, and the second is doing very marginal business. Both hold on primarily because the families own outright the stores' real estate and equipment, and family members continue to work in the stores. There are some single-store supermarkets in Northern California run by Chinese Americans who purchased them from their former employers, who were independent operators, local chain companies, or national chain companies. The operation of the Centr-O-Marts—four in Stockton, one in Oakley, and two in Brentwood—is unique. They were purchased and operated by separate partnerships that later consolidated into a corporation, reversing the trend toward independent single-store operations. Nearly all these supermarkets tend to be 1970s vintage and are located in old neighborhoods. They are operated by families or partners who work long hours and hire only a few nonunion employees. Although there are a few exceptions, they eke out a profit by catering to local niche markets, generally grossing $70,000 to $150,000 a week in sales volume. The superstores, by comparison, generally gross $400,000 to $700,000 a week.

Several Chinese American independent and small chain supermarkets are still operating in towns and cities of central and southern San Joaquin Valley. Most of them were established during the 1950s and are family or partnership operations.[1] Located primarily in ethnic and working-class neighborhoods, their sales volumes are large enough to make decent profits from their nonunion labor, but not high enough to attract national chain companies that require high sales volumes due to their costly overheads. In the past, some of these Chinese American supermarkets competed against national chain supermarkets like Safeway, but they never reached prominence, like Bel Air and Jumbo in Sacramento.[2] The national chain companies eventually withdrew because of stagnant or shrinking local markets. In rural communities, supermarkets often provide credit to their customers, with whom employees are on neighborly terms. Nonetheless, their annual sales in the early 1990s were considered "small change" compared to what large supermarkets in a competitive market could do.

Chinese American operators did not maintain their prominence or at least continue operating supermarkets because they never had plans to do so. The operators regarded supermarkets as a means for attaining financial security and prosperity for themselves. They entered the business to make as much money as possible as quickly as possible with little or no thought of dominating the retail food trade. When they were leaders in the grocery business from the postwar years to the 1960s, it was by accident rather than design. The circumstances were right, and they had low-cost labor. Most of them did not want to invest any more capital into their supermarkets than necessary after commencing operation. They remodeled their stores only to maintain profitability, not to keep up with industry trends. This was evident in the leveling of weekly sales volumes after the first year of business. Similarly, opening additional stores offered better prospects for increasing revenues than investing in improvements for existing stores that may have already reached their potential in neighborhood markets.

This critique is not an indictment for failure. On the contrary, the operators did what they set out to do and did it successfully. They made their money and quit. When studying entrepreneurship in America, it is natural to assume that entrepreneurs would want to continue expanding until they sell their enterprises or pass their enterprises to heirs. This assumption holds progress as the ideal. In other words, the means becomes the end, and expansion measures the means. For Chinese Americans, money was the end, and proprietorship was the means to the end. Proprietorship helped them earn money for the comforts of life and for measuring their status in their communities.

In contrast, national chain supermarkets stayed in business largely in part to support company executives who placed salaries, personal prestige, and power above profits for public shareholders. This is exemplified by their small net profit margins, usually about one percent or less.[3]

When Chinese Americans first entered the grocery business, they were interested only in making a living and improving their economic situations. They wanted some control over their endeavors because it was difficult to get ahead working for somebody else. They did not think too much about risk or failure, only believing optimistically that with hard work, they would succeed. They did not envision themselves building their small grocery stores into big supermarkets, let alone chain operations. Only later did they realize that with expansion they could gain greater profits, but to achieve competitiveness for competitiveness's sake was not on their minds.[4] For the Wong family of Bel Air, however, competitiveness was the end. They liked what they were doing; hence, Bel Air's continual innovation and growth until it was sold.

If there was any shortcoming in operating supermarkets, it was that most owners, partners, or shareholders did not give much thought to how they were going to end their proprietorships, only knowing that they would not be involved with them. This lack of long-term strategy, along with conservatism, was characteristic of the way most Chinese Americans ran their stores.

Chinese Americans regarded operating supermarkets as a very demanding enterprise. Nevertheless, as outlined in prior chapters, it was more rewarding than most other enterprises, including work in meat markets, produce stores, restaurants, and laundries. From the 1940s to 1960s, the owners, partners, and shareholders were able to recapture their capitalization costs and secure good profits soon after commencing business. They became accustomed to putting out a moderate one-time investment for startup and gaining quick returns. But the supermarket industry developed rapidly; consequently, starting up and operating supermarkets became increasingly expensive. By the 1970s, operators figured that the cost of capitalization for a new supermarket or for remodeling an old supermarket outweighed the potential returns in the short term. Complacent and conservative, they were unwilling to change their basic mode of operation and to invest more resources. Soon they lost much of their market share to more progressive operators, mostly the national chain companies. The latter capitalized on the window of opportunity that opened after the 1975 recession and on the housing boom during the second half of the 1970s. Before competitive pressures fell upon the second-generation supermarket operators, many of the first-generation operators lost business to new competitors, many of whom were their former apprentices.

Both generations of operators quit for personal reasons, too. They were getting older in age and did not have the energy or desire to continue. They felt that they had worked hard, made their money, and that it was time to retire.

The entry of Chinese Americans into the grocery business in Northern California can be traced back to two sources: Lee Gim's 1921 fortuitous start in Chung Sun Market in Colusa, and the invitation to Chinese Americans to operate meat and produce concessions in combination markets in Sacramento during the 1930s. In other locales, such as Southern California and Houston, Texas, Chinese Americans did not establish a strong presence in the grocery business until World War II, when they took over the grocery stores that Japanese Americans were forced to abandon. Even so, only the Chinese Americans in Northern California expanded their small grocery stores into single-store supermarkets and chain supermarkets, becoming prominent competitors from the postwar period to the mid-1970s. The majority of grocery stores, however, did not expand into supermarkets. While some of their operators were content simply to make enough money to be comfortable and secure, others who wanted to expand did not have the capital, labor, and expertise to do so. Many grocery store operators barely got by with an adequate amount of business.

Most Chinese Americans who expanded their grocery stores to supermarkets never operated more than one or two. Assuming that there was a harmonious relationship, owners or partners were either content with their small operations, or they did not have enough resources generated from one store to expand further. If they had the resources to remodel or expand, they weighed the work and time that would be necessary to recapture their investment and to realize their profits. They found the commitment was not worthwhile when they had already secured their financial future, and the risk unsound when they were no longer young and energetic and when competition was increasing.[5] Some supermarkets closed within a few years after opening because business was not good. The owners had chosen locations without potential, or locations with potential but where stores could not generate enough early profits to meet expenses. In other words, the local markets had not developed enough to support the supermarkets. Such was the case of the Panorama Markets in the early 1960s.[6]

The success of early entrepreneurs such as Lee Gim depended upon two factors. The first was the willingness of the Arata Brothers Wholesale Grocery (later renamed Valley Wholesale Grocery) to sell merchandise to them to stock their stores. Other wholesale grocery companies were not willing to sell to Chinese Americans, possibly because they harbored racial prejudice or were in collusion with their regular customers to keep newcomers out of the business. Credit was not an issue because Chinese Americans dealt in cash. This situation would persist for Chinese American grocers until the 1950s, when their prominence could not be ignored any longer and the wholesale grocery companies began courting their business. But for decades it was only the Arata Brothers that sold and gave credit to Chinese Americans. In other words, Arata Brothers was the linchpin that helped the founding and growth of Chinese American grocery stores and supermarkets. Lewis Kassis of Stop-N-Shop affirmed this fact.

> You know who helped the Chinese people? The Arata Brothers! He had the wholesale house and he wanted to keep more volume. He wasn't getting enough from the white people, running the business, he put a Chinese store right next to it. He supplied the merchandise.[7]

As described in this study, the other factor that helped Chinese American grocers succeed was low-cost labor. Low-cost labor was achieved when owners or partners worked long hours and employed immigrant employees. From the 1930s to the 1950s, Chinese American operators employed mostly immigrant employees who acquiesced to working long hours. In the early years, employers worked long hours alongside their employees, ameliorating any feelings of exploitation. All work was the same, and work continued until completed. In addition, the obligatory room and board for employees provided by employers reinforced the sense of mutual responsibility and ethnic solidarity, as did the hiring of kin and friends from the same or nearby villages in the old country. Thus, the employees were like dependable family members found in family-run grocery stores and supermarkets. But the relationship between employers and employees eroded as their socioeconomic circumstances improved. The mutual responsibility and ethnic solidarity that pundits often ascribe to the historical success of Chinese Americans may well have been mutual dependency and economic expediency, possible to undermine if better opportunities became available.

The use of low-cost labor was not new. During the latter half of the nineteenth century and early twentieth century, Chinese Americans had been willing to work at a lower wage rate than most other workers, much to the vexation of Euro-American laborers. This occurred in mining, railroad building, manufacturing, reclamation, agriculture, and other labor-intensive industries. When jobs were difficult to obtain because of competition from newer immigration groups willing to work for even lower wages, Chinese Americans resorted to self-employment by operating enterprises such as truck farms, restaurants, and laundries. When necessary, they hired other Chinese Americans at low wages. Because remuneration from a successful enterprise was much better than working for someone else, employees sought to start their own enterprises with savings from their labor. These enterprises would later include grocery stores and supermarkets. This pattern of profiting from low-cost labor continued until the labor unions persuaded employees to enroll in their organizations and coerced employers to sign labor agreements, thereby ending the cycle in the grocery business.

Management was a principal factor in the success and decline of Chinese American supermarkets. During the early years of supermarket development, management and operation were relatively simple. Because nearly all supermarkets were the about the same in size and inventory, Chinese American stores could outsell and outlast their competitors because of their low-cost labor. Their advantage was not without shortcomings. Management often complained that many of their employees, especially immigrants, tended to be lackadaisical and leisurely in performing tasks. This criticism, however, was countered by complaints from employees who accused management of insufficient supervision, exemplified by a lack of employee training.

High sales volumes mitigated whatever weaknesses and deficiencies were found in management and employees in the early supermarkets. As long as the owners made good profits and the employees received regular paychecks, everything was fine. A strong leader also helped keep things running smoothly by providing firm direction and adjudicating personnel differences. Problems arose when profits declined due to increased competition, and the strong leader abdicated his authority, retired or left the business, or passed away. Consequently, management became directionless, and bickering and self-interest surfaced among partners and employees, consuming the business.[8]

There were other weaknesses in the early Chinese American supermarkets. In partnerships, management was generally by consensus, but it was not unusual to find mistrust and jealousy among partners that not only arrested progress but also encumbered operations, especially after the departure of a strong leader. In addition, partners generally did not want to delegate authority to help them manage their stores, each guarding whatever small control he had. These weaknesses not only contributed to the decline of the supermarkets, but also resulted in a great deal of difficulty for owners or partners in their later attempts to sell their stores, which by then were unsound and unprofitable.[9]

Whereas the success of the early supermarkets was dependent primarily upon a strong leader, the success of the later supermarkets that expanded into chain operations was dependent on an effective managerial organization. At a time of increasing competitive pressures and rapid changes in the industry, a multiple-store company needed competent supervisors and managers to assume a division of responsibilities. Small mistakes could be compounded to the point where losses could not be recovered, possibly devastating the entire company. Owners or partners determined policy and direction, but efficacy required control by those in charge of daily operations. Unfortunately, some owners or partners wanted to micromanage particular aspects of an operation without consideration or coordination with their supervisors and managers, often interfering with them. Furthermore, they did not provide their managerial organizations with adequate resources and complete trust. Thus, a recipe for failure was in place, which caused companies to become uncoordinated and out of control. Some owners or partners understood their need for good help and organization, but unwittingly or carelessly placed their confidence on unqualified supervisors and managers who ran their stores to ruin.

Among all the Chinese American operators, only the Wongs of Bel Air got out of the business while their stores were in ascension and prosperous. They had a competitive spirit and enjoyed the challenge of operating and improving their supermarkets. They were concerned about the image of their stores, constantly reinvesting their revenues to stay in the forefront of innovation. When they sometimes failed, they got back on their feet and tried something else. "There is no reward without risk," Bill Wong said.[10] As a result, Bel Air became the preeminent chain operation in Northern California in the 1980s and early 1990s. The Wongs themselves were highly regarded in the local supermarket industry for their business acumen and their concern for their customers, employees, vendors, and suppliers. They were also highly regarded in the community for their charitable philanthropy and involvement in civic affairs.

The drive to be competitive was linked with good management, timing, and locations. The Wongs acknowledged the fact that they were not experts in all aspects of an increasingly large and complex operation. They were willing to delegate authority to capable people and to expend resources to build an effective managerial organization. Their success was also due to perseverance. Bel Air consistently featured full service, selection, and convenience throughout the vicissitudes of the economy and industry. When their finances improved, many families with busy working spouses preferred shopping at Bel Air, albeit with consideration to location, because of these features. The Wongs benefited from prime locations that were acquired when national companies defaulted on their commitment to occupy new shopping centers during the recession of the late 1970s. Developers solicited Bel Air to occupy their new prime-location shopping centers in burgeoning neighborhoods because the Wongs had a reputation for operating successful upscale supermarkets. The local markets of these middle- and upper-middle-class neighborhoods were scarcely affected by downturns in the economy.

The business life-span of Chung Sun Market appears near its end. The Lee family have lasted this long because they own the store's real estate and equipment, and family members continue to work long hours, thereby keeping their operating costs to a minimum. But the weekly sales and profits will very likely remain stagnant, if not gradually shrink. The question becomes whether Lee Gim's immediate heirs want to keep working so assiduously for modest returns. They are close to retirement and have achieved financial security. Their children are pursuing other career opportunities. Notwithstanding its up-to-date equipment, the Chung Sun Market is a throwback to supermarkets of the late 1960s in terms of size, and little can be done to enlarge the physical structure because of the limitations of the real estate. At best the Lees could maintain a small niche market because industry giants are only a twenty-minute drive away, an insignificant distance by today's standards. In earlier times, local businesses like Chung Sun Market were part of their community's identity. The customers were loyal. As the character of Colusa and other small communities becomes more homogenized, national chain supermarkets will be gaining an increasing share of expanding markets.

The Lees ought to be proud of the success and longevity of Chung Sun Market. They made a comfortable living for themselves and secured a future for their heirs. Chung Sun Market has done business continuously as a family operation for over eight decades, longer than any other Chinese American grocery operation in Northern California. It was one of the first grocery stores, if not the first, to open, and has outlasted all the other prominent operations that started later. When Chung Sun Market closes, it will indeed be a historic event.

Chinese American supermarkets hold an important place in history because they were ethnic enterprises selling non-ethnic merchandise in non-enclave markets. In addition, they were prominent competitors against national chains, local chains, and independent supermarkets for over thirty years. They helped Chinese Americans attain financial security, moving a step beyond operating or working in restaurants, laundries, and farms, where risk and toil were greater. The income from owning and working the supermarkets provided the resources for both employers and employees to enter middle- and upper-middle-class life and for their children to have the opportunity to pursue higher educations, other careers, or business ventures. These enterprises facilitated the assimilation of Chinese Americans into mainstream society. On the one hand, retail intercourse required social intercourse, which helped to erase prejudices and stereotypes held by both Chinese Americans and their customers. On the other hand, the success of Chinese American grocers in a mainstream enterprise exemplified the Horatio Alger model that American society values highly, thus gaining respect and admiration for them.

It is highly improbable that Chinese Americans or any other ethnic group will become leading competitors in the retail of American groceries again. The myriad of unique socioeconomic conditions that fostered the rise and prominence of Chinese American supermarkets are very unlikely to be repeated. It is very possible that an ethnic group could seize the opportunities of a nascent industry, riding the wave of growth and becoming successful. As the industry matures, however, they will probably have to deal with rising competition, costs, and complexities, and only those with plentiful resources and good management will remain successful.

APPENDIX

ALL OF THE LOCAL SUPERMARKET CHAINS in this study have gone out of business or have different ownership, except for Raley's, which continues to expand and prosper, opening new stores and acquiring other chains. At the end of 2001, the company had sales of $3 billion and about 17,000 employees at 148 stores: ninety-seven Raley's, eighteen Bel Air Markets, twenty-six Nob Hill Foods, and seven Food Source warehouse stores, located from the San Francisco Bay Area (but not in the city) to Taos, New Mexico.[1]

Raley's success is due to solid financing, good management, and aggressive marketing. Raley's management has made the right decisions at the right time, astutely recognizing and implementing promising trends in the industry. Its rise to prominence started during the mid-1960s when the company started closing small out-dated supermarkets, remodeling ones that still had potential, and building increasingly larger ones in shopping centers in new communities. Raley's has been committed to expansion, exemplifying the adages "big begets big" and "economy of scale."

The company is noted especially for its very successful advertising strategy. Before the 1970s, Raley's advertisements were similar to those of its competition, focusing on sale prices. Thereafter, in frequent advertisements on television and in radio and newspapers, Raley's has been proudly pitching the exclusiveness of specific products in its meat, produce, and other departments: "available exclusively at our stores." These products are deemed by Raley's, in the best interest of its customers, to be of the highest quality and from the best producers. Raley's also promotes good customer service. Consequently, shoppers feel that they are privileged to get special products and services at Raley's, even though its prices for other comparable groceries may be higher than those of its competitors. How effective the advertisements have been can be measured to some extent by how shoppers evaluate Raley's. A leading consumer magazine reported that shoppers gave Raley's stores the highest satisfaction rating in a 1999 regional and national survey of supermarkets.[2] And Raley's frequent sponsorship of community events further enhances its reputation in the locations where it does business.

A recent development in supermarket entrepreneurship appears similar to the ones in this study. It is the 99 Ranch Market chain of supermarkets and shopping plazas owned and operated by Asian Americans and Asians. The supermarkets are located primarily in the western United States: one in Kent, Washington; six south and east of San Francisco; nine in the Los Angeles area; three in Orange County; and one in San Diego. All are owned by their parent TAWA Company. There are also six other 99 Ranch Markets owned and operated by independent licensees in Honolulu, Hawaii; Las Vegas, Nevada; Doraville, Georgia; Phoenix, Arizona; and Jakarta, Indonesia. TAWA began with an individual market in 1984, subsequently diversifying into the development, leasing, and management of supermarkets and shopping plazas. In 1988, it began soliciting investors from Southern California, Taiwan, and other overseas countries to finance expansion in response to a rapidly growing middle-class Asian American population, especially immigrant, which was moving into established suburbs. Hence, the 99 Ranch Markets are located outside ethnic enclaves but in areas populated heavily by Asian Americans. In comparison, the Chinese American supermarkets expanded into new suburbs along with the general population that was booming for two decades after the war.

Unlike the Chinese American supermarkets that sell American food products to a general clientele, the 99 Ranch Markets sell primarily imported Asian food products to mainly Asian American suburbanites. The stores' personnel are predominantly foreign-born. Operated with up-to-date equipment, the stores are large, clean, and organized, and the service is good, very much like any modern American supermarket. These amenities tend to be nonexistent in the small food stores of Chinatowns and other old ethnic enclaves, the primary competition for the 99 Ranch Markets. Recently, the small food stores have begun upgrading their facilities and service, but a greater challenge to 99 Ranch Market is the increasing number of imitators. The prices of the 99 Ranch Markets tend to be considerably higher than those found in the small stores. In addition to their convenient locations, the stores' success is due to the use of both Asian and American methods of merchandising. The most noticeable aspects of Asian merchandising are the stocking of live seafood and the availability of prepared food, bakery, and other vendors in the stores. It is also apparent that the investors of 99 Ranch committed a considerable amount of capital into their supermarkets.

In developing and managing its 99 Ranch Markets, TAWA adheres to guiding doctrines that have been instrumental to its success. They include: "continuous innovation by absorbing new business concepts and management techniques, as well as updating equipment and technology; providing the best of service; earning public trust with honesty and integrity; and investing in human resources by reserving and training employees." Apparently, "honesty and integrity" in the operation of Asian food stores have been issues for shoppers, enough so that TAWA consciously addresses them.[3]

The 99 Ranch Markets and their satellite stores and restaurants in the shopping plazas have greatly reduced the number of Asian Americans who live outside of ethnic enclaves but go into them for purchases and services. Ethnic studies sociologists have postulated that Asian Americans who have moved up the socioeconomic ladder often return regularly to the old ethnic enclaves to stay connected to their roots. The social development associated with the 99 Ranch Markets and shopping plazas tests the validity of that theory.

NOTES

INTRODUCTION

1. *Sacramento's Chinese Directory* (Sacramento: Chinese Publishing House, circa 1960), 6–9; *Sacramento City Directory, 1960* (Los Angeles: Sacramento Directory Company, 1961), 120–21.

2. Fine Food, Wonder Food, Broderick, Freeway, State Fair, General, El Camino Super, and Elgen. Only seven stores were members of the Famous Food Markets at any time.

3. In this study, "Northern California" is the region from Stockton northward. The major Chinese American supermarkets were located in Sacramento, Stockton, and the Sacramento Valley. There were numerous operations in the central and southern San Joaquin Valley and along the coast south of San Francisco, but they were not as predominant.

4. Rose Hum Lee, *The Chinese in the United States of America* (Hong Kong: Hong Kong University Press, 1960), 252–53.

5. S. W. Kung, *Chinese in American Life: Some Aspects of Their History, Status, Problems, and Contributions* (Seattle: University of Washington Press, 1962), 184.

6. See *SN [Supermarket News] 1978, Distribution Study of Grocery Store Sales,* which states, "Note: Figures on grocery store numbers and market share are supplied by many newspaper organizations. Data may not be comparable from year to year due to differences in market area definitions or in methods of compilation. Reported sales shares are estimated by reporting sources. Methods of compilation vary, from formal surveys to checks with food representatives, brokers, other local sources or reflecting informed opinion. In some instances, as noted, percentages reflect place of most frequent purchase, as reported by consumers, rather than dollar volume" and "This report is presented as a convenient summary of the best available information on grocery store business in each market area. *Supermarket News* assumes no responsibility for the accuracy of figures supplied by reporting sources."

1 / SUPERMARKETS

1. Frank J. Charvat, *Supermarketing* (New York: Macmillan Company, 1961), 7–8, 14, 189–90; Randolph McAusland, *Supermarkets, 50 Years of Progress* (Washington, D.C.: Food Marketing Institute, 1980), 5; Hugh S. Peak and Ellen F. Peak, *Supermarket Merchandising and Management* (Englewood Cliffs, N.J.: Prentice-Hall, 1977), 7–9; "A supermarket is a departmentalized retail food store having four basic food departments— self-service groceries, meat, produce, and dairy—plus any number of other departments, with the establishment doing a minimum yearly volume of $500,000 [est. 1954]" (Charvat, 7).

2. McAusland, 5.

3. Ibid.

4. Charvat, 18.

5. Charvat, 7–8, 15; J. Tevere MacFadyen, "The Rise of the Supermarket," *American Heritage*, vol. 36, no. 6 (October/November 1985): 27.

6. Charvat, 15–17.

7. McAusland, 10, 11, 13.

8. Peak, 16. Cost-effectiveness: producing optimum results for the expenditure.

9. McAusland, 22.

10. Charvat, 196–97. The definitions of a supermarket and chain operation varied somewhat, depending on the publication and the period of time. The *37th Annual Report of the Grocery Industry,* supplement to the *Progressive Grocer, April 1970* (New York: Progressive Grocer, 1970), gives these definitions:

> Supermarket: any store, chain, or independent doing $500,000 or more per year.
>
> Superette: any store doing from $150,000 to $500,000 a year.
>
> Small Store: any store doing less than $150,000 a year.
>
> Independent: an operator of 10 or fewer retail stores.
>
> Chain: an operator of 11 or more retail stores.
>
> Cooperative Retailers: retailers (generally independents) who are stockholder members of cooperative wholesale buying groups, such as Certified Grocers, Associated Grocers.
>
> Voluntary Group Retailers: retailers who belong to voluntary merchandising groups sponsored by wholesalers and who operate under a common name such as IGA, Red & White, Spartan, Super Valu, Clover Farm.

The *SN [Supermarket News] 1982, Distribution Study of Grocery Store Sales* gives these definitions:

> Supermarket: A complete, departmentalized grocery store with minimum annual sales of $1,000,000.

Chain: A company which operates four or more stores in total. A chain store
unit is a store operated by such a company.

Independent: A firm which operates from one to three stores.

Unaffiliated independent: Operator of from one to three stores having no affiliations with any organization and buying entirely from wholesalers or suppliers
on an independent basis.

Cooperative: Independent grocers who jointly own and operate their own wholesale organization.

Voluntary: A group of independent grocery stores jointly sponsored by an independent wholesaler.

The *SN [Supermarket News] Distribution Study of Grocery Store Sales, 1990* (New
York: Fairchild Publications, 1990) gives these definitions:

Supermarket: A supermarket is any full-line, self-service grocery store with
sales volume of $2 million or more annually.

Chain: A company which operates eleven or more stores in total. A chain store
unit is a store operated by such a company.

Independent: A firm which operates from one to ten stores.

11. Charvat, 25; McAusland, 25, 28; MacFadyen, 45.

12. Charvat, 25.

13. McAusland, 27, 29; MacFadyen, 24.

14. Peak, 20–21.

15. Charvat, 28; Peak 21.

16. Charvat, 28–29; McAusland, 33, 38, 39.

17. U.S. Bureau of the Census, *U.S. Census of Housing, 1960.* Vol. I, *States and Small
Areas.* Part 1, *United States Summary* (Washington, D.C.: U.S. Government Printing
Office, 1963), xliii.

18. Charvat, 5, 44; McAusland, 52.

19. U.S. Bureau of the Census, *U.S. Census of Population, 1960.* Vol. I, *Characteristics
of the Population.* Part 1, *United States Summary* (Washington, D.C.: U.S. Government
Printing Office, 1964), 1: xvii, 1:25, 1:163.

20. Charvat, 3, 29, 191.

21. *U.S. Census of Population, 1960.* Vol. I, *Characteristics of the Population.* Part 1,
United States Summary, 227.

22. Charvat, 31–41.

23. McAusland, 58.

24. Charvat, 47–48; McAusland, 60; MacFadyen, 27.

25. McAusland, 65, 68.

26. Charvat, 55–57.

27. Ibid., 85–86.

28. Ibid., 87.

29. Ibid., 101, 147.

30. McAusland, 83; Peak, 26–28; *37th Annual Report, Progressive Grocer, April 1970,* 50, 52.

31. *37th Annual Report, Progressive Grocer, April 1970,* 48, 57.

32. McAusland, 83; Peak 28; *37th Annual Report, Progressive Grocer, April 1970,* 52.

33. Peak, 26.

34. Charvat, 150–51.

35. Ibid., 182–84, 187.

36. Ibid.

2 / COMMUNITY, EMPLOYMENT, AND ENTERPRISE

1. U.S. Bureau of the Census, *U.S. Census of Population, 1960,* Vol. I, *Characteristics of the Population,* Part 6, *California* (Washington, D.C.: U.S. Government Printing Office, 1961), 6–58; *U.S. Census of the Population, 1960, Subject Reports, Nonwhite Population by Race,* Final Report PC(2)-1C (Washington, D.C.: U.S. Government Printing Office, 1963), 215.

2. U.S. Bureau of the Census, *Fifteenth Census of the United States, 1930,* Vol. III, *Population,* Part 1, *Alabama-Missouri* (Washington, D.C.: U.S. Government Printing Office, 1932), 266; U.S. Bureau of the Census, *Sixteenth Census of the United States, 1940, Population,* Vol. II, *Characteristics of the Population,* Part 1, *United States Summary and Alabama-District of Columbia* (Washington, D.C.: U.S. Government Printing Office, 1943), 567; *U.S. Census of the Population, 1950, Subject Reports, Nonwhite Population by Race,* Report P-E No. 3B, (Washington, D.C.: U.S. Government Printing Office, 1953), 3B–64; *U.S. Census of the Population, 1960, Subject Reports, Nonwhite Population by Race,* Final Report PC(2)-1C, 217. The 1950 population figure is for the Sacramento Standard Metropolitan Area (SMA), which includes the city of Sacramento and nearby urban areas. In 1960 the census grouped these areas as the Sacramento Standard Metropolitan Statistical Area (SMSA).

3. *U.S. Census of Population, 1960,* Vol. I, Part 6, *California,* 6–58; *Sixteenth Census of the United States, 1940,* Vol. II, Part 1, *U.S. Summary and Alabama-District of Columbia,* 644, 669; *U.S. Census of the Population, 1950, Subject Reports, Nonwhite Population by Race,* Report P-E No. 3B, 3B–64; *U.S. Census of the Population, 1960, Subject Reports, Nonwhite Population by Race,* Final Report PC(2)-1C, 217.

4. *U.S. Census of the Population, 1950, Subject Reports, Nonwhite Population by Race,*

Report P-E No. 3B, 3B–64; *U.S. Census of the Population, 1960, Subject Reports, Nonwhite Population by Race,* Final Report PC(2)-1C, 217.

5. Mely Giok-lan Tan, The Chinese in the United States: Social Mobility and Assimilation (Taipei: Oriental Cultural Service, 1971), 39–40.

6. Sucheng Chan, "The Exclusion of Chinese Women, 1870–1943," in *Entry Denied: Exclusion and the Chinese Community in America, 1882–1943,* ed. Sucheng Chan (Philadelphia: Temple University Press, 1991), 120–32, 137–39.

7. Tan, 30, 40–41.

8. Lee, 261, 266–68; Him Mark Lai, Joe Huang, and Don Wong, *The Chinese of America, 1785–1980* (San Francisco: Chinese Cultural Foundation, 1980), 60.

9. Lai, 76–77; Kung, 182, 184.

10. John T. C. Fang, *The Chinese Community in Sacramento* (Sacramento: Chinese Publishing House, 1961), 38–39; *U.S. Census of the Population, 1960, Subject Reports, Nonwhite Population by Race,* Final Report PC(2)-1C, 249; *Sacramento's Chinese Directory,* 6–9; U.S. Bureau of the Census, *1963 Census of Business,* Vol. II, *Retail Trade Area Statistics,* Part 1, *U.S. Summary and Alabama to Illinois* (Washington, D.C.: U.S. Government Printing Office, 1966), 6–28; *U.S. Census of Population, 1960,* Vol. I, Part 6, *California,* 6–127.

11. U.S. Bureau of the Census, *Fifteenth Census of the United States, 1930, Population,* Vol. V, *General Report on Occupations* (Washington, D.C.: U.S. Government Printing Office, 1933), 95–97; Kung, 181.

12. Lai, 59–60.

13. L. Eve Armentrout Ma, "The Big Business Ventures of Chinese in North America, 1850–1930," in *The Chinese American Experience: Papers from the Second National Conference on Chinese American Studies (1980),* ed. Genny Lim (San Francisco: Chinese Historical Society of America and Chinese Culture Foundation, 1984), 101–12.

3 / BEGINNINGS

1. Jimmie Lee (sixty-one)and Leland Lee (seventy-one), sons of Lee Gim, the founder of Chung Sun Market (Colusa, California), taped interview, Sacramento, California, 17 November 1997. Chung Sun (Chungsan) was the Cantonese name of the district from which Sun Yat-sen came and which was renamed in honor of him.

2. Ibid.

3. Ibid. In the 1930s, Lee Gim purchased a panel truck and hired a delivery driver.

4. Ibid. Although many of the partners were immigrants, ownership of land was possible despite the alien land laws. These laws prohibited noncitizens from owning land in California because some of the immigrants derived U.S. citizenship from their

U.S. citizen fathers. In other words, their immigration papers claimed that their fathers were U.S. citizens. Some partners were American-born.

5. Ibid.

6. Ibid.

7. Leland Lee, taped interviews, Sacramento, California, 25 November 1997, 10 August 1998, and telephone interviews, 23 August 1998, 22 September 1998; Sohan L. Sidher, "The Changing Role of the Sacramento Independent Grocery Wholesalers 1920–1960" (Master's thesis, Sacramento State College, 1964), 38.

8. Jimmie Lee and Leland Lee interview, 17 November 1997.

9. George Quan, Jr. (seventy), past president of the Sacramento Chinese Food Dealers Association, past president of the Northern California Grocers Association, taped interviews, Sacramento, California, 29 July 1997, 12 August 1997, 23 September 1997, and 13 February 1998.

10. George Quan interview, 29 July 1997.

11. Ibid.

12. Ibid. Although Quan does not remember precisely, Eye Street Bridge Market was probably 3,000 to 4,000 square feet in sales floor space when it first opened. The market was expanded and remodeled in subsequent years.

13. Ibid.

14. Ibid.

15. George Quan interviews, 29 July 1997, 12 August 1997.

16. George Quan interview, 12 August 1997.

17. George Quan interview, 29 July 1997.

18. Bill Wong (eighty), member of the Wong family of Bel Air Market, eldest son of Wong Gim, taped interview, Sacramento, California, 20 April 1998, 14 July 1998. Bill Wong's father most likely purchased "papers" stating he was the son of a U.S. citizen. Through derivation, he was also an U.S. citizen, which allowed him to purchase property in California, a privilege denied to people who were not citizens.

19. Bill Wong interviews, 20 April 1998, 14 July 1998.

20. Bill Wong interview, 20 April 1998. Walter Fong would eventually establish the Farmers Market supermarket chain, opening forty stores in Sacramento and Northern California. But not all forty-plus stores were operating in a given time; that is, while new supermarkets opened, unprofitable ones were closed.

21. Bill Wong interview, 20 April 1998.

22. Ibid.

23. George Wong (seventy-four), president of Bel Air Market, past president of the Northern California Grocers Association, past president of the California Grocers Association, taped interview, Rocklin, California, 24 April 1998; telephone interview, 6 October 1998.

24. Ibid.

25. Bill Wong interview, 20 April 1998.

26. George Wong interview, 24 April 1998.

27. Susie Chan (sixty-two), daughter of Sam Wah You, taped interviews, Stockton, California, 16 December 2001, 5 January 2002.

28. Ibid.

29. Louis Lee (ninety), head of operations for Centr-O-Mart from 1946 to 1982, taped interview, Stockton, California, 29 December 2001.

30. Ibid.

31. Susie Chan interviews, 16 December 2001, 5 January 2002; Louis Lee interview, 29 December 2001.

32. Paul C. P. Siu, *The Chinese Laundryman: a Study of Social Isolation* (New York: New York University Press, 1987), 82.

33. George Quan interview, 29 July 1997; *Sacramento City Directory, 1919* (Sacramento: Sacramento Directory Company, 1919), no pagination; *Sacramento City Directory, 1927* (Sacramento: Sacramento Directory Company, 1927), 839, 861.

34. Betty Hanson, *Raley's, A Family Store* (Sacramento: Raley's Superstores, 1989), 9–21, 32, 41–42.

In 1989, Raley's Superstores was the twenty-fifth largest retail chain in the United States, grossing $1 billion with fifty-six stores.

4 / GOLDEN TIMES

1. Leland Lee taped interviews, 25 November 1997, 10 August 1998; telephone interviews, 23 August 1998, 22 September 1998.

2. Bill Wong interviews, 20 April 1998, 14 July 1998; George Quan, Jr. interviews, 29 July 1997, 12 August 1997, 23 September 1997, 13 February 1998.

3. George Quan interview, 13 February 1998.

4. Gene Adkins, *California's Retail Food Industry: A Breakdown of Competition* (Sacramento, California: Assembly Office of Research, 1977), 17–18.

5. George Quan interviews, 29 July 1997, 12 August 1997, 13 February 1998.

6. George Wong taped interview, 24 April 1998; telephone interview, 6 October 1998.

7. Joe Tang (seventy-five), president of Tang Associates, independent consultant to food processors, taped interview, Sacramento, California, 27 October 1998; George Quan interviews, 29 July 1997, 13 February 1998; Leland Lee interview, 25 November 1997; Jimmie Lee and Leland Lee interview, 17 November 1997.

8. Joe Tang interview, 27 October 1998; George Wong interview, 24 April 1998; Bill Wong interview, 14 July 1998.

9. George Quan interview, 13 February 1998.

10. Leland Lee interviews, 10 August 1998, 22 September 1998; Joe Tang interview, 27 October 1998; George Wong interview, 24 April 1998.

11. Adkins, 7.

12. Bill Wong interview, 14 July 1998; McAusland, 99.

13. Leland Lee interview, 25 November 1997; George Quan interview, 23 September 1997.

14. George Quan interview, 23 September 1997.

15. Leland Lee interview, 25 November 1997.

16. Ibid.

17. Jimmie Lee and Leland Lee interview, 17 November 1997. In Colusa there has never been more than four or five grocery stores and a like number of supermarkets. During the past seven decades, grocery stores and supermarkets have come and gone, including a national outlet, Safeway Store, and a local independent operation, Purity Market. The Lees did not enlarge Chung Sun Market until 1956, when they were fairly certain that a larger store with its bigger overhead would be profitable.

18. Jimmie Lee and Leland Lee interview, 17 November 1997; Leland Lee interview, 25 November 1997; George Chan (sixty-five), American-born, former employee of Palm Market (Auburn, California), Giant Foods Market (Sacramento), Albertsons (Sacramento), Corti Brothers (Sacramento), taped interview, Folsom, California, 15 April 1998. The author's father purchased a share and entered into the partnership of Fine Food Market in 1956 or thereabouts, when one of the partners retired.

19. Leland Lee interview, 25 November 1997.

20. Jimmie Lee and Leland Lee interview, 17 November 1997; Leland Lee interview, 10 August 1998.

21. Jimmie Lee and Leland Lee interview, 17 November 1997; Leland Lee interview, 25 November 1997.

22. *Sacramento Bee,* November 1958–1966.

23. Jimmie Lee and Leland Lee interview, 17 November 1997; Leland Lee interviews, 25 November 1997, 10 August 1998; Joe Tang interview, 27 October 1998.

24. Ralph Cassidy Jr., *Competition and Price Making in Food Retailing* (New York: Ronald Press Company, 1962), 267–68; Herbert R. Northrup, Gordon R. Storholm, and Paul A. Abodeely, *Restrictive Labor Practices in the Supermarket Industry* (Philadelphia: University of Pennsylvania Press, 1967), 15; *35th Annual Report of the Grocery Industry,* supplement to the *Progressive Grocer, 1969* (New York: Progressive Grocer, 1969). The specific profit margin and sales volume figures for Northern California supermarkets were not available. During this period, they may not have been recorded and published.

25. Jimmie Lee and Leland Lee interview, 17 November 1997; Leland Lee interview, 23 August 1998. The labor unions were unable to persuade employees to join because

supermarket employees were almost all family members; this was the case, for example, in Chung Sun Market.

26. Gene Yee (seventy-three), past president of the Central Coast Grocers Association, past president of the Bay Area Grocers Association, past chairman of the California Grocers Association, taped interviews, Sunnyvale, California, 26 March 1999, 1 April 1999; *San Jose Mercury News,* November 1969.

27. Gene Yee interviews, 26 March 1999, 1 April 1999.

28. Ibid.

29. Ibid.

30. Ibid.

31. George Quan interview, 29 July 1997.

32. Ibid.

33. Ibid.

34. Ibid.

35. Ibid.

36. Bill Wong interview, 20 April 1998.

37. Bill Wong interviews, 20 April 1998, 14 July 1998.

38. Bill Wong interview, 20 April 1998.

39. Ibid.

40. Bill Wong interview, 14 July 1998.

41. Bill Wong interview, 20 April 1998.

42. Bill Wong interviews, 20 April 1998, 14 July 1998; George Wong interview, 24 April 1998.

43. Ibid.

44. Bill Wong interview, 20 April 1998; George Wong interview, 24 April 1998.

45. Henry Fong (sixty-eight), former employee of Yolo Grocery (a supermarket in Woodland, California, in which Lee Gim invested), State Fair Market (one of the seven Famous Food Markets in Sacramento), Jumbo Market (Sacramento), interviews, Sacramento, California, 1 October 1997, 4 December 1998.

46. Ibid.

47. Ibid.

48. Ibid.

49. Susie Chan interviews, 16 December 2001, 5 January 2002; Louis Lee interview, 29 December 2001.

50. Louis Lee interview, 29 December 2001.

51. Louis Lee interview, 29 December 2001. The Hob Nob stores were located in Hayward, Cupertino, Sunnyvale, Milpitas, and San Jose; the Farmers Market stores were located in Anderson, Redding, Red Bluff, Oroville, Chico, and Enterprise.

52. Susie Chan interviews, 16 December 2001, 5 January 2002; Louis Lee interview, 29 December 2001.

53. Bill Wong interview, 14 July 1998.

54. Siu, 24–26.

55. *Sacramento Bee*, November 1961–1972; Bill Wong interview, 14 July 1998; George Quan interview, 13 February 1998.

56. Bill Wong interview, 20 April 1998.

5 / DECLINE AND PASSING

1. George Quan interviews, 29 July 1997, 12 August 1997, 23 September 1997, 13 February 1998.

2. George Quan interview, 13 February 1998; Jimmie Lee and Leland Lee interview, 17 November 1997; Leland Lee interviews, 25 November 1997, 10 August 1998, 23 August 1998, 22 September 1998.

3. George Quan interview, 13 February 1998.

4. Leland Lee interview, 25 November 1997; Joe Tang interview, 27 October 1998.

5. Leland Lee interview, 25 November 1997; Joe Tang interview, 27 October 1998.

6. Leland Lee interview, 25 November 1997.

7. Leland Lee interview, 10 August 1998; Bill Wong interviews, 20 April 1998, 14 July 1998.

8. Leland Lee interview, 25 November 1997.

9. Ibid.

10. Ibid.

11. Ibid.; George Quan interview, 23 September 1997.

12. Leland Lee interview, 25 November 1997.

13. Ibid.

14. Joe Tang interview, 27 October 1998.

15. Ibid.; Bill Wong interview, 14 July 1998. The exact number of stores operating in the Farmers Market chain was less than forty. The number varied during the company's peak in the mid-1970s because in a given year, a few stores opened while a few closed. A new store was designated with a sequential number.

16. Joe Tang interview, 27 October 1998; Bill Wong interview, 14 July 1998; Earl Joe (seventy-one), former employee of Walter Fong's Save-a-Lot Market, former manager of a Farmers Market for twenty years, one of the family owners of Panorama Markets, taped interviews, Sacramento, California, 4 March 1999, 23 March 1999.

17. Joe Tang interview, 27 October 1998; Bill Wong interview, 14 July 1998; Earl Joe interview, 4 March 1998.

18. Leland Lee interview, 10 August 1998.

19. Jimmie Lee and Leland Lee interview, 17 November 1997; Leland Lee interview, 10 August 1998.

20. Ibid.

21. George Quan interview, 13 February 1998.

22. Ibid.

23. Ibid.

24. Joe Tang interview, 27 October 1998.

25. Henry Fong interview, 4 December 1998.

26. Ibid.; Joe Tang interview, 27 October 1998.

27. Ibid.

28. Henry Fong interview, 4 December 1998.

29. Gene Yee interviews, 26 March 1999, 1 April 1999.

30. Ibid.

31. Bill Wong interview, 14 July 1998.

32. Ibid.

33. Susie Chan interviews, 16 December 2001, 5 January 2002; Louis Lee interview, 29 December 2001.

34. Louis Lee interview, 29 December 2001.

35. Ibid.

36. Susie Chan interviews, 16 December 2001, 5 January 2002.

37. Louis Lee interview, 29 December 2001; Susie Chan interviews, 16 December 2001, 5 January 2002.

38. Leland Lee interview, 10 August 1998.

39. Joe Tang interview, 27 October 1998.

40. George Quan interview, 23 September 1997; Joe Tang interview, 27 October 1998.

41. Adkins, 12, 17, 31–32.

42. Ibid., 15.

6 / EMPLOYEES AND SALESMEN

1. Henry Fong interview, 1 October 1997; William (Bill) Lew (seventy-three), American-born, former employee of Wonder Food Market (one of the seven Famous Food Markets in Sacramento), Jumbo Market (Sacramento), taped interview, Sacramento, California, 19 November 1998.

2. Henry Fong interview, 1 October 1997; Earl Joe interviews, 4 March, 1999, 23 March 1999.

3. Henry Fong interview, 1 October 1997; Earl Joe interview, 4 March 1999.

4. Henry Fong interview, 1 October 1997.

5. Joe Tang interview, 27 October 1998.

6. Henry Fong interview, 1 October 1997; Bill Lew interview, 19 November 1998.

7. Henry Fong interview, 1 October 1997; Leland Lee interviews, 10 August 1998, 23 August 1998.

8. George Quan interviews, 12 August 1997, 23 September 1997.

9. Henry Fong interview, 1 October 1997.

10. Ibid.

11. Ibid.

12. Ibid.

13. Leland Lee interview, 10 August 1998; Henry Fong interview, 1 October 1997.

14. Ibid.

15. Art Yim (eighty-three), a manufacturer's representative from 1955 to 1991, taped interviews, San Francisco, California, 12 March 1999, 19 March 1999.

16. Art Yim interview, 19 March 1999.

17. Henry Fong interview, 1 October 1997; Joe Tang interview, 27 October 1998.

18. Joe Tang interview, 27 October 1998.

19. Ibid.

20. Henry Fong interview, 1 October 1997; Bill Lew interview, 19 November 1998; Earl Joe interview, 4 March 1999.

21. Ibid.

22. Bill Lew interview, 19 November 1998; Earl Joe interview, 4 March 1999.

23. George Chan interview, 15 April 1998. All subsequent quotations in this chapter are from this interview.

7 / CHINESE MANAGEMENT AND LABOR UNIONS

1. Gary G. Hamilton and Kao Cheng-shu, "The Institutional Foundations of Chinese Business: The Family Firm in Taiwan," *Comparative Social Research*, vol. 12 (1990): 148–49.

2. Ibid., 143–44.

3. Ibid., 145.

4. Ibid., 146–47.

5. Siu-lun Wong, "The Chinese Family Firm: A Model," *The British Journal of Sociology*, vol. 36, no. 1 (March 1985): 60–61.

6. Ibid., 61–62.

7. Ibid., 63–68.

8. Wellington K. K. Chan, "The Organizational Structure of the Traditional Chinese Firm and Its Modern Reform," *Business History Review*, vol. 56, no. 2 (summer 1982): 219–20.

9. Ibid., 220–21.

10. Ibid., 231–35.

11. Leland Lee interviews, 10 August 1998, 23 August 1998. The labor union enrolling the partners was the Retail Clerks Union Local 588; the general manager was not allowed to participate in the pension plan.

12. Henry Fong interview, 1 October 1997.

13. Walter Fogel, "Union Impact on Retail Food Wages in California," *Industrial Relations*, vol. 6, no. 1 (October 1966): 79; Northrup, Storholm, and Abodeely, 30–36.

14. Northrup, Storholm, and Abodeely, 37–38. The author witnessed the use of people hired by the Retail Clerks Union to walk the picket lines in Sacramento during the late 1970s. The union never considered having store employees picket the supermarkets in which they were employed.

15. Northrup, Storholm, and Abodeely, 44.

16. Leland Lee interview, 10 August 1998; George Quan interviews, 12 August 1997, 23 September 1997.

17. California State Council of Retail Clerks, *Thousands of People Like You*, 1945, 1–19.

18. Ibid., 14; Henry Fong interview, 1 October 1997. Information regarding unionization was gathered from interviews with employers and employees who described the situation during the 1940s and early 1950s.

19. Leland Lee interview, 10 August 1998.

20. Northrup, Storholm, and Abodeely, 51–59: Fogel, 91–92; Leland Lee interview, 10 August 1998. Lee provided the cost figures for the 1950s. Fogel and Northrup, Storholm, and Abodeely do not mention the costs of the benefit coverage in the labor agreements. To get an idea of how much non-wage compensation cost an employer, in 1990 the hospital and medical care package cost $271 a month per employee, not covering his family and not including dental care, eyeglasses, and psychiatric treatment. Pension contribution from the employer was over $1 for each hour worked by the employee during the late 1980s. Included in the benefit agreements in the 1980s was a half-hour consultation with an attorney free of charge each year. These benefits applied to Retail Clerks Union Local 588 in the Sacramento and Northern California area.

21. Northrup, Storholm, and Abodeely, 71.

22. Ibid., 89.

23. George Chan interview, 15 April 1998.

24. Leland Lee interview, 10 August 1998.

25. Bill Lew interview, 19 November 1998.

26. Ibid., 19 November 1998.

27. George Chan interview, 15 April 1998.

28. George Quan interview, 12 August 1997; Leland Lee interview, 10 August 1998; Henry Fong interview, 1 October 1997; Earl Joe interviews, 4 March, 1999, 23 March 1999.

8 / STOP-N-SHOP

1. Lewis Kassis (eighty-eight), taped interviews, Sacramento, California, 22 August 2000, 29 August 2000.

2. Lewis Kassis interview, 29 August 2000.

3. Ibid.

4. Lewis Kassis interview, 22 August 2000.

5. Frank Kassis, "History of the A. G. Kassis Enterprise," unpublished typescript, 25 October 1982, Sacramento, California; Lewis Kassis interview, 22 August 2000.

6. Frank Kassis, "History."

7. Ibid.

8. Ibid.

9. Lewis Kassis interviews, 22 August 2000, 29 August 2000.

10. Frank Kassis, "History"; Lewis Kassis interviews, 22 August 2000, 29 August 2000.

11. Frank Kassis, "History"; Lewis Kassis interview, 22 August 2000.

12. Lewis Kassis interviews, 22 August 2000, 29 August 2000.

13. Lewis Kassis interview, 29 August 2000.

CONCLUSION

1. Him Mark Lai, "Chinese Regional Solidarity: Case Study of the Hua Xian (Fa Yuen) Community in California," in *Chinese America: History and Perspectives, 1994* (San Francisco: Chinese Historical Society of America, 1994), 35–37.

2. Joe Tang interview, 27 October 1998.

3. Adkins, 6.

4. George Quan interview, 23 September 1997.

5. Rose Yee (ninety), wife of Joe Yee, who operated Independent Market and Grand Central Market (grocery stores), and Grant Union Market and Grand View Market (supermarkets) from 1929 to 1973, taped interview, Sacramento, California, 22 March 1999.

6. Bill Wong interview, 14 July 1998; Earl Joe interviews, 4 March, 1999, 23 March 1999.

7. Lewis Kassis interview, 22 August 2000.

8. Leland Lee interview, 25 November 1997.

9. Ibid.

10. Bill Wong interview, 14 July 1998.

APPENDIX

1. "New Raley's Bakery Planned in West Sac," *Sacramento Bee,* 31 August 2001, D1.

2. "Supermarkets: Food Fight," Consumer Reports, vol. 65, no. 9 (September 2000), 17.

3. www.99ranch.com.

BIBLIOGRAPHY

Adkins, Gene. *California's Retail Food Industry: A Breakdown of Competition.* Sacramento, California: Assembly Office of Research, 1977.

Anderson (California) Valley News. November 1960.

California State Council of Retail Clerks. *Thousands of People Like You.* 1945.

Cassidy, Ralph Jr. *Competition and Price Making in Food Retailing.* New York: Ronald Press Company, 1962.

Chan, Janet B. L., and Yuet-wah Cheung. "Ethnic Resources and Business Enterprises: A Study of Chinese Businesses in Toronto." *Human Organization,* vol. 44, no. 2 (summer 1985): 142–54.

Chan, Sucheng. *This Bittersweet Soil: The Chinese in California Agriculture, 1860–1910.* Berkeley: University of California Press, 1986.

———. *Asian Americans, an Interpretive History.* Boston: Twayne Publishers, 1991.

———. *Asian Californians.* San Francisco: MTL, 1991.

———. "The Exclusion of Chinese Women, 1870–1943." In *Entry Denied: Exclusion and the Chinese Community in America, 1882–1943,* ed. Sucheng Chan, 94–146. Philadelphia: Temple University Press, 1991.

Chan, Wellington K. K. "The Organizational Structure of the Traditional Chinese Firm and Its Modern Reform." *Business History Review,* vol. 56, no. 2 (summer 1982): 218–35.

Charvat, Frank J. *Supermarketing.* New York: Macmillan Company, 1961.

Chen, Gavin M., and John A. Cole. "The Myths, Facts, and Theories of Ethnic Small-Scale Enterprise Financing." *The Review of Black Political Economy,* vol. 16, no. 4 (spring 1988): 111–23.

Chen, Jack. *The Chinese of America.* San Francisco: Harper and Row, 1981.

Chinese Directory of Sacramento and Vicinity. San Francisco: Chinese Commercial Bureau, 1949.

Chinn, Thomas W. *A History of the Chinese in California: A Syllabus.* San Francisco: Chinese Historical Society of America, 1984.

Chiu, Ping. *Chinese Labor in California, 1850–1880.* Ann Arbor, Michigan: Edwards Brothers, Inc., 1963.

Fang, John T. C. *The Chinese Community in Sacramento.* Sacramento: Chinese Publishing House, 1961.

Fogel, Walter. "Union Impact on Retail Food Wages in California." *Industrial Relations,* vol. 6, no. 1 (October 1966): 79–94.

Gong, Tim Yuen. "A Gold Mountain Man's Memoir." Trans. Marlon K. Hom. In *Chinese America: History and Perspectives, 1992.* San Francisco: Chinese Historical Society of America, 1992.

Hamilton, Gary G. "Ethnicity and Regionalism: Some Factors Influencing Chinese Identities in Southeast Asia." *Ethnicity,* vol. 4, no. 4 (December 1977): 337–51.

Hamilton, Gary G., and Kao Cheng-shu. "The Institutional Foundations of Chinese Business: The Family Firm in Taiwan." *Comparative Social Research,* vol. 12 (1990): 135–51.

Hanson, Betty. *Raley's, A Family Store.* Sacramento: Raley's Superstores, 1989.

Harrington, Michael. *The Retail Clerks.* New York: John Wiley and Sons, Inc., 1962.

Hsu, Francis L. K. *Americans and Chinese, Passages to Differences.* Honolulu: University of Hawaii Press, 1981.

Hsu, Madeline. "Gold Mountain Dreams and Paper Son Schemes: Chinese Immigration Under Exclusion." In *Chinese America: History and Perspectives, 1997.* San Francisco: Chinese Historical Society of America, 1997.

Kassis, Frank. "History of the A. G. Kassis Enterprise," typescript, 25 October 1982.

Kung, S. W. *Chinese in American Life: Some Aspects of Their History, Status, Problems, and Contributions.* Seattle: University of Washington Press, 1962.

Lai, Him Mark. "Chinese Regional Solidarity: Case Study of the Hua Xian (Fa Yuen) Community in California." In *Chinese America: History and Perspectives, 1994.* San Francisco: Chinese Historical Society of America, 1994.

Lai, Him Mark, Joe Huang, and Don Wong. *The Chinese of America, 1785–1980.* San Francisco: Chinese Cultural Foundation, 1980.

Lee, Rose Hum. *The Chinese in the United States of America.* Hong Kong: Hong Kong University Press, 1960.

Lew, Ling. *The Chinese in North America: A Guide to Their Life and Progress.* Los Angeles: East-West Culture Publishing Association, 1949.

Li, Peter S. "Ethnic Business Among Chinese in the U.S." *The Journal of Ethnic Studies,* vol. 4, no. 3 (fall 1976): 35–41.

Light, Ivan H. *Ethnic Enterprise in America: Business and Welfare Among Chinese, Japanese and Blacks.* Berkeley: University of California Press, 1972.

Liu, Kwang-ching. "Chinese Merchant Guilds: A Historical Inquiry." *Pacific Historical Review,* vol. 57, no. 1 (1988): 1–23.

Ma, L. Eve Armentrout. "The Big Business Ventures of Chinese in North America, 1850–1930." In *The Chinese American Experience: Papers from the Second National Conference on Chinese American Studies (1980)*, ed. Genny Lim, 101–12. San Francisco: Chinese Historical Society of America and Chinese Culture Foundation, 1984.

MacFadyen, J. Tevere. "The Rise of the Supermarket." *American Heritage*, vol. 36, no. 6 (October/November 1985): 22–47.

McAusland, Randolph. *Supermarkets: 50 Years of Progress*. Washington, D.C.: Food Marketing Institute, 1980.

McGowan, Joseph A. *History of the Sacramento Valley*. Vol. 2. New York: Lewis Historical Publishing Company, 1961.

Mark, Diane Mei Lin and Ginger Chih. *A Place Called Chinese America*. Dubuque, Iowa: Kendall/Hunt, 1993.

Minnick, Sylvia Sun. *Samfow: The San Joaquin Chinese Legacy*. Fresno, California: Panorama West Publishing, 1988.

Nee, Victor, and Herbert Wong. "Asian American Socioeconomic Achievement: the Strength of the Family Bond." *Sociological Perspectives*, vol. 28, no. 3 (July 1985): 281–306.

Ng, Franklin. "The Sojourner, Return Migration, and Immigration History." In *Chinese America: History and Perspectives, 1987*. San Francisco: Chinese Historical Society of America, 1987.

Northrup, Herbert R., Gordon R. Storholm, and Paul A. Abodeely. *Restrictive Labor Practices in the Supermarket Industry*. Philadelphia: University of Pennsylvania Press, 1967.

Peak, Hugh S., and Ellen F. Peak. *Supermarket Merchandising and Management*. Englewood Cliffs, New Jersey: Prentice-Hall, 1977.

Perkins, William E. "Symposium on Ethnic Enterprises in America, Review Essay II." *The Journal of Ethnic Studies*, vol. 1, no. 4 (winter 1974): 73–82.

Red Bluff City Directory, Supplement Edition, 1965. Chillocothe, Ohio: Mullin-Kille Company, 1965.

Red Bluff City Directory, 1967. Chillocothe, Ohio: Mullin-Kille Company, 1967.

Red Bluff City Directory, 1969. Eugene, Oregon: Johnson Publishing, 1969.

Redding City Directory. San Francisco, Los Angeles, and Monterey Park, Calif.: R. L. Polk and Company, 1952, 1960, 1965, 1970.

Redding, Enterprise, Anderson, Cottonwood City Directory. Monterey Park and South El Monte, Calif.: R. L. Polk and Company, 1973, 1974, 1977.

Redding (California) Record-Searchlight. November 1961.

Retail Clerks Local Union, No. 588, Sacramento. *Articles of Agreement*, 1938.

Rhoads, Edward J. M. "The Chinese in Texas." *Southwestern Historical Quarterly*, vol. 81, no. 1 (July 1977): 1–36.

Sacramento Bee. November 1940–1980.

Sacramento's Chinese Directory. Sacramento: Chinese Publishing House, circa 1960.

Sacramento City Directory. Sacramento, Los Angeles, and Monterey Park, Calif.: Sacramento Directory Company, 1919–1970.

Sacramento City Directory. Dallas: R. L. Polk and Company, 1980.

San Jose City Directory. Los Angeles and Monterey Park, Calif.: R. L. Polk and Company, 1960, 1965, 1966, 1970.

San Jose Mercury News. November 1951–1970.

Sidher, Sohan L. "The Changing Role of the Sacramento Independent Grocery Wholesalers, 1920–1960." Master's thesis, Sacramento State College, 1964.

Siu, Paul C. P. *The Chinese Laundryman: a Study of Social Isolation.* New York: New York University Press, 1987.

SN [Supermarket News] 1978, Distribution Study of Grocery Store Sales. New York: Fairchild Publications.

SN [Supermarket News] 1982, Distribution Study of Grocery Store Sales. New York: Fairchild Publications.

SN [Supermarket News] 1990, Distribution Study of Grocery Store Sales. New York: Fairchild Publications.

SN [Supermarket News] 1995, Distribution Study of Grocery Store Sales. New York: Fairchild Publications.

Soper, Will. "Supermarkets." *American History,* vol. 18, no. 1 (March 1983): 40–47.

Stockton City Directory. San Francisco, Los Angeles, Monterey Park, and South El Monte, Calif.: R. L. Polk and Company, 1948, 1950, 1960, 1970.

Stockton City Directory. Dallas, Texas: R. L. Polk and Company, 1980.

Stockton Record. November 1950–1978.

Sue, Stanley, and Harry H. L. Kitano. "Stereotypes as a Measure of Success." *Journal of Social Issues,* vol. 29, no. 2 (1973): 83–98.

Sung, Betty Lee. *Chinese American Manpower and Employment.* New York: Praeger Publishers, 1976.

———. *Mountain of Gold: The Story of the Chinese in America.* New York: Macmillan Company, 1967.

Sunnyvale City Directory. Monterey Park, California: R. L. Polk and Company, 1964, 1968.

Sunnyvale (California) Daily Standard. November 1961.

"Supermarkets: Food Fight." *Consumer Reports,* vol. 65, no. 9 (September 2000): 11–17.

Takaki, Ronald T. "Symposium on Ethnic Enterprise in America, Review Essay I." *The Journal of Ethnic Studies,* vol. 1, no. 4 (winter 1974): 69–72.

Tan, Mely Giok-lan. *The Chinese in the United States: Social Mobility and Assimilation.* Taipei, Republic of China: Oriental Cultural Service, 1971.

Bibliography · *187*

35th Annual Report of the Grocery Industry, supplement to the *Progressive Grocer, 1969.* New York: Progressive Grocer, 1969.

37th Annual Report of the Grocery Industry, supplement to the *Progressive Grocer, April 1970.* New York: Progressive Grocer, 1970.

Tsai, Shih-shan Henry. *The Chinese Experience in America.* Bloomington: Indiana University Press, 1986.

Uneke, Okori. "Ethnicity and Small Business Ownership: Contrasts Between Blacks and Chinese in Toronto." *Work, Employment, and Society,* vol. 10, no. 3 (September 1996): 529–48.

U.S. Bureau of the Census. *Fifteenth Census of the United States, 1930.* Vol. III, *Population.* Part 1, *Alabama-Missouri.* Washington, D.C.: U.S. Government Printing Office, 1932.

———. *Fifteenth Census of the United States, 1930, Population.* Vol. V, *General Report on Occupations.* Washington, D.C.: U.S. Government Printing Office, 1933.

———. *Sixteenth Census of the United States, 1940.* Vol. I, *Population, Number of Inhabitants.* Washington, D.C.: U.S. Government Printing Office, 1942.

———. *Sixteenth Census of the United States, 1940.* Vol. I, *Retail Trade:* Part 1, *United States Summary.* Washington, D.C.: U.S. Government Printing Office, 1943.

———. *Sixteenth Census of the United States, 1940.* Vol. II, *Characteristics of the Population.* Part 1, *United States Summary and Alabama—District of Columbia.* Washington, D.C.: U.S. Government Printing Office, 1943.

———. *Census of Population, 1950.* Vol. II, *Characteristics of the Population.* Part 5, *California.* Washington, D.C.: U.S. Government Printing Office, 1952.

———. *U.S. Census of the Population, 1950, Subject Reports, Nonwhite Population by Race.* Report P-E No. 3B. Washington, D.C.: U.S. Government Printing Office, 1953.

———. *U.S. Census of Population, 1960.* Vol. I, *Characteristics of the Population.* Part 6, *California.* Washington, D.C.: U.S. Government Printing Office, 1961.

———. *U.S. Census of the Population, 1960, Subject Reports, Nonwhite Population by Race.* Final Report PC(2)-1C. Washington, D.C.: U.S. Government Printing Office, 1963.

———. *U.S. Census of Housing, 1960.* Vol. I, *States and Small Areas.* Part 1, *United States Summary.* Washington, D.C.: U.S. Government Printing Office, 1963.

———. *U.S. Census of Population, 1960.* Vol. I, *Characteristics of the Population.* Part 1, *United States Summary.* Washington, D.C.: U.S. Government Printing Office, 1964.

———. *1963 Census of Business.* Vol. II, *Retail Trade Area Statistics.* Part 1, *U.S. Summary and Alabama to Illinois.* Washington, D.C.: U.S. Government Printing Office, 1966.

Wang, L. Ling-chi. "Symposium on Ethnic Enterprise in America, Review Essay III." *The Journal of Ethnic Studies,* vol. 1, no. 4 (winter 1974): 83–88.

Wong, Charles Choy. "The Continuity of Chinese Grocers in Southern California." *The Journal of Ethnic Studies,* vol. 8, no. 2 (summer 1980): 63–82.

Wong, Morrison G. "Changes in Socioeconomic Status of the Chinese Male Population in the United States from 1960 to 1970." *International immigration Review,* vol. 4, no. 4 (winter 1980): 511–24.

Wong, Siu-lun. "The Chinese Family Firm: a Model." *The British Journal of Sociology,* vol. 36, no. 1 (March 1985): 58–72.

INDEX

A & P, 18. *See also* Supermarket development, early

Albers, William H., 18

Albers Super Market, 19. *See also* Supermarket development, early

Albertson's, 111, 126, 127–29

Alpha-Beta, 18, 111. *See also* Supermarket development, early

Alpine Market, 130

Amalgamated Meat Cutters Union, 138, 140, 142

A-1 Meat Company, 62

Arata Brothers Wholesale Grocery, 52, 156–57. *See also* Valley Wholesale Grocery

Auburn Grocery, 80

Bank of Canton, 46

Bel Air, 4, 57–60, 74, 76, 94, 95, 107, 124, 153, 155, 159–60; employee and customer appreciation, 89; expansion of, 88; hiring, 88–89; incorporation, 61; philosophy, 58; sale of, 112–13; service and innovation, 86–87; ventures and investments, 87

Big Bear Store, 18, 21. *See also* Supermarket development, early

Bi-Rite, 147

Broderick Market, 81, 84, 93–94, 102

Businesses and occupations, early Chinese American, 4–5

Cardinal Grocery, 66, 85

Centr-O-Mart, 4, 95, 153; decline of, 113–14; ethnic employees, 63; expansion of, 91; first, 62–63; grocery wholesale, 63; investing in, 91–92

Chan, George, 126–31

Cherry pickers (shoppers), 97. *See also* Loss leaders

China: conditions in Toishan and Hoiping, 64

Chinese Food Dealers Association, 66

Chung Sun Grocery (Market), 9, 53, 56, 80, 81, 153, 160; customer credit, 49–50; employees, 50; family-run, 52; modest beginnings, 49–50; new store capitalization, 51; partnerships, partners, shareholders, 51; resiliency, ominous signs, 106

Community, Chinese American: bicultural American-born, 42–43; economic reward, 94; experiences with dominant population, 43; historical record, 12–15; immigration, 34–37; job opportunities, 45; mixed experi-

CAPTIONS

Jacket photo: Interior of the Eye (I) Street Bridge Market, Broderick, California, c. 1939. Courtesy of George Quan Jr.

CPSIA information can be obtained at www.ICGtesting.com
Printed in the USA
BVOW081517140413

318062BV00002B/34/P